"Over the years, I have come across a number of books about spirituality and politics. Almost all of them have left me unsatisfied. It seemed as if they were generally preaching to the choir and offering tentative and impractical solutions. *America's Next Great Awakening* is an exception, largely because of its timing. It recognizes that the polarization of society has reached a crisis point, exactly the condition necessary for a new Awakening. Furthermore, it acknowledges the role that atheists will play in the coming years. This is not a book only for the choir."

—Jeffrey Mishlove, PhD, host and producer of PBS's *Thinking Allowed* and *New Thinking Allowed*, author of *Roots of Consciousness*

"In *America's Next Great Awakening*, Christopher Naughtons proves the critical bridge-voice our nation needs to rediscover what actually unites it, which is the vitality of the individual search. As Christopher reckons, we as a nation are capable of navigating disparate beliefs and outlooks, as we have in the past, through reclaiming our core ideal: that every individual is a seeker, and only through honoring the search—and what we owe to it and each other—can we fulfill the meaning of *e pluribus unum*, from many one."

—Mitch Horowitz, PEN Award-winning author of *Occult America* and *Uncertain Places*

"Christopher's insights remind us how women, people of color, Native Americans, and those less connected to power have dramatically shifted America's spirituality and consciousness."

—**Nancy Webster Kirkpatrick**, author of *True Tales from the Edgar Cayce Archives: Lives Touched and Lessons Learned from the Sleeping Prophet*

"The never-ending tension between the Great Awakenings and the Enlightenment is a thread running through Christopher's book, not to mention American history, showing up, again, loudly in our current cultural and political discourse. He demonstrates why cyclical polarization is both the bane of our national existence as well as the grist of our evolution."

—**William Hoffman**, historian, attorney-at-law

"In a rare, big-picture look, Christopher Naughton identifies the source and the potential solution to multiple convergent crises in modern America. We are living through a 'great gate' in history, says Naughton, evocative of the American Revolution, the Civil War, and WWII. However, the tension of opposites does not spell our downfall; instead it could result in the emergence of a higher synthesis and, ultimately, the realization of America's sacred purpose: unity in diversity. An important book for anyone interested in the nation's diverse spiritual history and potential."

—**Glenn Aparicio Parry**, author of two award-winning books, *Original Politics: Making America Sacred Again* and *Original Thinking: A Radical ReVisioning of Time, Humanity, and Nature*

"I have yet to read anything that outlines the religious, ideological, and spiritual aspects of our great leaders . . . as *America's Next Great Awakening* has."

—**Tod Gohl**, author of *Saving America's Citizens*

"Naughton . . . traces the connections between centuries of mysticism, New Age thought, and contemporary atheism that suggest a potential path forward for the United States . . . [and] offer[s] realistic insights into religious evolutions that Americans may find themselves facing in the near future. . . . [A] thoughtful and thought-provoking look at where American religious identity is going."

—*Kirkus Reviews*

America's Next Great Awakening
by Christopher W. Naughton
© Copyright 2023 Christopher W. Naughton

ISBN 978-1-64663-870-3

Published by

◤köehlerbooks™

3705 Shore Drive
Virginia Beach, VA 23455
800-435-4811

A NEW AMERICAN REVOLUTION
IN CONSCIOUSNESS

America's Next Great Awakening

WHAT THE CONVERGENCE OF MYSTICISM,
RELIGION, ATHEISM AND SCIENCE MEANS
FOR OUR NATION. AND YOU.

Christopher W. Naughton

VIRGINIA BEACH
CAPE CHARLES

To Valerie,
whose love, support, and smarts
inspire me always

TABLE OF CONTENTS

For everything that rises must converge.

Pierre Teilhard de Chardin

The seven pointed star on the front cover and noted throughout the book is reminiscent of the Bennington Flag— one of the earliest known American flags with thirteen stars and thirteen stripes. It may have preceded the well-known circular field of thirteen stars on the Revolutionary War flag. More likely, it was created for use in the War of 1812 and for the fiftieth anniversary of the Declaration of Independence, 1826. Unlike other American flags, the Bennington flag sports seven pointed stars as opposed to the usual five pointed stars.

While the pentagram, or five pointed star, symbolizes man, the seven pointed star (or, alternately, septagram or heptagram) has accumulated many levels of meaning over the centuries. It has been interpreted as a bridge of the realm between worlds.

One of the oldest recorded meanings given to this star is found within the mystical Jewish Kabbalistic tradition, where it represents the power of love and the sphere of victory. It is also found within Christian tradition as a symbol of protection, the seven points representing the perfection of God and the seven days of creation. In Islam, the heptagram is used to represent the first seven verses in the Koran. Alchemists used the seven pointed star to represent the seven elements of the world. On the flag of the Cherokee people, the seven pointed star symbolizes peace.

To Freemasons the seven pointed star relates to the seven rungs of Jacobs Ladder, the evolved "seven-fold man" whose seven steps of learning gains him greater insight into the omniscience of the Great Architect of the Universe.

The seven pointed star is also a common sight within neo-paganism, where it is known as the "Faery" or "Elven" star. A group in San Francisco during the 1980s called "The Elf-Queen's Daughters" adopted this strongly feminist title, a group consisting of both men and women who believed themselves to be incarnated elven spirits in human form, sent to bring about an acceleration of consciousness on Earth.

A New Great American Awakening?

Our best chance of summoning what Abraham Lincoln called
"the better angels of our nature" may lie in recovering the sense
and spirit of the Founding era and its leaders.

Jon Meacham

In order to evolve, the United States must return
to its core spiritual template.

Caroline Myss

The only true America is the coming spiritual Republic.

Andrew Jackson Davis

At last count, in this young century alone, the words *soul* and *America* have concurrently cropped up in dozens of magazine articles, book titles, documentaries, films, and other media—mostly in the last few years.

Small wonder. Regardless of where one sits on the spectrum of belief, religion, or "none of the above," a consistent sentiment persists: there is grave concern for the future of the United States.

Admittedly, using the term *awakening* or anything resembling *awake* is stepping into a minefield. In the last few years, conspiracy-based groups believe that America is facing existential crises that will trigger a "Great Awakening," which in turn will bring down an evil deep state. On the other hand, those who demonstrate overt political correctness and hypersensitivity in matters of race, religion, and class equality have been contemptibly described as "woke." While the convergence of mysticism, religion, atheism, and science addressed here is set apart from such notions, something is bubbling up from within the American psyche that is seemingly felt by all.

In American history, from Great Awakenings to the Age of Enlightenment, religious, spiritual, and intellectual movements have shaped the nation's consciousness. The ideologies that sprang from those experiences have preceded and coexisted with national crises, sometimes serially fending one another off and at other times overlapping, if not intertwining, ultimately resulting in a better America. Our present time calls for something as dynamic, if not more so.

To some, history is completely linear. It doesn't repeat. But perhaps it rhymes. That latter notion is attributed to Mark Twain, even if he never uttered the words. Regardless, the idea is not unique. Native American Indian cultures did not see time as linear, instead believing nature unfolds in a circle. Others see the evolution of history as a series of elevating, concentric circles that expand and ascend—as if coming to the same place on the circle, but a step or two up an evolutionary helix. Still others believe that America experiences existential crises every eighty years or so—the American Revolution, the Civil War and World War II—and now eighty years later a new generation of Americans must demonstrate the wisdom and courage reminiscent of those specific preceding generations in order to move past current predicaments. If an authentic new Great American Awakening is in the offing, perhaps it will rhyme with historical precedent.

Evolutionary transformation is no longer a luxury, no longer optional. For the first time in the history of humanity, a transformation of consciousness is a necessity.[1] If this planet is to survive and evolve, then America—a microcosm of the world and one of diverse faiths, cultures, races, colors, national origins, ethnicities, and genders—a constitutionally limited, democratic republic extolling freedom for all must evoke these founding ideals as never before. *That is her destiny, should she be willing to accept it.* Especially now, with the existential threats of autocracy, climate crisis, and more.

To do so, the nation must tap into its spiritual core and experience a new revolution in consciousness. If not, the world could easily fall into a new dark age—culturally, politically, militarily, ecologically. We may see America's problems as political, monetary, racial, ecological, or religious in nature. But the core of America's crisis is essentially one in consciousness.

Is the nation poised for such a shift? Is raising the collective consciousness of the nation the *only* way out of this predicament?

CONTEXT

America is experiencing a polarization and moral depression unlike anything we have endured in over a hundred years—far worse than the malaise of post-assassination/Watergate/Vietnam-era America, as memorialized in a Jimmy Carter speech. By most assessments, the country is the most divided it has been since the Civil War. Throughout the nation and the world, authoritarianism and autocracy creep forward. The damage and threat of climate change unfolds before our eyes. Seeming norms have been turned on their heads. The institutions of America are, by any political assessment, eroding.

No time is without its perils, its fear-inducing crises, but most Americans who have been alive since the mid- to late-twentieth century would likely agree that this is an age of unpredictability and instability that most of us figured we'd *never* experience in our lifetime. One historical commentator says it best: "Although each generation believes that it lives on some kind of precipice, I have never before seen Americans angrier, more divided, and less possessed of confidence in our common future."[2] Most cannot recall a time when the nation has been so challenged from within.

That may be so in our lifetimes—but it's hardly new to the American story. Consider:

✳ George Washington, the commanding general, leading a fledging nation-to-be against the world's preeminent power, which still held sway with a significant number of loyal colonists in America; his was an act of monarchical defiance that would surely have led him and his compatriots to the gallows if they were not militarily successful;

✳ Abraham Lincoln, who had to surreptitiously travel through unfriendly territories in the dead of night to assume the mantle of the presidency in a White House south of the Mason Dixon line—seven Southern states having already seceded, four more soon to join them, followed by almost 700,000 deaths and the bloodiest war in US history;

✳ Franklin Delano Roosevelt, paralyzed but not defeated by polio, facing down a global depression and the rising specter of world-wide authoritarianism as evidenced by Nazi Germany, fascist Italy, Imperial Japan, and communist Russia, not to mention right-wing coup attempts against him at home;

✳ Lyndon Johnson, inheriting the office from a young, vigorous president who'd been assassinated by a questionably known shooter, facing international (Vietnam) and national (race riots, anti-war demonstrations, etc.) crises, followed by successive assassinations of American progressive leadership.[3]

We Americans, in the toughest times, have always found our way. Something deep within the American soul, in the most fundamental beliefs about ourselves, has ultimately prevailed.

WHAT COULD EMERGE?

The United States has evolved through a largely untold, subsumed religious and spiritual history.

By most historical accounts, there have been two overarching

Great Awakenings in America, seen largely as emotive religious events with widespread ramifications. Significant catalysts that changed American thinking and spirituality, they had the look and feel of passionate Christian evangelical movements. These awakenings generated inspired action that arguably helped create and later save a nation. Without the First Great Awakening, there may not have been an American Revolution; without the Second Great Awakening, many of the monumental social changes in race, suffrage, labor, and education brought about by the Civil War it helped trigger may never have come about—or at the very least, their manifestation would have been delayed.

Remnants of these two historical markers inhabit some space in America's next Great Awakening.

But something moving more deeply from within America's core is emerging. It stems from ancient Egypt, via the democracies of Greece and the republics of Rome, up through esoteric traditions in Europe, then setting foot on these shores and inspiring the most enlightened of our founders. It is also infused with the arcane roots of ancient Judaic, African American, and Native American Indian influences. Together these influences have sparked a uniquely American form of consciousness whose very being is transcendental in nature. It has run silently, sometimes almost imperceptibly, beneath the loud emotional outbursts of religious, largely Christianized America. It lacks the revivalist fervor of a Jonathan Edwards, the institutional biblical authority of a Dwight L. Moody, the presidential conferral of approval of a Billy Graham, the moral certitude of a Jerry Falwell, James Dobson, or Pat Robertson.

But its imprint on the American soul is undeniable.

An authentic, alternative consciousness that helped mold the American Enlightenment is rising again, in new form. If America is to realize its sacred purpose—unity in diversity—an inner awakening that spans belief systems and religions (including atheism), transcends ideologies, and honors scientific realities must emerge. Will democracy survive? Or will world leadership pass to China, Russia, or other autocracies?

America inaugurated its own way of fighting wars, its own unique form of government, its own sport in baseball, its own musical expressions in jazz and rock 'n roll. Should it be so surprising that the nation found a unique spiritual voice, tied in part to both traditional, ardent religious expression as well as mystical and esoteric philosophies—and that it did so by creating a diverse, incorporeal ecosystem, allowing beliefs to exist side by side in toleration of, if not always in harmony with, one another? America was and is a multifaceted spiritual landscape that would have overjoyed the founders because no one religious perspective has taken hold and dictated to all others.

Since colonial times, America has been a free-flowing interchange for new spiritual ideas. In the 1600s, many came to escape religious persecution in their home countries. English Quaker William Penn established Philadelphia as a town where all religious faiths could live together. By 1682, Mennonite, Amish, and Lutheran church offshoots coexisted in the city. Soon thereafter, Catholics, Jews, and others settled and thrived in the region. Mystically oriented communities found refuge in the nearby countryside, suggesting America was an experiment that worked, establishing fresh attitudes for future generations.

The ideas and concepts of Freemasonry also found root in fertile American soil. Emerging out of the Reformation, it was not a religion but rather a freethinking intellectual and holistic salon, a radical spiritual brotherhood filled with liberal ideas about how people of different religious faiths could work well together within a nation. Today America is still a great laboratory of religious experiment, of spiritual exploration, of conscious awakening.

This awakening—should it come to fruition—will be far more

powerful than the outward, pray-in-the-open, emotive Great Awakenings of the past. It will incorporate the very best that those awakenings had to offer; but this new Great Awakening will be more than the veneration of a singular perspective espousing one predominant religious belief. It will be, in a sense, a convergence of distinct counterpoints that have long resided in the American soul.

Einstein suggested, "The problem cannot be solved by the same consciousness that created it." Revival of a fundamental theology will not resolve the nation's historic divisions. This awakening comes from our intuitive depths—perhaps, dare I say, from an optimal future. Timeless, it can stir the souls of individuals, the nation, and a global collective consciousness in an era of desperate need.

Is the answer to current crises—maybe the only answer—a spiritual awakening? A prominent American historian suggests that may be the best way out of our current political dilemma.[4] The convergence of atheism, religion, mysticism, and science is opening up new highways of awareness that have the potential to dwarf any of America's Great Awakenings of the past.

To reap the blessings of liberty, the times call for a revolution in consciousness, largely emulating those who embodied an enlightened awareness and transcendental vision—with all of their warts—and whose dedication saw us through the American Revolution, the Civil War, the World Wars and more recent watershed events. Not perfect people, not by a long shot, these men and women—both engineers and by-products of their eras—tracked closely to intellectual, ecumenical, and spiritual enlightenment, not conventional thinking or religiosity. Their stories reveal the seeds of hope.

In the end, both in American myth and history, two qualities have ultimately shone through: the resourcefulness and inner goodness at the core of this country. Americans have *always* found a way, even in the most trying crises. Is this yet another chapter that ultimately defines our nation and helps transform the world?

Now is the moment to call on the essence of our historical great awakenings, along with the esoteric, enlightened wisdom found in the American soul. It's in our DNA. The time is now. And we have the keys.

CHAPTER ONE

The Power of National Myth

While the stars remain, and the heavens send down dew
upon the earth, so long shall the Union last. . . .
The whole world united shall never prevail against her.

George Washington's "Angelic Vision" at Valley Forge

The delegates, carried away by his enthusiasm, rushed forward.
John Hancock scarcely had time to pen his bold signature
before the quill was grasped by another. It was done.

Manly P. Hall, from *The Secret Destiny of America*

STORIES OF A NATION'S DESTINY

They are the stories we tell ourselves.

Myths attempt to define our perspective of reality. Throughout human history, they are told. And retold. Not because they're factually true but because their symbology reveals a deeper truth. "A myth is a story that's often considered sacred," says Prof. David Leeming of the University of Connecticut, "but essentially it's a story in which the events that take place don't take place normally in our everyday lives."[5] Myth plays an integral role in understanding who we are. And who are we but the stories we tell ourselves about ourselves and believe?[6]

Mythology was at the heart of everyday life in ancient Greece and Rome. Greeks regarded mythology as a part of their history. Modern scholars study myth in an attempt to shed light on religious and political institutions of ancient civilizations and to gain understanding of the nature of mythmaking itself.[7] A recent theory establishes similarities shared by many myths, suggesting they have a common origin, passed down across thousands of generations. Myths often share similar incidents, characters, or narrative structures, whether they derive from classical Greece or the ancient mythologies of Egypt, Mesopotamia, Japan, or India.[8]

A parallel theory stems from Sigmund Freud's one-time protégé psychologist Carl Jung. Both men took myth seriously. Jung believed that myths and dreams were expressions of the collective unconscious, in that they express core ideas that are part of humanity as a whole. Jungian analysis of classical mythology suggests gods and goddesses express archetypes and symbols common to human thinking everywhere.[9] In Jung's vocabulary, myths express wisdom encoded in all humans, expressing universal concerns. For Jung, this common origin explained why myths from societies at opposite ends of the earth are often strikingly similar.

Joseph Campbell, author of the popular book and PBS series *The Power of Myth*, proposes that "every myth . . . is psychologically symbolic. Its narratives and images are to be read, therefore, not literally, but as metaphors."[10] Whereas those of a scientific or a purely rational bent look at myth as denoting something false or lacking realism, Campbell asserts that myths offer a greater truth than anything in the realm of mere logic. "Myth is much more important and true than history," he once said. "History is just journalism and you know how reliable that is."[11]

Campbell popularized the notion of the monomyth, or the hero's journey: a template of stories that is common across cultures, irrespective of those cultures' connectivity or lack thereof. The monomyth involves a hero who goes on an adventure, is victorious in a decisive crisis, and comes home changed or transformed.[12]

Myths, according to Campbell, "instill and maintain a sense of awe and mystery before the world and provide a symbolic image for the world." He goes on to say myths also "maintain the social order by giving divine justification to social practices and above all harmonize human beings with the cosmos, society, and themselves."[13]

The origins and the reasons why man has created myth still fascinate and perplex. We have myths that describe the origin of the world, the creation and fall of humans, an end of the universe, sometimes coupled with the hope for a new world.[14] One main lineage of myth asks the eternal questions: *Where do we come from? Why are we here? Where do we go?* The answers suggest we are descendants of the gods, who on their part have evolved from early generations and ultimately from the universe itself.[15]

The same questions may be asked of a country. National myths speak a symbolic, archetypal language, sometimes louder than the acts that inspired the myths. These stories reveal our country's inherent nature. Two such stories, stemming from the forming of the American republic, are buried within the national collective. They say something about who we are. And, perhaps, who we are to become.

FIRST STORY:
"THE UNKNOWN SPEAKER"
AND A TWENTIETH-CENTURY PRESIDENT

The scene: Independence Hall, Philadelphia, Pennsylvania, July 4, 1776. In the middle of intense debate concerning whether the colonies should vote as one and set America free from the British Empire, a man—a stranger—walks up to the podium. No one is sure who he is. No one is even sure how he gained entrance into the room.

According to Jefferson, it was late in the afternoon before the delegates gathered their courage to the sticking point. The talk was about axes, scaffolds, and the gibbet, when suddenly a strong, bold voice sounded.

"They may stretch our necks on all the gibbets in the land; they may turn every rock into a scaffold; every tree into a gallows; every home into a grave, and yet the words of that parchment can never die! . . .

"They may pour our blood on a thousand scaffolds, and yet from every drop that dyes the axe a new champion of freedom will spring into birth! The British King may blot out the stars of God from the sky, but he cannot blot out His words written on that parchment there. . .

"Sign that parchment! Sign, if the next moment the gibbet's rope is about your neck! . . . Sign, and not only for yourselves, but for all ages, for that parchment will be the textbook of freedom, the bible of the rights of man forever. . .

"As I live, my friends, I believe that to be His voice! Yes, were my soul trembling on the verge of eternity, were this hand freezing in death, were this voice choking in the last struggle, I would still, with the last impulse of that soul, with the last wave of that hand, with the last gasp of that voice, implore you to remember this truth—God has given America to be free."

The unknown speaker fell exhausted into his seat. The delegates, carried away by his enthusiasm, rushed forward. John Hancock scarcely had time to pen his bold signature before the quill was grasped by another. It was done.

The delegates turned to express their gratitude to the unknown speaker for his eloquent words. He was not there.

Who was this strange man, who seemed to speak with a divine authority, whose solemn words gave courage to the doubters and sealed the destiny of the new nation? Unfortunately, no one knows. . . .

He speaks of the "rights of man," although Thomas Paine's book by that name was not published until thirteen years later.

He mentions the all-seeing eye of God which was afterwards to appear on the reverse of the Great Seal of the new nation.

In all, there is much to indicate that the unknown speaker was one of the agents of the secret Order, guarding and directing the destiny of America.[16]

＊ ＊ ＊

Where does this story come from? Who was the unknown speaker, this "orator," this "mysterious man" who was the ultimate patriot? Don't look for answers in history books or biographies. You won't find it mentioned by any who witnessed the signing that July 4, 1776.

But one individual—the fortieth president of the United States—immortalized it as an American story.

"THE TEFLON FOR THE TEFLON PRESIDENCY"

The father of modern American conservatism, he was the president most revered by evangelicals, those direct descendants of America's Great Awakenings. Despite being a traditionalist icon, despite the adulation from his Christian base, the man engaged in esoteric practices for much of his life, more than, as far as is known, any modern president. He is responsible for keeping a virtually hidden account of American destiny alive in the nation's book of dreams.

As a Hollywood actor, Ronald Reagan is generally remembered for his B movies: *Bedtime for Bonzo, Hellcats of the Navy* (with wife Nancy

Davis), and dozens more. He is likely best known for *Knute Rockne: All-American*, a 1940s film in which he utters the famous line "Win one for the Gipper." Although he never reached the heights of a serious leading man, Reagan's ultimate starring role was that of president of the Screen Actors' Guild. In the 1950s, as his politics turned more conservative, General Electric tapped him as spokesman. He was well suited for speeches and presentations, talents that would later pay off handsomely on the campaign trail.

But for all that Reagan is remembered for, little is said about the arcane phenomena that swirled about his life. Lucille Ball once recounted a story from the 1950s of Ron and Nancy arriving late for a dinner party in honor of actor William Holden, "out of breath and excited," claiming they had just seen a UFO.[17] In 1974, while returning from a gubernatorial campaign event by air, Reagan and his group on board their Cessna witnessed an unidentified object flying past their plane at a high rate of speed.[18]

Throughout their personal and professional lives, the Reagans relied upon numerology and astrology. When the couple were making their way in Hollywood, "they sought out Carroll Righter, the Philadelphia lawyer who had become the 'gregarious Aquarius' astrologer advising Cary Grant and Princess Grace, among others."[19] Later, Mrs. Reagan consulted astrologers, most famously Jeanne Dixon, during her husband's years as governor of California. It was Dixon who recommended the most propitious times for important events, once time-shifting Reagan's gubernatorial swearing-in from twelve noon until after midnight.[20]

The most controversial consultant was San Francisco astrologer Joan Quigley, who spent seven years conferring with First Lady Nancy Reagan. Quigley had veto power over presidential press conferences, advised when it was safe to travel, and exerted almost complete control of the president's speech timetables and even the most optimal times for summits.[21] Quigley precisely timed the announcement of Anthony Kennedy as Supreme Court justice nominee[22] and briefed the Reagans on Gorbachev's horoscope before a major summit.

One time, when the president's take-off and landing schedule became incredibly convoluted, presidential advisor Don Regan demanded to speak with the astrologer directly.[23] While serving in the White House, Regan would slough off questions about the president's affinity for "lucky numbers." But eventually the irked advisor got fed up with the Reagans' abstruse philosophy, revealing, "Virtually every major move and decision the Reagans made during my time as White House chief of staff was cleared in advance with a woman in San Francisco who drew up horoscopes to make certain that the planets were in a favorable alignment for the enterprise."[24] Writing in his tell-all book *From Wall Street to Washington*, Regan says it became "too burdensome to deal with all of the 'occult prognostications.'"

But others believed Reagan's reputation was a direct result of Ms. Quigley's uncanny timing for the events in his life; she knew how to play those astrological angles to Reagan's advantage. Quigley claimed she was the one providing "the Teflon for the Teflon presidency."[25] As for the president, he had firmly come to believe in the Aquarian legacy of Ganymede, the humanitarian water bearer of the zodiac most associated with the future, freedom, equality, and utopian vision. Reagan's ideals arguably resemble an American Aquarian age: the shining city on the hill, the world's best last hope, a nation with a secret destiny of freedom for all humanity.

Maybe, then, it's not surprising Reagan adopted and later publicly shared the saga of the unknown speaker. Somewhere along the way, he must have happened upon the theosophical storyteller whose account of the signing of the Declaration shows up time and again in Ronald Reagan's speeches about America's purpose and destiny.

CALIFORNIA DREAMING

In 1919, a young man left his native Canada for Southern California. There he reunited with his bohemian mother, who was a chiropractor and member of the Rosicrucian Fellowship.

Living in Santa Monica, Manly Palmer Hall was immediately drawn to the arcane world of mysticism, Theosophy, esoteric philosophies, and their underlying principles. Hall delved deeply into "teachings of lost and hidden traditions, the golden verses of Hindu gods, Greek philosophers, Christian mystics and the spiritual treasures waiting to be found within one's own soul."[26] Over a seventy-year career, the author, speaker, and astrologer wrote more than 150 volumes of esoteric work and gave thousands of lectures, including two at Carnegie Hall. In 1934 he founded the Philosophical Research Society in western Los Angeles. He called it a "mystery school" dedicated to "Truth Seekers of All Time."[27]

Hall published what would become the cornerstone of his legacy in 1928—*The Secret Teachings of All Ages: An Encyclopedia Outline of Masonic, Hermetic, Qabbalistic and Rosicrucian Symbolical Philosophy*, an exemplar of the increasingly influential metaphysical movement of the 1920s. His opus was a "massive codex to the mystical and esoteric philosophies of antiquity."[28] Exploring subjects from Native American mythology to Pythagorean mathematics to the geometry of ancient Egypt, this "encyclopedia arcana" remains the unparalleled guidebook to ancient symbols and esoteric thought.[29] Hall's book challenged assumptions about society's spiritual roots and made people look at them in new ways.[30] *The Secret Teachings* won the admiration of figures ranging from Bela Lugosi to General John Pershing to Elvis Presley. *New York Times* best-selling novelist Dan Brown (*The DaVinci Code*) cites it as a key source of his esoteric plots.[31]

In 1944, Hall produced a short work called *The Secret Destiny of*

America. The United States, in his view, was a society that had been planned and founded by secret orders to spread enlightenment and liberty to the world.[32] It was in this book where Hall recounted the story of the unknown speaker. Where did Hall discover the tale that inspired a president? It originally appeared in George Lippard's *Washington and His Generals; Or, Legends of the Revolution* in 1847. According to *American National Biography*, Lippard "wrote many semi-fanciful 'legends' of American history, mythologizing the founding fathers and retelling key moments of the American Revolution so vividly that several of the legends . . . became part of American folklore."[33] Lippard acknowledged inventing the story: "The name of the Orator . . . is not definitely known. In this speech, it is my wish to compress some portion of the fiery eloquence of the time."[34] It later appeared in the publication *The Theosophist* in May 1938 where Hall likely first saw the story.

The tale may not have ventured much beyond occult circles except for one fact: from the 1920s until his death in 1990, Hall wrote in Los Angeles, the same hometown as the struggling actor and future president. *The Secret Teachings of All Ages* and *Secret Destiny of America* secured Hall's early entrance into inner Hollywood circles, opening doors that made him a monumental figure behind the "new age."[35] Somehow the young Reagan must have bumped into the author's work—they may have even met—because the language Reagan uses in the retelling of the speech of the unknown speaker is unmistakably that of Hall's.

Reagan referenced the story several times, including in a 1957 commencement speech at his alma mater, Eureka College. He shared it at the first Conservative Political Action Conference (now known as CPAC) convention in 1974 and again in a *Parade* magazine article during the first year of his presidency and at a Fourth of July celebration at the Statue of Liberty in 1986. Reagan's version of the story is faithful to the original: "When they turned to thank the speaker for his timely words, he couldn't be found and to this day no one knows who he was or how he entered or left the guarded room.'"[36] For the president, the life of the story took on a greater dimension. But like Manly P. Hall before him, Reagan never attempted to attribute the genesis of the story or speculate on who the unknown speaker might have been. Nor, for that matter, did Reagan ever drop Hall's name.

The myth Ronald Reagan shared with America reflects a resplendent Aquarian optimism. It boasts of a nation's unique destiny to lead mankind in the conscious awakening of freedom for all. The unknown speaker is the sole voice in what would otherwise be a Greek chorus, providing other characters with the insight they need. He expresses to the audience what the main characters cannot say or do, revealing their hidden fears or secrets. In this apocryphon, does the unknown speaker represent the conscience of America? Its courageous inner voice? Would Carl Jung call him an American archetype, speaking from the country's timeless, collective unconscious?

SECOND STORY:
WASHINGTON'S ANGELIC VISION

On a cold, cloudless day in the horrific winter of 1778 at Valley Forge, George Washington retired to his tent. He later emerged, ashen. He spoke to an officer and was overheard by one of his generals. He had just experienced an otherworldly event: a vision in which an angel showed him three trials and tribulations that would face the republic. The first, in which the country was presently engaged, being its war for independence with Great Britain; the second was an incendiary civil war; and a third one was yet to come, at some time well off into the future.

Washington is to have said of the experience:

Presently I heard a voice saying, "Son of the Republic, look and learn," while at the same time my visitor extended an arm eastwardly. I now beheld a heavy white vapor at some distance rising fold upon fold. This gradually dissipated, and I looked upon a strange scene. Before me lay spread out in one vast plain all the countries of the world: Europe, Asia, Africa and America. I saw rolling and tossing between Europe and America, the billows of the Atlantic, and between Asia and America lay the Pacific.

Then once more, I beheld the villages, towns and cities springing up where I had seen them before, while the bright angel, planting the azure standard she had brought in the midst of them, cried with the loud voice: "While the stars remain, and the heavens send down dew upon the earth, so long shall the UNION last." And taking from his brow the crown on which blazoned the word "UNION," he placed it upon the Standard while the people, kneeling down, said "Amen."

. . . The scene instantly began to fade and dissolve, and, I at last saw nothing but the rising, curling vapor at first beheld. This also disappeared, and I found myself once more gazing upon the mysterious visitor, who, in the same voice I had heard before, said, "Son of the Republic, what you have seen is thus interpreted; Three great perils will come upon the Republic. The most fearful for her is the third. But the whole world united shall not prevail against her. Let every child of the Republic learn to live for his God, his land and the Union." With these words the vision vanished, and I started from my seat and felt that I had seen a vision wherein had been shown to me the birth, progress, and destiny of the United States.[37]

"Washington's Vision" is a narrative presented as the reminiscences of one Anthony Sherman, who allegedly served as general in George Washington's army at Valley Forge. Sherman claimed he overheard Washington tell an officer of the prophetic vision for America. The passage of more than 150 years has since obscured the origins and purpose of this narrative, leading some who encounter it now to believe that it is a true account of an incident from Washington's life rather than a fictional tale created for political purposes long after Washington's death.[38]

The source of the story? Charles Wesley Alexander wrote it under the pseudonym Wesley Bradshaw. Sherman reportedly shared his secret with Alexander on July 4, 1859. The story was first published in April 1861 at the outbreak of the Civil War. A more infamous version appeared later in the popular newspaper *The National Tribune*.[39]

But here, now, are the facts.

Although an officer named Anthony Sherman did serve in the Continental Army, he was at Saratoga under the command of Benedict Arnold at the end of 1777. Therefore, he wasn't with Washington's forces at Valley Forge during the winter of 1777–78, so it's likely suggestive or mere coincidence that Alexander chose that name for his narrator. Also, "Bradshaw" had written "sketches" of other historical figures that stretched the bounds of credulity. Finally, aside from the content of the tale itself, it was reputedly shared by a ninety-nine-year-old man, some eighty years after the event!

As the Civil War began, the story was widely shared by the press. At the time, former US secretary of state and then Massachusetts senator Edward Everett commended it as "teaching a highly important lesson to every true lover of his country."[40] But in Everett's estimation there was no attempt to put forth the "dream" as authentic.

"Washington's Vision" has been reprinted many times since

Washington's Vision: The First Union Story Ever Written

it originally appeared in 1861. It was published that year in *The Philadelphia Inquirer* and *Pittsfield Gazette*, and the following year in the *New Hampshire Sentinel*. In 1864, "Washington's Vision" appeared in a pamphlet courtesy of the Lilly Library at Indiana University. It was later reprinted in *The Theosophist* periodical, ironically in the same 1938 edition as the aforementioned "The Speech of the Unknown Speaker." Grand Army of the Republic's popular *Stars and Stripes* published it in 1950.

The 1961 television series *One Step Beyond*, a contemporary of *The Twilight Zone*, gave credence to the story in an episode called "Night of Decision." The story gained renewed currency in 2001 after the events of September 11. Noted contemporary evangelical and New Age authors have alluded to the story as factually true.[41] And now that it's on the internet, "Washington's Vision" will never die.[42]

THE "POLITICAL RELIGION OF OUR NATION" OR DESTRUCTION FROM WITHIN

The apocryphal story of Washington's Vision suggests an ultimately promising destiny for the United States. But what is said may be as uplifting as what's not said is haunting: if "the whole world united shall not prevail against her," what about a house divided? What of destruction from within?

The shadow side of Alexander's story is reminiscent of Abraham Lincoln's warning uttered before the Young Men's Lyceum of Springfield, Illinois, in January 1838,[43] some twenty-three years before his presidential inauguration and the Civil War:

> At what point shall we expect the approach of danger? By what means shall we fortify against it? Shall we expect some transatlantic military giant, to step the Ocean, and crush us at a blow? Never! All the armies of Europe, Asia and Africa combined, with all the treasure of the earth (our own excepted) in their military chest; with a Buonaparte for a commander, could not by force, take a drink from the Ohio, or make a track on the Blue Ridge, in a trial of a thousand years. At what point then is the approach of danger to be expected? *I answer, if it ever reaches us, it must spring up amongst us. It cannot come from abroad. If destruction be our*

lot, we must ourselves be its author and finisher [emphasis mine].
As a nation of freemen, we must live through all time, or die by
suicide.[44]

Lincoln understood the roots of the founders' conscious creation of a
land that, separated from the Old World by oceans, had staked out its
own unique destiny—an amalgam of the world, an experiment in
awareness to see if peoples of varying origins could live together
in relative peace, under the umbrella of a constitutionally limited
democratic republic.

In that same 1838 address, Lincoln refers to the Constitution
and rule of law as "the *political religion* of our nation."[45] He feared a
"mobocratic spirit" where vigilante bands of self-declared "good
citizens" would take the law into their own hands. Lincoln warned that
if American citizens tolerated such abuses, the nation would descend into
anarchy and call upon a despot, "a Napoleon, Caesar or Alexander the
Great[,] for rescue and salvation."

To prevent that downward spiral, Lincoln said, "As the
patriots of seventy-six did to the support of the Declaration of
Independence, so to the support of the Constitution and Laws, let
every American pledge his life, his property, and his sacred honor." In
Lincoln's estimation, "to survive as a democracy we must transcend our
racial, religious, regional, and party affiliations and embrace together
under one unifying political religion: the Constitution and the rule of
law."[46]

NATIONAL MYTHS OF TRUTH

If we give that mystery an exact meaning we diminish the experience
of its real depth. But when a poet carries the mind into a context
of meanings and then pitches it past those, one knows
that marvelous rapture that comes from going past

all categories of definition. Here we sense the function of metaphor that allows us to make a journey we could not otherwise make, past all categories of definition.

Joseph Campbell from *Thou Art That*

Once again, we come to face-to-face with the import of metaphor and myth. Both stories are fraught with challenge and danger. Yet they come with promise: a nation predestined for greatness that could never fall from without, only from within.

Stories of the unknown speaker and Washington's angelic vision symbolize the higher octave of America's calling to pursue our better angels and in the process become a more perfect union. For all of the nation's shortcomings, today, in the midst of chaos and uncertainty, those positive myths still call out to us from the core of the American soul.

Will tapping into that core elicit a new Great Awakening?

— ✳ —

CHAPTER TWO

Of Great Awakenings
and "Founding Mystics"

We need spiritual revival. . . .
[O]ur nation needs a spiritual awakening
and it starts with prayer.
Franklin Graham

We need a moral and spiritual awakening in this country. . . .
[It] is necessary to redeem our country, but a spiritual awakening
takes courage. And a spiritual awakening takes love.
Marianne Williamson

REVIVAL: COME AGAIN?

For all that ails the nation today—from the tragedy of 9/11 to mass shootings, the opioid epidemic, racial violence, crime, corporate greed, income inequality, the January 6 Capitol riot, and historic polarization that we haven't seen since the Civil War—citizens of the country rue the divide, the perils of dissension, the specter of violence, and the erosion of long-standing norms and institutions. In short, there is consensus worry over the possible end of a nearly 250-year experiment in democracy, and the freedoms and bounty that have come with it.

Regardless of political or spiritual belief, common underlying sentiment appears to be self-evident: *something has got to change.* There is a universal sense that an inner shift is necessary. In order for American democracy to survive and, beyond that, to thrive, something demonstrable, if not dramatic, must occur.

In evangelical circles, the suggested remedy heard for generations has been "America needs revival. Bring revival to this nation." Their aspiration is for a religious revival on the scale of the historic Great Awakenings. For those of agnostic or atheistic leanings, the hope may be for a new, scientifically based Age of Reason, a humanistic renaissance in thinking, politics, science, the arts, and human interrelationship. For those who consider themselves spiritual but not religious, the answer might be a quantum leap in both personal and collective consciousness: self-realization on a Jungian or *A New Earth* Eckhart Tolle–like scale. In all cases, an inner awakening points to a shift in consciousness that leads to evolutionary change.

No one quarter appears to have all the answers: the fundamentalist notion of going back to "my religion is better than yours" has seen its day. Atheism incurious about the non-locality or genesis of consciousness appears stagnant. A solely inward-looking, meditative, New Thought approach may lack the courage or initiative of our Transcendentalist forbears to bring about social change. And to paraphrase Stephen Hawking, science alone will never reveal the "mind of God."

The convergence of these perspectives, however, might suggest a way through our current crises.

THE EVOLUTION OF THE AMERICAN SOUL

As difficult as it is to put into any kind of language, the soul of the country is varied and deep; one could argue that religious pluralism *is* the religion of the United States. But from the nation's beginning, two poles, two predominant spiritual forces, emerged. They have morphed but today remain as adversarial as ever. Their conflict poses a grave challenge to the nation—but also provides the grist of antithesis to help move it forward.

The ideologies of the Great Awakening and the Enlightenment

are those two foundational forces of the American soul. By many accounts, they are two of the greatest influences on the American Revolution and the Declaration of Independence. The former is more fundamentally religious in its outlook; the latter, though inherently rationalistic, nevertheless embraced a pan-spiritual, perennial wisdom. They dominated the early belief landscape of the New World. Sibling rivals, they were often at odds: two contravening forces, two streams of consciousness, two ways of seeing God, the universe, and one's fellow man. Though they were sparring partners, they sometimes overlapped, and at critical moments in American history they converged, ushering in major change.

Today, as in the past, some degree of convergence and reconciliation appears necessary in order for the nation to heal and move forward on its initial vision.

GREAT AWAKENING VS. THE ENLIGHTENMENT

By most historians' accounts, there have been two prominent Great Awakenings in the nation's history—the first occurring prior to the American Revolutionary War, the second preceding the American Civil War. Some historians see myriad smaller awakenings throughout American history.

With its emotional intensity and fervent religiosity, the First Great Awakening took its cue from Puritanism, its ideological ancestor that first blossomed in 1600s New England. Early religious life in America is perceived as a fire-and-brimstone Puritanism, best embodied by the theology of Cotton Mather.[47] But the First Great Awakening would eclipse its predecessor.

Puritanism in precolonial America fell into disfavor. Aside from internal adversity, the Puritans' single, strict religious code could not withstand the onslaught of varying belief systems flooding in with new immigrants, and by the eighteenth century, the Christianity of the Great Awakening and philosophy of the Enlightenment had become the colonies' predominant spiritual influences.[48]

Where Puritanism extolled the virtuous life, steady and steadfast in its fundamentalism, the Great Awakening was grounded in feeling and faith and fostering a new understanding of a person's one-on-one relationship with God. It was no longer necessary to access the divine through the vicar, minister, or priest. Also, the preaching associated with these awakenings simultaneously gave listeners a sense of awe, personal guilt, and their need for salvation through Jesus Christ. The movement captured the imagination of the New World and arguably contributed to the emotional charge that sparked the revolution.

The Great Awakening was also a response to the Enlightenment's skeptical rationalism and Deism. The Enlightenment largely rejected religious orthodoxy, superstition, and the emotive outpouring of early evangelicalism.[49] It emphasized observation and experimentation. A scientific spirit and reasoning dominated its approach, leading scientists to deeply examine natural law.

The Enlightenment, however, was in no sense areligious. Its liberal approach to spirituality went well beyond institutional doctrines and dogma. The known initiators of the Enlightenment, including Newton, Locke, and Voltaire, held nontraditional, sometimes esoteric perspectives of being and the universe. These men more or less followed a "perennial wisdom," questioning the widely accepted Christian knowledge of how things came to be. They sought to spread new ideas based on investigation, openness, and tolerance. They were also openly influenced by Native American wisdom and opposed to converting them.

The Great Awakening and the Enlightenment stirred the minds of American colonists to start thinking for themselves. Colonists realized that they were a unique culture, capable of ruling and leading themselves, both politically and religiously. Mindsets about particular societies, religious affiliations, as well as the colonists' relation to their mother country changed.

And nothing stirred the souls of American settlers more than firebrands with "awakened" gifts of oratory.

GEORGE WHITEFIELD, ROCK STAR

In the firmament of the First Great Awakening, his star shone brightest. Without him, the American story would never have revealed the likes of Dwight L. Moody, Billy Graham, Oral Roberts, or thousands of other incendiary Christian preachers.

George Whitefield (pronounced as and sometimes spelled "Whitfield") was an ordained Anglican deacon achieving both success and notoriety in 1730s England. Whitefield's great interest in theater as a young man enlivened his preaching. He would often portray the lives of biblical characters by singing, dancing, and screaming, attracting legions of followers. Crowds materialized and hung on his every word.[50] Many in England's ecclesiastical hierarchy found Whitefield pedantic and emotional. His antics threatened their established order. But they could not deny his charisma.

Brothers Charles and John Wesley (the latter called the father of modern-day Methodism) took Whitefield under their wing. Barred from Anglican pulpits, they preached in barns, homes, and outdoor locations. In 1735 the Wesleys set sail for Savannah, Georgia, a "haven for persecuted religious sects and penniless debtors."[51] Later they invited Whitefield to join them in the New World. After a short stop with his mentors in Georgia, Whitefield set out on an American tour, starting in the colonies' most celebrated city, Philadelphia. There, he and his searing messages would surpass his greatest influences.

Although largely forgotten today except in evangelical circles, no one had a greater impact on religious awakening in eighteenth-century America. Whitefield mesmerized thousands—a true "headliner" of his day. He left his mark wherever he went. He toured the colonies seven times in the years prior to the Revolutionary War, delivering sermons that left his huge audiences spellbound and penitent with souls "awakened" (thus the phrase "Great Awakening").[52] With a booming voice that could be heard by huge crowds, once Whitefield started speaking, the frenzied mobs stilled. When Whitefield preached, eyewitnesses described "the awe and attention" of audiences.[53]

In Philadelphia, those desiring to experience him were so prevalent that he had to take his act outdoors—more than 8,000 people showed up. He even impressed a young Benjamin Franklin, "who describes in his autobiography the immediate and dramatic effects of Whitefield's preaching on colonists . . . in 1739."[54] In Franklin's lifetime, Whitefield was "the most charismatic man to speak the English language. . . . Many thought, *He spoke as never a man spoke*, before him. So charmed were people with his manner of address, that they shut up their shops, forgot their secular business, and laid aside their schemes for the world."[55]

Whitefield's main message to the throngs was for each person to experience a "new birth." Sarah Edwards, wife of future famed evangelist Jonathan Edwards, exclaimed, "[Whitefield] makes less of the doctrines than our American preachers generally do and aims more at affecting the heart. He is a born orator. A prejudiced person, I know, might say that this is all theatrical artifice and display, but not so will anyone think who has seen and known him."[56]

Although far from being an abolitionist, Whitefield also brought his famed revival to slave and Black freedmen communities. He was so well received there that some historians cite this as the genesis of African American Christianity. In all, the spiritual revival Whitefield ignited, the Great Awakening, became one of the most formative events in American history. In his life he would preach 18,000 times to perhaps 10 million listeners. The last sermon on his initial tour, given at Boston Commons before 23,000 people, was the largest known gathering in the New World to that time.[57]

American religion would never be the same.

SINNERS IN THE HANDS OF AN ANGRY GOD

July 8, 1741, stands out as a catalyst in American religious history.

The man of the hour? Not Whitefield, nor a Wesley, but the preacher known as Jonathan Edwards. On that day, before a large gathering in Enfield, Connecticut, Edwards—not even originally scheduled to speak—strode to the stage. He began to preach. And what a day of preaching it would be.

Speaking to the crowd, Edwards didn't pull any punches. God was displeased with his creation. The unrepentant—the outwardly wicked who rejected God, even those who were merely complacent—faced fearful judgment. Those who hadn't experienced an inward renewal or "awakening," as had many who had been converted during this time, were considered servants of the devil and therefore doomed. In his historic sermon "Sinners in the Hands of an Angry God," Edwards likened corrupt sinners to vermin suspended over the fiery pits of hell: "The wrath of God burns against them, their damnation does not slumber; the pit is prepared, the fire is made ready, the furnace is now hot, ready to receive them; the flames do now rage and glow. The glittering sword is whet, and held over them, and the pit hath opened its mouth under them."[58]

In Edwards's most enduring image, God dangles the sinner like "a spider, or some other loathsome insect," over this fire. Each of these metaphors reiterates how puny, weak, and disgusting the sinner is in the sight of God: there's no room for pride or justification. Sinners simply cannot be respectable or admirable—they must be "born again."[59]

Edwards's message includes themes that many Christian preachers use to this day: that all people are born sinners; that without salvation, sin will send a person to hell; all people can be saved if they confess their sins, seek forgiveness, and accept God's grace; all people can have a direct and emotional connection with God; and religion shouldn't be formal and institutionalized, but rather casual and personal.

But predestination—the belief that God's decision of whether one was heaven-bound or not had already been made—also reigned in early American Christian theology. Faced with the virtually insurmountable threshold of the preached message, the innate depravity of mankind, the teeming crowds often issued plaintive cries: "How then can we be saved? Tell us, please tell us!"[60]

Within this emotive field burned a fundamentalism not found in mainstream religion. Although these events brought huge and diverse segments of the populace together, they were often critiqued for their scenes of excessive emotional distress.[61] As Jonathan Edwards put in a letter to Thomas Prince, a pastor in Boston, "It was a very frequent thing to see a house full of outcries, faintings, convulsions and such like, both with distress and also with admiration and joy."[62]

The ambivalence of these evangelical events was not lost on the man who had come to know and admire George Whitefield—the curious yet cautious Benjamin Franklin. Personally, he liked the evangelist and acknowledged his impact on colonists, saying, "It was wonderful to see the Change soon made in the Manners [behavior] of our Inhabitants; from being thoughtless or indifferent about Religion, it seem'd as if all the World were growing Religious; as if from going to spiritually indifferent it seemed like the whole world was turning religious."[63] But Franklin also held certain reservations about "how much they admir'd and respected him, notwithstanding his common Abuse of them, by assuring them they were naturally half Beasts and half Devils."[64]

AWAKENING: A UNIFYING FORCE

The Great American Awakening in the mid-eighteenth century was full of sound and fury. Religious tent revivals. Fire and brimstone. Getting right with God. The likes of the Wesleys, Whitefield, Edwards, Gilbert Tennent, and James Davenport kindling a religious fervor never before seen in North America, if not the world. With electric simultaneity, the fervent preaching experienced in Philadelphia was shared by colonists in Enfield, Connecticut; Savannah, Georgia; Boston, Massachusetts; Charleston, South Carolina; and New York City.

Prior to these revivals, the colonies hadn't experienced such interconnectivity. The impact of bringing forth large crowds in state after state over a period of decades is inestimable. Despite the unworthiness heaped upon the masses, these charismatic "men of God" bound together the people of a yet unborn nation, generating some of the unifying passion that helped make the American republic possible.

To this day, the topic of the First Great Awakening brims with controversy for its lasting impact on American Christianity, particularly evangelicalism. The Great Awakening may have shed itself of the monarchical caste system of God to ruler to man, but it preserved several key elements from traditional, staid Christianity ("Old Light" religion), albeit with greater emotional intensity: biblical literacy, Christian supremacy, fear of hell, and salvation through belief in Jesus as savior and only son of God. Despite rejecting an "Old Light" approach, "New Light" adherents "retained sufficient composure to band together against such irredeemably lost souls as Muslims, Catholics and Jews."[65]

For all of the Great Awakening's enthusiasm and ability to bond the people of an emerging country, behind and beneath these loud, passionate expressions of religious fervor lay a more esoteric, contemplative, less boisterous counterpart, with its roots deep in a primordial spirituality that far preceded America's birth.

THE "INNER LIGHT"

Next unto God, Love is the Cause of Causes, itself without any Cause.
Francis Bacon, *Cupid and Coelum, On Principles and Origins*

Even as its influence swept over the American colonies, the First Great Awakening wasn't the sole spiritual force leading up to the revolution—perhaps, despite appearances, not even the dominant one.

Americans were beginning to dismiss the political, moral, and religious authority of the mother country, increasingly questioning the authority of mainstream religion inherited from the Old World. They found their own pathway to God and simultaneously questioned the divine right of the king. Both the Great Awakening and the Enlightenment promoted these ideas, the former unabashedly religious and the latter unorthodox, blending rationalism with a distinctly different spiritual heritage.

And nothing stood outside the bounds of orthodoxy more than Deism.

Deism is often cited as the cornerstone consciousness for the Age of Reason and the Enlightenment. Though its roots hearken back to ancient Egypt, Deism's inspiration can be found in the humanist tradition of the Renaissance and the revived interest in ancient Greece and Rome. But it is not a religion. Deism has no tenets, doctrines, bishops, popes, or church, and not much of a God to speak of. The classic notion of Deism is that God created the universe but then stopped interfering in the daily affairs of men. God is the "clockmaker" who wound up the universal clock and went home.

When Voltaire, a famed Deist, was accused of being godless, he responded: "It is perfectly evident to my mind that there exists a necessary, eternal, supreme, and intelligent being. This is no matter of faith, but of reason."[66] Deists of the time saw nature as the primary means of understanding the world, and when they referred to a deity, it was chiefly in terms of "Chief Architect," "grand designer," or "Providence."[67]

In ecumenical matters, Voltaire went far beyond his Great Awakening counterparts by tolerating other religious expression and ethnicities: "It does not require great art, or magnificently trained eloquence, to prove that Christians should tolerate each other. I, however, am going further: I say that we should regard all men as our brothers. What? The Turk my brother? The Chinaman my brother? The Jew? The Siam? Yes, without doubt; are we not all children of the same father and creatures of the same God?"[68]

Many key Enlightenment thinkers were deistic in their understanding of the divine. But Deism's heavily rationalistic approach tells an incomplete story of the spirituality behind the founders of the American Enlightenment. Influenced by an ancient heritage, their spiritual concepts, insights, practices, and "new thought" forms blossomed in the oxygen of the New World. In addition to Deism, their consciousness was largely grounded in esoteric philosophies that frequently transcended religion itself: Unitarianism, Freemasonry, Rosicrucianism, and the *inner light* of Quakerism. These perspectives often involved the leveling of all religions, seeing them as "different paths to the mountaintop."

Or would that be to the apex of a pyramid?

A HIDDEN MYSTICAL CORE?

While many endorse the notion that the founders were religious men and Christians, these are largely inaccurate conclusions. To be certain, most of the founders followed a spiritual path.[69] But almost to a person, they steadfastly opposed the idea of "a Christian nation." Steven Waldman, former *Newsweek* editor in chief and founder of BeliefNet, suggests America owes its religious freedoms to men and women with unorthodox views of God.[70] Mitch Horowitz, author of *Occult America*, indicates the founders had a mystical bent, leading them to seek "direct contact with spirit and the spirit world, without an intermediary religion or religious figure. That is, direct contact with the sacred outside of any prescribed religion."[71]

In his groundbreaking book *The American Soul: Rediscovering the Wisdom of the Founders*, Jacob Needleman asks, somewhat rhetorically, "Does America have a hidden mystical core?" The spirituality of some of America's earliest settlers, e.g. William Penn (whose mysticism is the subject of several biographies), George Fox, and the Quakers, "burned with a strangely intense light: *that of the inner life; silence, conscience.*"[72] They believed men should follow their inner guidance rather than the external rules of orthodoxy.

Quakers generally treated people equally, regardless of race, gender, or social status. These enlightened concepts merged fluidly with many of the Founding Fathers' affiliation with Freemasonry.[73] In addition to Quakerism, Needleman cites a "strong current of communal mysticism that took root in early colonial America," especially in communities in and around Philadelphia:

> Many of the ideals Americans now considered definitive of our nation were introduced and developed by these mystical communities. . . . For example the ideas of human equality and independence in these communities are rooted in the notion that God, or "the inner light," exists within every human being, and that the aim of life revolves around the endeavor and the necessity for every man or woman to make conscious contact with this inner divine force. This interior divinity—in William Penn's language, "the inner Christ"—is the source of true happiness, intelligence and moral capacity, and is meant to be the guide and ultimate authority in the conduct and assessment of our lives and obligations.[74]

It is precisely this demonstration of conscious awareness, a recognition of the inner light or inner Christ, that "initiated a divine contract when [the founders] created this nation. One that honors the natural laws of the human spirit,"[75] creating the understanding that America was as much an idea as a place.

But that notion didn't originate with European-born Americans.

"MORE A MYSTIC THAN A THEOLOGIAN"

Chased from his English homeland because he deemed the Church of England to be corrupt, he soon discovered his Puritan brethren in the New World were equally suspicious of his evolving ideas—spiritual and otherwise.

Roger Williams was a well-received preacher in 1630s Massachusetts, first in Boston and then in Plymouth. But he tangled with the colony's governor, principally because he established a relationship with the native Narragansett Indians and believed the colonists should purchase land from them, not steal it. For holding these and other erroneous, "diverse, new and dangerous" positions,[76] he was tried for sedition and heresy. Williams slipped away to form his own colony, meeting with and befriending various Indian tribes along the way.

The Narragansett Indians greeted him warmly in what today is Rhode Island. Finding a peaceful and suitable tract of land and believing he and his fellow settlers had been divinely led to this place, Williams purchased it from the natives and called it Providence.

Williams wanted his settlement to be a haven for "liberty of conscience." In his mind, civil government had no right to interfere with issues of religious belief. He is considered the first in modern history to create a government where citizenship and matters of conscience were separate, providing religious liberty. It was the advent of the separation of church and state. His colony became a refuge for people who were persecuted for their beliefs, including Baptists, Quakers, and Jews. Williams believed there needed to be a "wall or hedge of separation between the Garden of the Church and the Wilderness of the World,"[77] a concept that would be adapted by an even more famous, latter-day colonist.

Curiously, Williams attributed his inspiration for separation of church and state to the Indians. He believed that Native Americans would "never think of imposing personal religious values on civil society.[78] He interpreted their behavior as showing a distaste for telling others what to do, particularly in matters of the heart and spirit.[79] Their harmonious, egalitarian societies with little or no concept of personal property were enormously appealing to Williams, as was the fact that they were not beholden to kings or monarchs, and their political leaders acted democratically, in concert with the will of the community—lest they be removed.[80]

A century later, these ideas found favor with colonists who would eventually lead the American Revolution. Benjamin Franklin demonstrated an affinity for Native Americans because Williams had a great influence on him. The thread that connects Williams with the Founding Fathers is that "they all valued what they learned from their encounters with Native Americans: lessons about personal liberty, natural rights, economic equality, and religious and political freedom."[81]

Williams is fondly remembered because his advocacy for Native Americans impacted his novel approach to nature, religion, and government. He is considered "more of a mystic than a theologian; he was inclined towards the spirit rather than the letter of religion. His recognition of the 'indwelling God of Love in a world of material things' anticipated Emerson and the Concord school, as well as Unitarian, Unity, and other 'new thought' movements of the twentieth century."[82]

The profound influence of Native American spirituality on the United States is covered more deeply in Chapter 9's "Remember the Future." But the indebtedness of colonists to the Native American Indian for inspiring a template for government, equality, freedom of conscience, and diversity is historically evident. These "new Americans" owed much to Native Americans when they sought the unencumbered atmosphere of a new land unrestrained by convention, where they could think, believe, act—and breathe—freely.

THE OXYGEN OF
FREE-THINKING SPIRITUALITY

In fire it ended. And then, began.

Joseph Priestley's spiritual perspectives, religious commentary, and support of the American and French Revolutions incensed the rabble of his hometown of Birmingham, England, in 1791. Despite his considerable scientific reputation, his invention of carbonated water, his writings on electricity, and his discovery of several "airs" or gases (the most famous being oxygen), his scientific investigation into "why things

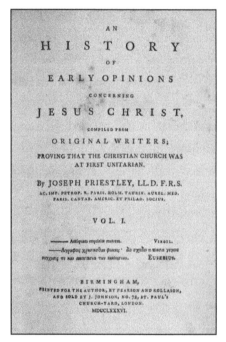

A History of Early Opinions Concerning Jesus Christ by Joseph Priestly

burn" ironically ended when an angry mob marched to his home and laboratory, then to his church, and torched them all. Disappointed in his country, he left England and began a new life in America. There, he believed, was a land open to the principles of the Enlightenment, providing the space for his scientific and spiritual exploration. He did not know how right he was—America was primed for his message.

Priestley's theology and scientific mind were intrinsically connected.

He wrote 150 texts and books, consistently trying to fuse Enlightenment rationalism with Christian theism in his metaphysical works.[83] One of them, *The Corruption of Christianity*, states that Jesus existed as a historical figure and was more or less what the New Testament made of him: a reformist and a rabbi who wanted to internalize the conscience but was not interested in the outward formalism of Orthodox Judaism.

The Jewish establishment and the Roman authorities crucified him, and a "Jesus cult" sprang up, following "the Way"—i.e., the noble intentions of this man.[84] Priestley's view was that the core story of Jesus had been distorted over time by formal religion. Emphasis on the miracles, original sin, and predestination found in Christianity took precedence over the good works laid out by Jesus himself.

From these assertions, Priestley became an early co-founder of the Unitarian church, or Unitarian "persuasion," in England and is its effective founder in the New World.[85] Some Unitarian communities initially sprang up during the Reformation in Eastern Europe before taking root in Britain and America. Unitarian philosophy was a blend of scientific rationalism and unitary, monotheistic theology, maintaining a concept of the oneness of God. From its inception, Unitarianism considered its Christology most similarly matched to that of the "original Christians," closer to the monotheism of Judaism or the concept of oneness in Islam. Along with its scientific and natural law approach, it attracted many of the freethinking rationalists of the day—including a number of noted founders.

"I TRUST THERE IS NOT
A YOUNG MAN NOW LIVING . . .
WHO WILL NOT DIE A UNITARIAN"

In the years before the American Revolution, Priestley struck up a warm friendship with fellow scientist and *philosophe* Benjamin Franklin in

London. In fact, Priestley's *History of Electricity* preserved Franklin's account of his famous kite and lightning experiments. Coming to America after the war, Priestley moved in a cosmopolitan circle of friends that included Franklin and fellow revolutionaries Thomas Jefferson, John Adams, and Thomas Paine.[86]

When Jefferson visited Philadelphia, he often attended Reverend Priestley's Unitarian congregation. He concurred with many of Unitarianism's principles, endorsing free will and rejecting original sin and eternal punishment in hell. Unitarians believe that the authors of the Bible were inspired by God but subject to human error—that no religion can claim an absolute monopoly on the Holy Spirit or theological truth. They also do not enforce belief in creeds or dogmatic formulas as a way of salvation. Although there is flexibility in the nuances of basic truths for the individual Unitarian, general principles of faith have been recognized as a way to bind the group in some commonality.[87]

In short, Unitarianism has always taught that reason, rational thought, science, and philosophy coexist with faith in God and that the life and teachings of Jesus Christ constitute the exemplar for living one's own life.

Spiritually, Unitarianism was within Jefferson's comfort zone because it aligned with Deism's principles and rational religion.[88] Though Jefferson never became an official member of any church, late in life he wrote to Unitarian minister Benjamin Waterhouse with his approval of, and future hopes for, Unitarian philosophy:

> The population of my neighborhood is too slender, and is too much divided into other sects to maintain any one preacher well. I must therefore be contented with being a Unitarian by myself. . . . I rejoice that in this blessed country of free inquiry and belief, which has surrendered its creed and conscience to neither kings

nor priests, the genuine doctrine of one only God is reviving, and I trust that there is not a young man now living in the United States who will not die a Unitarian.[89]

His hopeful prophecy did not come to fruition, at least not in his lifetime, but Jefferson boldly stated, "I confidently expect that the present generation will see Unitarianism become the general religion of the United States."[90]

"NOT, IN ANY SENSE, FOUNDED ON THE CHRISTIAN RELIGION"

Thomas Jefferson's commitment to religious freedom and the separation of church and state are reflected in his own beliefs and writings.[91] Along with James Madison, Jefferson fought against state financial support of churches in Virginia and for any house of worship to disseminate their literature as they pleased. Jefferson adapted Roger Williams's phrase, citing a "wall of separation between church and state" in his 1802 letter to the Danbury Baptists of Connecticut and later in an 1808 letter to Virginia Baptists. In those correspondences, Jefferson confirmed the Baptists' right to pray and think as they chose: "Believing with you that religion is a matter which lies solely between man and his god, that he owes account to none other for his faith or his worship . . . ."[92]

Jefferson's Virginia Statute of Religious Freedom served as a model for the religious freedom found in the Constitution's First Amendment. It was "meant to comprehend, within the mantle of its protection, the Jew and the Gentile, the Christian and the Mohammeden, the Hindoo and Infidel of every denomination."[93] Jefferson's innate curiosity led him to explore diverse religious and philosophical fonts, and he specifically wished to avoid the dominance of any single religion.[94]

Jefferson's approach was reminiscent of the Treaty of Tripoli with the Barbary pirates during John Adams's presidency, while Jefferson was vice president. Article 11 of the treaty was authored by Joel Barlow, an ardent Jeffersonian Republican, who wrote:

> As the Government of the United States of America is not, in any sense, founded on the Christian religion; as it has in itself no character of enmity against the laws, religion, or tranquility, of Mussulmen [Muslims]; and as the said States never entered into any war or act of hostility against any Mahometan [Mohammedan] nation, it is declared by the parties that no pretext arising from religious opinions shall ever produce an interruption of the harmony existing between the two countries.[95]

This article channels the wisdom of Jefferson's mentor John Locke, who insisted that Muslims and all others who believed in God be tolerated in England. Campaigning for religious freedom, Jefferson followed in the footsteps of his idol, demanding recognition of the religious rights of Jews and Muslims as well as pagans and followers of other faiths, thus creating what has aptly been described as "one nation under many gods." The Fifth Congress voted unanimously for the Treaty of Tripoli.

Jefferson actually owned a Koran, the holy book of Islam. In 2007, Muslim US congressman Keith Ellison placed his hand on Jefferson's Koran when he took his oath of office.[96]

ALL CLAIM THE SAGE
OF MONTICELLO

As the young nation matured, Jefferson became the precocious advocate of what would be called a "civil religion," the moral foundation of a truly free and united people.[97] Before he died, in a letter to John Adams he named the Unitarian Joseph Priestley and Conyers Middleton, an English Deist, as his religious inspirations.[98]

Authors, historians, conspiracy theorists, the religious, and the irreligious all have something to say about Jefferson's spirituality, perhaps to serve their own agendas. Was he simply a Deist? Jefferson's deity was not a clockmaker god—he believed that God actively engaged in time, sustaining creation on an ongoing basis.[99] A Christian? In his letters to Dr. Benjamin Rush, a friend and avowed Christian of his day, Jefferson considered the teachings of Jesus as having "the most sublime and benevolent code of morals which has ever been offered to man"[100] but questioned Jesus's divinity. An atheist? Far from it, though his unorthodox beliefs led many to define him as such, especially when it suited their purposes (e.g., during presidential elections). A Freemason? That's been debated for more than two centuries. While no documents suggest formal membership, it is known that he attended meetings at a prestigious lodge in France and that he marched in a Masonic procession in Charlottesville, Virginia. Similarly, there is no documented evidence that he was a Rosicrucian, but there are intriguing hints. Among them are his supposed use of a secret Rosicrucian communication code and his Rosicrucian-inspired, Kabbalistic design for building the University of Virginia.[101]

Jefferson's private beliefs may never be fully understood—or appreciated—except to say they were eclectic and diverged widely from the orthodox religion of his era. According to Jon Meacham in *American Gospel*, "Neither conventionally devout nor wholly unbelieving, Jefferson surveyed and staked out an American middle ground between the ferocity of evangelizing Christians on one side and the contempt for religion of secular philosophies on the other. The right would like Jefferson to be a soldier of faith, the left an American Voltaire."[102]

Whatever his personal beliefs ultimately were, Jefferson departed this life leaving clues. He made certain that he would be remembered for spiritual conscience. As our third president and author of the Declaration of Independence, he invoked the Supreme Being three times in that timeless, inspired document. When he wrote his epitaph, he cited the Virginia Statute for Religious Liberty (1779) above all his other accomplishments, save for penning the Declaration of Independence (1776) and founding the University of Virginia.

In the end, Jefferson most likely emulated one of his other great influences, Sir Francis Bacon, in following the Middle Way—a forerunner to what is now the fastest growing "religion" in the nation: the "spiritual but not religious."[103]

AMERICA'S MERLIN

When it came to matters of the spirit, Benjamin Franklin did not follow the script.

Franklin openly admired George Whitefield's evangelizing and kept a Bible in the top drawer of his desk at all times, making notations in the margins. But he attended Unitarian churches, believed in reincarnation, and touted astrology in his *Poor Richard's Almanac.* Franklin was so supple in matters of religion that he drove a frustrated John Adams to write, "The Catholics thought him almost a Catholic. The Church of England claimed him as one of them. The Presbyterians thought him half a Presbyterian, and the Friends believed him a wet Quaker."[104]

In a word, Franklin—like many of his founding colleagues—was a chameleon. His faith could not be pigeonholed. Franklin reserved the right to change his mind. It's no wonder that, much like Jefferson, diverse religions and persuasions throughout the ages have used Franklin for their own purposes.

Hailing from Boston, Franklin was raised Puritan. He was expected to read the Bible and practice aspects of Puritan faith as a young boy.[105] Franklin's parents originally intended him to join the ministry, but his questioning mind led him to doubt many of the Christian beliefs he had been taught. He moved from Massachusetts to Philadelphia largely due to his distrust in the region's Puritan fundamentalism. By his own estimation, he could not get out of Boston soon enough.

Franklin rejected his birth religion because "it was more interested in dogma than a moral life."[106] His difficulty with established religion "had to do with its incapacity to help individuals be of service to each other and its tendency to set people against each other, rather than to support the formation of community,"[107] thus "serving to divide us and make us unfriendly to one another."[108] He spoke and interacted with people of varying persuasions and, being politically adept, reserved judgment of others' beliefs. But clearly over the arc of his life he was far more comfortable with Deism, Unitarianism, Freemasonry, and Rosicrucianism, whose influences were all within his orbit.

While Franklin was running a business as a young man in Philadelphia, some men approached him with information they thought would irrefutably demonstrate the ills of Deism. In his autobiography he explains, "Some books against Deism fell into my hands. It happened that they wrought an effect on me quite contrary to what was intended by them; for the arguments of the Deists, which were quoted to be refuted, appeared to me much stronger than the refutations; in short, I soon became a thorough Deist."[109]

Deism's principle tenet, a natural theology based on reason, drew Franklin in; he saw "God as an eternal, transcendent force with divine intelligence, as the first cause; the architect behind the universe and natural laws."[110] Though Deism could be dryly logical—the God who created man and then left him on his own—the Deism of the early founders was broader than this two-dimensional caricature. Franklin came to epitomize the expanded version.

In 1731 Franklin became a Freemason. Within three years he was the grand master of all of Pennsylvania's Masons.[111] Although his Rosicrucian affiliation cannot be proven, he notably published the books of Johann Conrad Beissel, founder of Ephrata, Pennsylvania, the first Rosicrucian community in the New World. Franklin frequently visited this mystically oriented enclave.[112] The community was known for its "spreading of 'Ageless Wisdom' in America, and after its disbanding, most of its metaphysical library passed into Franklin's keeping."[113]

Franklin, like Thomas Jefferson, George Washington, and John Adams, was known to worship on occasion at Priestley's Unitarian church[114] but declined to align himself with any denomination. His creed was practical and simple: "I never doubted, for instance, the existence of the Deity; that he made the world, and govern'd it by his Providence; that the most acceptable service of God was the doing good to man; that our souls are immortal; I esteem'd the essentials of every religion; and, being to be found in all the religions we had in our country, I respected them all."[115] If others wanted to believe that Jesus was the only son of God, Franklin had no objection, especially if it made Jesus's teachings better respected.[116]

For all of his esoteric leanings, it was Franklin's appeal to conventional Christianity that may have saved the First Constitutional Convention of 1787. Meeting four years after the Revolutionary War officially ended, the convention was tasked to create a constitution that could be accepted and adhered to by all thirteen original colonies—and those that would follow. As with Jefferson's Declaration of Independence years earlier, no one was under the illusion that this Madison-inspired document would sail through unmolested. But after days of endless argument and stagnation, the convention's success appeared doubtful. With the nascent country hanging in the balance, Franklin called upon the bickering representatives from the colonies to pray, saying:

In the beginning of the Contest with Great Britain, when we were sensible of danger we had daily prayer in this room for the divine protection. Our prayers, Sir, were heard, & they were graciously answered. All of us who were engaged in the struggle must have observed frequent instances of a superintending providence in our favor. Have we now forgotten that powerful friend? I have lived, Sir, a long time, and the longer I live, the more convincing proofs I see of this truth—that God Governs in the affairs of men.[117]

Whether merely a ploy to appeal to the constituents' religious orthodoxy or, more likely, something that Franklin genuinely believed, the impasse broke, and America's Constitution became the law of the land. Several years later, the first ten amendments would be added, further guaranteeing the personal rights of its citizens, regardless of the state in which they lived or the religion they had adopted.

"A NEW AND MORE PERFECT EDITION"

Benjamin Franklin's belief in the continuity of life after death parallels Hermetic and perennial wisdom and echoes Rosicrucian and Freemason philosophies built on the metaphor of the human soul and successive lifetimes. Each incarnation is the opportunity to build upon the previous one, in its polishing of the human soul.[118]

Observing the great frugality of nature, which the deity designed to ensure that nothing once created was lost, Franklin supposed that something similar applied to souls: "Thus finding myself to exist in the world, I believe I shall, in some shape or form, always exist; and with all the inconveniences human life is liable to, I shall not object to a new edition of mine; hoping however that the errata of the last may be corrected."[119] This stance was true even early on in Franklin's life when, as a young man in 1728, he composed his own mock epitaph, which read:

THE BODY OF B. FRANKLIN PRINTER;

LIKE THE COVER OF AN OLD BOOK,

ITS CONTENTS TORN OUT,

AND STRIPT OF ITS LETTERING AND GILDING,

LIES HERE, FOOD FOR WORMS.

BUT THE WORK SHALL NOT BE WHOLLY LOST:

FOR IT WILL, AS HE BELIEV'D, APPEAR ONCE MORE,

IN A NEW & MORE PERFECT EDITION,

CORRECTED AND AMENDED

BY THE AUTHOR.

HE WAS BORN ON JANUARY 6, 1706.

DIED 17__[120]

To Franklin, life could take on many forms, even after the body expired. H. W. Brands in *The First American* quotes Franklin saying,

> A man is not completely born until he is dead. When then should we grieve that a new child is born among the immortals? We are spirits. That bodies should be lent to us, while they can afford us pleasure, assist us in acquiring knowledge or in doing good to our fellow creatures, is a kind and benevolent act of God. When they become unfit for these purposes and afford us pain instead of pleasure, instead of an aid become an encumbrance, it is equally kind and benevolent that a way is provided by which we may get rid of them. Death is that way.[121]

In Franklin's universe, death was not to be feared. When he was recovering from yet another malady in his eighties, his daughter exclaimed, "Oh thank goodness! May you live another ten years!" To which her father replied, "I should hope not!"[122]

When asked what form of government would work best for the young nation, Franklin's famous answer was "A republic, if you can keep it." Founding Father, diplomat, innovator, unorthodox believer, and visionary, perhaps that is why today some call him "America's Merlin."[123]

THE "SLY FOX"

Late in George Washington's second term, a group of clerics wrote him. They wanted answers.

Earlier in his life, Washington attended the Anglican Church. Later he became a vestryman in an Episcopal church. His wife, Martha, was known to be devout, reading sermons from the pulpit. That may have been the extent of Washington's conventional Christianity. His public statements spoke in broad, Deistic terms, referring to God as Providence, which was not a biblical term but was often associated with Washington's Deist, Freemason, and Unitarian compatriots. He very rarely mentioned Jesus and after the revolution did not receive Communion.[124] He often wrote as an outsider to the faith. In one letter to Lafayette he writes, "I'll give Christians that way to heaven that they find easiest."[125] And despite the many artistic renderings depicting it to be so—whilst alongside his horse—he was not known to kneel to pray.[126]

The clergymen who doubted Washington's Christian faith sent him a list of questions in hopes that he would clear up his stance on God and religion. When it came to answering as to whether he was a Christian or not, he simply skipped over it. Because of it, Jefferson referred to Washington as "the sly fox." Circumstances surrounding Washington's death should have later confirmed some of the clerics' doubts. The lack of religious context is striking: no religious words were spoken; no prayer; no asking for forgiveness; no farewell message; no hope for meeting in heaven. No call for a minister even though there was plenty of time to do so.[127]

Despite his upbringing and the strict religiousness of his wife, George Washington's spiritual proclivities can best be described as eclectic. In addition to attending Anglican and later Episcopal churches with Martha, Washington frequented Quaker, Jewish, Methodist, and Unitarian services. On one occasion, in his own words he attended "the Presbyterian meeting in the forenoon and the Romish Church in the afternoon."[128]

Just as he abhorred sectarian bickering within his cabinet, Washington had little stomach for religious factionalism and went to great lengths to repair relations between Catholics and Protestants. In his day Roman Catholics were a religious minority and viewed with great suspicion. He wrote to Thomas Carroll, the first Catholic bishop in the new United States, lauding Catholics for their patriotism and assuring Carroll of the church's place in the nation: "All those who conduct themselves as worthy members of the Community are equally entitled to the protection of civil Government." Washington socialized

Washington as Freemason

with prominent Catholics while he lived in Mount Vernon and during his presidency. He even donated money towards the construction of a Catholic church in Baltimore.[129]

Revealing his stand for ecumenism, ethical principles, and social duty, George Washington became a member of the Mason brotherhood. He was initiated into the Masonic Lodge of Fredericksburg, Virginia, in 1752[130] and became America's most prominent thirty-third-degree Freemason. Little is known about his adherence to strict Masonic practices such as the secret handshakes and code words, but he clearly accepted Masonic ritual. In his public pronouncements, Washington emphasized that America was founded on the precept of religious freedom, which is a core ecumenical, Freemason concept. In his vision for the nation, he went well beyond mere tolerance of differing beliefs. He saw religious variety and independence as a blessing to and strength of the new nation.[131]

NO TOLERANCE FOR TOLERATION

One story may best reflect Washington's attitude towards religious liberty and ideals.

Shortly after Rhode Island ratified the US Constitution in 1790, Washington and much of his cabinet visited the state and met with the town of Newport's leading citizens. Some of them were members of local religious denominations present in the city, including those of the Jewish faith.[132] One of the officials of Yeshuat Israel, the first Jewish congregation in Newport, expressed concern to Washington. He wanted a guarantee of "liberty of conscience."

Days later, the president responded by letter to members of the synagogue, addressing the notion of religious tolerance. Quoting the Old Testament, Washington wrote, "Every one shall sit in safety under his own vine and fig tree, and there shall be none to make him afraid." And then further:

It is now no more that toleration is spoken of, as if it were the indulgence of one class of people that another enjoyed the exercise of their inherent natural rights, for happily the Government of the United States gives to bigotry no sanction, to persecution no assistance, requires only that they who live under its protection should demean themselves as good citizens, in giving it on all occasions their effectual support.[133]

Washington was unequivocal: our spiritual independence is innate, a God-given—not government-given—right, though it is up to government to safeguard such rights. Further, Washington made it clear that minority religions were full members at the table of the United States.

"THAT DIABOLICAL HELL . . . OF PERSECUTION"

Another founder who rejected the notion of tolerance was the nation's fourth president, James Madison, architect of the Constitution. One of Madison's key contributions to the founding of the new nation was the sacrosanct protection of religious liberty. Although likely a Mason with deistic tendencies, Madison, unlike many of his contemporaries, kept his personal religious views to himself. The greater force behind his work appears to be on behalf of those seeking guarantee of freedom for their spiritual expression. In that regard Madison did not disappoint.

Several years prior to the revolution, as a young lawyer Madison rode to a prison in Culpeper County, Virginia, where six Baptist preachers had been jailed—all for preaching and publishing their religious views, which were at odds with the mainstream Anglicanism of the region.[134] He was appalled. "That diabolical Hell[-]conceived principle of persecution rages among some," he wrote to his friend William Bradford. "This vexes me the most of any thing whatever."[135] This event fueled his passion and action for defense of religious liberty that lasted well into his eighties.

Months before the Declaration of Independence was written,

published, and passed, the new Commonwealth of Virginia created its own constitution. The document contained a Declaration of Rights with a clause on religious liberty, penned by George Mason. The original clause declared that "all men should enjoy the fullest toleration in the exercise of religion, according to the dictates of conscience."[136]

All well and good, right? Not for Madison. As Washington would later demonstrate in the Rhode Island synagogue matter, Madison believed the word *tolerance* implied that such freedom was a government-sponsored right, when in fact, according to Madison and the founders who shared the ideal, religious liberty—liberty of conscience—was an inalienable right. It was a natural right of man to believe in the God of his or her choice. Or none at all. Madison's insistence on its inclusion in Virginia's constitution amounted to a trial run for what would be the cornerstone of the US Constitution's First Amendment.

QUAKER, DEIST, COMMON SENSE

As it turned out, his pen was mightier than the sword.

Thomas Paine published *Common Sense* in January 1776, just months before the revolution. It eventually sold more than 150,000 copies, unheard of in his day. Writing his arguments in simple and understandable form, Paine appealed to the masses. Incontrovertibly, it was the literary spark behind the American Revolution.

Paine was not an atheist as some have labeled him. He was raised a Quaker, which influenced his fierce commitment to radical equality and a hatred of privilege. Over time, he came to prefer Deism, finding his deity in "the divine geometry of nature." He believed that a revolution in religion would follow a revolution in politics.[137]

Unlike *Common Sense*, Paine's other books, *The Rights of Man* and *The Age of Reason*, written after the French Revolution, disconcerted many. On one hand they constituted a strong defense of the liberty of the individual against the power of both church and state. People were created equal, Paine wrote, in the image of God—and any distinctions between kings and commoners were therefore a perversion of divine intent. At the same time, these books were "considered to be attacks on religion. Paine argued that people seeking knowledge of the divine needed to look not to scripture, but to creation. He referred to science as 'the true theology.'"[138]

Scientific discovery in the late eighteenth century, especially in astronomy, demonstrated the vastness of our solar system and the countless galaxies beyond. Reflecting on these empirical revelations, Paine said: "To believe that God created a plurality of worlds, at least as numerous as what we call stars, renders the Christian system of faith at once little and ridiculous." After all, why would God have singled out one small planet, and the inhabitants of one earthly tribe, to favor with special attention?[139]

Paine's popularity crested with the American Revolution, deteriorating over time. Even some of his staunchest allies distanced themselves because of his stance on religion; only a handful of people showed up to his funeral in 1809 to pay their respects.

ONE BITE FROM AN APPLE

He was no lover of Thomas Paine, and was likely the most religiously devout of the founders.

A dedicated churchgoer, John Adams believed that the Bible was the best of all books. He believed that Christianity was an indispensable guarantor of public morality. Although Adams may have fashioned himself as a true believer, he didn't act like one. He refuted Catholicism and other basic tenets of Christian orthodoxy, including Calvinism, which emphasized the depravity of man. Adams rejected the First

Great Awakening's premises of original sin and the doctrine of predestination.[140] He proclaimed, "I refuse to accept that one bite from an apple damned the whole human race, without any actual crimes committed by any of them."[141] The theory of atonement—that God sacrificed his son to save humanity from its sins—was not part of Adams's theology.[142] Eventually Adams joined a liberal Unitarian church that emphasized Christ's teachings rather than his divinity.

The American religious story in one sense remains true: our country was and is a nation built on religious diversity and pluralism. Those that politically and militarily fought for independence from Great Britain did not hold identical spiritual views. However, "if census takers had set up broad categories labeled 'Atheism,' 'Deism and Unitarianism,' 'orthodox Protestantism,' 'orthodox Roman Catholicism,' and 'Other' and if they had interviewed Monroe, Franklin, Washington, Adams, Jefferson, and Madison, they would undoubtedly have placed every one of these six Founding Fathers . . . under the category of 'Deism and Unitarianism.'"[143]

"LET THINE EYE BE SINGLE"

It's little wonder that when it came time to choose the Great Seal of the United States, its symbolism was tied to the esoteric.

A common bond among many—although certainly not all—of the founders was their membership or interaction with the Masonic Brotherhood. Its early influence on the founders' thinking cannot be underestimated. The hallmark of the Masonic Brotherhood at the time was radical ecumenism, the belief that all faiths have value. That notion is mostly commonplace today but was definitely a revolutionary idea at the time. At least eight and as many as twenty-one signers of the Declaration of Independence were Masons.[144]

At the time of America's founding, the Masonic lodges were very different from the social clubs many have become today. They developed common values and purposes among members as well as deep bonds of loyalty. Free-masonry was considered a spiritual force which sought to improve men morally and spiritually through association with other idealistic men who wanted to improve the quality of life around them. Its members studied the principles involved in attaining a universal brotherhood of man, emphasizing the truths of morality, justice, patriotism, and the necessity of brotherly love to achieve those universal ideals.

The traditional secrecy preserved in the lodges would have allowed members to communicate and organize the uprising that would become the revolution with little fear of exposure. This has long been the most accepted explanation for Masonry's role in the founding of our nation. But secrecy alone doesn't explain why it provided the structure of the US Constitution, or why the distinct brand of federalism created by the Constitution is identical to that of the Masonic Grand Lodge created in 1723.[145]

Many historians note that the Constitution and the Bill of Rights both seem to have been heavily influenced by the Masonic "civil religion" focus on freedom, free enterprise, and a limited role for the state.[146] The reason so many founders were Masons was because it appealed to their deep-seated belief in free will, democracy, and the brotherhood of man.

Not only were the Founding Fathers influenced by the ecumenism as promulgated by the Masons, but they also appropriated a means of visually conveying these metaphysical principles.

Adams, Jefferson, and Franklin were originally charged with the creation of the Great Seal. When it was finally finished, its roots were obvious. On the reverse side is the Freemason-inspired pyramid symbol. Today it graces the back of our one-dollar bill, as it has for decades.

According to radio talk personality and author Thom Hartmann,

"The eye atop the Egyptian pyramid is a design handed down by our Christian-mystic founding fathers."[147] Corinne McLaughlin of the Center for Visionary Leadership and author of *Spiritual Politics* has said the reverse of the Great Seal "is a powerful symbol of the soul of America," with roots in European Rosicrucianism and Freemasonry: it is the

Eye of Providence, Reverse of the Great Seal of the United States

All-Seeing Eye of God, the Eye of Providence, sitting atop the pyramid. Above and below are the words *Annuit Coeptus* ("God Favors Our Undertakings") and *Novus Ordo Seclorum* ("New Order of the Ages").[148]

The founders' preoccupation with ancient Egyptian symbolism—from obelisks to pyramids to the eye of Horus—speaks of one root source or origin. The eye also calls to mind a rather obscure New Testament reference: "Let thine eye be single and thy whole body shall be full of light" (Matthew 6:22).

Pilloried through the centuries by orthodox, traditional, and evangelical religious figures—not to mention Illuminati conspiracy theorists—Masonry is a pale reflection of what it once was. At the time of the revolution, Masonic brothers pledged to support one another and provide sanctuary if needed. The fraternity embodied European Enlightenment ideals of liberty, autonomy, and God as envisioned by Deist philosophers.[149]

While the Masons captured the allegiance of much of the early republic's elite, the group fell under widespread suspicion. The William Morgan Affair of 1826 (when a former Mason broke ranks and promised to expose the group's secrets) signaled its eventual downfall. Morgan was allegedly abducted and presumed killed by Masons, and the scandal proved a low point in the public image of the fraternal order.[150] The Masons' nineteenth-century association with the Confederacy further hastened its demise.

BUT FOUNDING . . . "MYSTICS"?

Admittedly, the notion of "Founding Mystics" is anathema to some. The word *mystic* and its corollary concepts come with a lot of baggage. There's certainly no suggestion that our founders cloistered themselves, consistently looking for and recognizing the divinity in their fellow man. Certainly they were not that kind of mystic.

But the notion of mysticism or what constitutes being a mystic has changed dramatically over the centuries. In light of the broad, worldwide investigation of mysticism—beginning with William James's examination over a century ago—our approach to and appreciation of the mystical has changed. The mystics that history now venerates often play against type. They were not only inwardly focused but also outwardly expressive. They were pragmatic in the sense that they took the value of their inner awakenings and became men and women of action.

Did the founders acknowledge or have an appreciation for the transcendent beyond religious dogma? Did they acknowledge spiritual truths beyond the intellect? Are they the prototype of a modern mystic today who seeks the sacred outside the bounds of organized religion and yet walks and interacts within the world?

Are their proclivities the template for today's "spiritual but not religious"?

There is more than enough evidence to suggest that innumerable founders were this kind of mystic: proponents of an inwardly directed, all-inclusive spirituality that many of them envisioned, practiced, and protected. These beliefs and practices shaped their desire for a nation free of state religion, a nation where diverse spiritual expression was encouraged—something far beyond mere tolerance. Without freedom of conscience, there was no foundation upon which to build a nation. "The Religion then of every man," Madison wrote, "must be left to the conviction and conscience of every man to exercise it as these may dictate."[151]

America was envisioned as a new land—culturally, politically, and spiritually. The founders were conscious of the impact their actions would have on future generations, what Washington referred to as "unborn millions."[152] Although neither the First Great Awakening nor the Enlightenment could be relegated to merely one category, it could be argued that proponents of the former represented more of the "engine" of passion and emotion behind the revolution, and it was the visionaries of the latter who largely steered it with their conscience and reasoning.

That combination helped forge the nation but also set the stage for the next step in the republic's evolution: an internal showdown that still colors the American soul today.

— ✳ —

CHAPTER THREE

Great Awakening 2.0 and the Transcendental Highway

A state of mind that sees God in everything is evidence of growth in grace and a thankful heart.

Charles Grandison Finney, 1830s

The highest revelation is that God is in every man.

Ralph Waldo Emerson, 1832

"LIKE A WAVE OF ELECTRICITY GOING THROUGH ME . . . IN WAVES OF LIQUID LOVE"

Standing atop a hillside in Upstate New York with a breeze blowing lightly through his hair, the man who came to define America's Second Great Awakening, the Reverend Charles Grandison Finney, surveyed his audience. His eyes—"large and blue, at times mild as an April sky, and at others, cold and penetrating as polished steel"—peered out upon the crowd; he stepped forward.[153] In his grand baritone, he exhorted the gathering: "Salvation is the beginning of a life of good works here on earth! Man can achieve his own salvation. God is not angry! God is merciful and loving. Therefore, go forth, and *do* as well as *believe!*"

Before a handful of students, faculty, and friends, Ralph Waldo Emerson—a contemporary of Finney's and the man who would come to epitomize the Transcendentalist movement—stepped upon the stage at Harvard Divinity School, from which he had graduated years earlier. Students had asked him to address the theological challenges facing the next generation of clergy. Foregoing any artificiality of religious language, Emerson likened divinity to nature, underscored intuition as the direct connection to the divine, and declared that Jesus Christ "belonged to the true race of prophets because he saw with an open eye the mystery of the soul."[154]

Finney and Emerson came to realize that moving the faithful forward with new interpretations of divinity is never an easy feat. Indeed, it often proves dangerous to the prophet. They both abandoned the voice of safety, of the status quo, which seemingly stands guard at the gate of human evolution. They received adulation and scorn for their insights and came to symbolize two intertwining spiritualities that were as different in nature as they were similar in impact.

Both the Second Great Awakening and the Transcendentalist movement would open America to intense national self-examination.

By the time Finney and Emerson appeared on the scene, the succeeding generation had taken up the reins of government from the original revolutionaries. John Quincy Adams, son of the second president, ascended to the executive office in 1825. After America finally ridded itself of the British by the end of the War of 1812, no strong, natural, and present enemy lay outside the country's boundaries. The British, French, and Spanish specters had largely disappeared. Manifest Destiny, the "God-given right" of an America spanning from the Atlantic to the Pacific, was within the grasp of the young nation. Save for the frontier and the American Indian, there were no immediate threats. With no significant external "other," the nation soon came face-to-face with the enemy within.

Finney, a Presbyterian preacher, utilized the talents he had polished as a trial lawyer. As a young attorney, he experienced what he called "a mighty baptism of the Holy Ghost," which "like a wave of electricity going through and through me . . . seemed to come in waves of liquid love." The next morning, he informed his first client of the day, "I have a retainer from the Lord Jesus Christ to plead his cause and I cannot plead yours." Leaving the practice of law, Finney began conducting revivals in Upstate New York. One of his most popular sermons, based on his essay, was "Sinners Bound to Change Their Own Hearts."[155]

Listeners needed look no further than the title of Finney's tract to see that this was not their father's Great Awakening. Here was a message of hope and opportunity. Religion was not only revived; it was transformed. God was not filled with vengeance for his creation. Gone were the warnings that man was "predestined" to salvation or damnation. The amazing assurance that life on earth had its own rewards and was not just a way station on the road to heaven or hell touched people's hearts. And they rushed to hear it.[156]

The crux of Finney's position was that human nature is not intrinsically sinful and that human beings are not "passive in regeneration." Rather, human beings have the ability to choose righteously when the truth is presented to them in language they can understand. He based his views about sin and salvation on his reading of the Bible and rejected the authority of a church to apply a doctrinal overlay on the scriptures. "I was quite willing to believe what I found taught in the Bible," he said— even when it contradicted the Presbyterian doctrines, in particular those of predestination and original sin.[157]

The new movement's rejection of the strict Calvinism of Jonathan Edwards helped create a tapestry of uniquely American religions. Imported from the Old World, these religions experienced a series of mitoses, continuing to evolve and split off. This created a fertile ground of multiple American spiritual expressions—the exact outcome the founders thought healthy in building a diverse, democratic nation.

At the start of the revolution, the largest denominations were Congregationalists (the eighteenth-century descendants of Puritan churches), Anglicans (known after the revolution as Episcopalians), and Quakers. By the early 1800s, however, Evangelical Methodism and Baptists became the fasting growing religions in the nation. Thereafter, new religions emerged, from Adventism and Mormonism[158] to a spate of "New Thought" religions that would blossom later in the nineteenth century. This resurgence strengthened appreciation for diversity and prevented the possibility that any one religion would dominate, fundamentally altering the face of American religion.

"NEW MEASURES" AND A DEMOCRATIC MOOD

An area around central New York and along the Erie Canal provided the launching pad for the Second Great Awakening. It became known as the Burned-Over District because of its association with Pentecostal fervor and conversion. Finney's God may have been less angry than Edwards's God, but Finney's approach was not without its own melodramatic outpourings.

The "new measures" of circuit-rider evangelical preachers—from James McGready to Peter Cartwright, Francis Asbury, Lorenzo Dow, and Lyman Beecher—included emotional tactics that led to fainting and weeping, like the "anxious bench," a precursor to today's altar call.[159] Large crowds under the big tent shared an overtly zealous religious experience. Huge, ecstatic camp meetings saw people speaking in tongues, falling down, shaking, shouting, and crying out in display of or in the manner of a more active evangelical form of Christianity. Early in the movement, a young man who attended a 20,000-person revival at Cane Ridge, Kentucky, captured the spirit of these camp meeting activities and what was to come:

> The noise was like the roar of Niagara. The vast sea of human beings seemed to be agitated as if by a storm. I counted seven ministers, all preaching at one time, some on stumps, others on wagons. . . . Some of the people were singing, others praying, some crying for mercy. A peculiarly strange sensation came over me. My heart beat tumultuously, my knees trembled, my lips quivered, and I felt as though I must fall to the ground.[160]

This was not religion for just the elite, either. One of the distinguishing factors between the First and Second Great Awakening was the "democratic" mood of the latter's gatherings. The itinerant preachers who traversed the terrain in Ohio, Kentucky, Indiana, and Tennessee came from among the common people. This helped circuit riders establish rapport with the frontier families they hoped to convert. The Second Great Awakening was a democratized religious experience not only because it rejected predestination (i.e., anyone had a chance of salvation) but also because women and Black Americans were able to participate in these revivals far more than in the preceding awakening.

Case in point: Jarena Lee. Born in Cape May, New Jersey, in 1783 a poor, free Black woman, she experienced conversion in her teens by Richard Allen, founder of the African Methodist Episcopal (AME) Church. Considering herself "a wretched sinner" who had contemplated suicide a number of times, Lee spent three months in prayer and repentance. She then felt worthy of baptism.[161] Soon after, she began hearing voices telling her, "Go preach the Gospel! Preach the Gospel! I will put words in your mouth." But Allen said that there was no provision for women to preach in the AME Church. Still, Lee persisted. "If the man may preach, because the Savior died for him, why not the woman, seeing he died for her also? Is he not a whole Savior, instead of half of one?"[162]

It took years, but Lee got her chance. Attending a service where a man was preaching from the book of Jonah, she perceived that he had "lost the spirit." Spontaneously, she took over:

When in the same instant, I sprang, as by altogether supernatural impulse, to my feet when I was aided from above to give an exhortation on the very text which my brother Williams had taken. I told them I was like Jonah; for it had been then nearly eight years since the Lord had called me to preach his gospel to the fallen sons and daughters of Adam's race, but that I had lingered like him, and delayed to go at the bidding of the Lord, and warn those who are as deeply guilty as were the people of Ninevah.

I now sat down, scarcely knowing what I had done, being frightened. I imagined, that for this indecorum, as I feared it might be called, I should be expelled from the church. But instead of this, the Bishop [Allen] rose up in the assembly, and related that I had called upon him eight years before, asking to be permitted to preach, and that he had put me off; but that now he as much believed that I was called to that work, as any of the preachers present.[163]

Lee became the first woman authorized to preach in Great Awakening revivals. Traveling thousands of miles to Ohio and later to Canada, she passed through dangerous slaveholding towns to sermonize. Though ostracized, she stood up to church leaders of her day, asserting the right to preach using her God-given gift. In rebuttal to questioning of her female ministry, she responded, "Did not Mary *first* preach the risen Savior?"[164]

By the 1830s, at about the same time Finney and Emerson were causing spiritual fusses of their own, Jarena Lee wrote *The Life and Religious Experience of Jarena Lee*, becoming the first African-American woman to publish an autobiography in the United States. Shortly thereafter, she joined the American Antislavery Society and then republished her autobiography in the next decade. Lee passed away during the American Civil War.

EVANGELICAL LIBERATORS

For all of the conservatism associated with the Second Great Awakening and its predominant influences on modern evangelicalism, the movement was out front in addressing America's original sin: slavery. In many ways, its religious fervor catalyzed the radical abolition movement of the 1830s. Preacher William Lloyd Garrison was one of the first to loudly advance the notion of slaveholding as sin. Garrison embraced fiery evangelist Lyman Beecher's vision of reform and became one of the nation's most eloquent proponents of abolition.

Almost three decades before the Civil War, two prominent New York City evangelical merchants, Arthur and Lewis Tappan, funded Garrison's newspaper in Boston, *The Liberator*. Noted for his boldness and strident journalism, Garrison announced in his new publication, "I do not wish to think, or speak, or write, with moderation. . . . I am in earnest—I will not equivocate—I will not excuse—I will not retreat a single inch—AND I WILL BE HEARD."[165] Garrison believed America stood "on a great precipice, ready to plunge into darkness," charging that slavery was at the very root of the American dilemma. He declared it to be "the bellwether of America's fidelity to its covenant with God."[166]

Ironically, as Garrison's call for abolition amplified, a growing number of Christian churches, especially those in the South, began favoring certain passages in scripture to justify slavery. As Garrison started winning the enthusiastic support of many he had "once condemned as irreligious, including Quakers, Unitarians and Freethinkers,"[167] he came to realize he could not wholly rely on his evangelical compatriots to further the cause of emancipation. On one occasion, Garrison searched in vain for a church or hall in Boston in which to speak. Former mentor Lyman Beecher refused to assist him, fearing Garrison had gone too far in his radical approach and dismissing Garrison's calls for abolition as "misguided."[168] Even Charles Finney, for all his egalitarianism, rebuffed a protégé who attempted to integrate religious services after the Civil War. He said, "You err in supposing the principle of abolition and amalgamation are identical."[169]

Nevertheless, many Northern Christian churches were, socially, on the move. They not only engaged in efforts to end slavery but also initiated other social reforms. Second Great Awakening reforms shaped the temperance movement and inevitably women's rights and suffrage as well; women constituted a large part of these volunteer societies. The Female Missionary Society and the Maternal Association, highly active in New York, were astutely organized and financially sophisticated women's organizations. Social activists also began efforts to reform prisons and care for the handicapped and mentally ill. In many cases, social activism merged with evangelical conversion.

Many participants in the revival meetings believed that reform was part of God's plan. In order to achieve salvation, the faithful not only had to repent of their own sins but also had to help move society towards both personal and societal liberation from sin.

THE MORE THINGS CHANGED . . .

Although their God may have been kinder and gentler than that of the First Great Awakening, the evangelicals of the Second Great Awakening held on to critical aspects of their predecessors. Lyman Beecher reminded his flock of its inherent sinful nature and "decried the moral decay of society and warned that if reformation did not occur, the nation's doom was assured."[170] Man was still a prisoner to his body and its drives: "The will is, in a sense, enslaved by the carnal and worldly desires," Finney said in his *Lectures on Revival of Religion*, "hence it is necessary to awaken men to a sense of guilt and danger, and thus produce an excitement of counter feeling and desire which will break the power of carnal and worldly desire and leave the will free to obey God."

Themes of sin, repentance, redemption, and salvation dominated camp meetings as well. Finney convinced his audiences of their personal guilt and need for a savior. Those who did not accept Jesus Christ as their personal savior would suffer damnation, eternal separation from God. [171]

The doctrine of being "saved" solely through Christ not only survived from earlier times; its role expanded. The second coming of Jesus became a central theme. Talk of millennialism, apocalypse, revelation, and rapture, relatively new concepts within Christianity, became an open-tent staple that still predominates evangelical circles today.

There was something else the Second Great Awakening shared with its eighteenth-century antecedent: rejecting the skepticism, Deism, Unitarianism, and rationalism of the American Enlightenment.[172] Finney spurned the secular arguments set forth by the Universalists that questioned the morality of a God who punishes sin with eternal abandonment. He viewed God's government as righteous in its punishment of those who, in the face of the truth, reject Christ and follow the way of evil. Finney also decried the perennial wisdom that ran through one of Transcendentalism's forbears, Freemasonry, which he called, referencing Ephesians, "the unfruitful works of darkness."[173]

In the end, the Second Great Awakening would impact the nation in ways similar to its forerunner in the previous century—holding on to the fundamental, all the while igniting monumental change. The Second Great Awakening accelerated the coming of the Civil War and associated social upheaval. At the same time, this evangelical awakening ran concurrent with an esoteric spiritual awakening that was ready to burst.

"I AM DIVINE. THROUGH ME, GOD ACTS."

Though the speech was delivered to but a small gathering in 1838, its impact was immense. Ralph Waldo Emerson's "Harvard Divinity School Address," as it became known, would shift the spiritual landscape of the youthful nation, creating fissures in its religious development and fostering a distinctly American cultural identity.[174] Because of the address, many mainstream and conservative religious thinkers of the day condemned Emerson. Their almost universal reaction took him by surprise. As for Harvard, Emerson would not be invited back to speak for another thirty years.

As a former Unitarian minister, Emerson came to represent something beyond the type of "liberal Christianity" that Unitarianism had become. In a way, his Harvard address was a prophecy, a symbol of spiritual evolution that went beyond Western religious traditions: it heralded the leveling of all religions, inferred the divinity of nature as proof of God's providence, and, long before the advent of a Carl Jung or Joseph Campbell, characterized Jesus as the Everyman on his own hero's journey. The Harvard Divinity School Address underscored the Emersonian philosophy that each person's unique spiritual journey transcends bodies, lifetimes, births, and deaths—evolving both within and outside time and space.

Emerson had "argued similar points in earlier speeches and essays . . . [but] never before had he offered such a direct challenge to mainstream Christianity."[175] Emerson's take on the divinity of the man Jesus in July 1838—and how it pertains to each of us—is likely what stirred the hornet's nest of criticism:

> Jesus Christ belonged to the true race of prophets. He saw with open eye the mystery of the soul. Drawn by its severe harmony, ravished with its beauty, he lived in it, and had his being there. Alone in all history, he estimated the greatness of man. *One man was true to what is in you and me* [emphasis mine]. He saw that God incarnates himself in man, and evermore goes forth anew to take possession of his world. He said, in this jubilee of sublime emotion, "I am divine. Through me, God acts; through me, speaks. Would you see God, see me; or, see thee, when thou also thinkest as I now think."[176]

Little wonder the clerics of his day—even so-called liberal Unitarians—

were angry. Emerson went well beyond arguing the notion that the divine speaks from within each of us: to him, Jesus was a way-shower, perhaps *the* way-shower, but ultimately no different than the rest of us. That concept demonstrated the root of a radically "democratic sentiment," one "antithetical to a tradition that took Jesus as the exemplar [or exception] rather than one example among many."[177] As with Jefferson before him, Emerson would be labeled an atheist, not for his lack of belief in a God but for his nonconforming views of spirituality and religion, particularly Christianity.[178]

But the backlash did not deter him. Three years after the Divinity School address, Emerson wrote his spiritual opus, "The Over-Soul." Often overshadowed by his "Self-Reliance" essay of the same vintage, "The Over-Soul" examines the soul's immortal nature, how we mistake our ego-body for our true self and how at some level all human souls are connected and God exists within the human soul:

> We live in succession, in division, in parts, in particles. Meantime within man is the soul of the whole; the wise silence; the universal beauty, to which every part and particle is equally related, the eternal ONE. And this deep power in which we exist and whose beatitude is all accessible to us, is not only self-sufficing and perfect in every hour, but the act of seeing and the thing seen, the seer and the spectacle, the subject and the object, are one. We see the world piece by piece, as the sun, the moon, the animal, the tree; but the whole, of which these are shining parts, is the soul.[179]

A quote by Albert Einstein a century later uncannily parallels Emerson's sentiment: "A human being is a part of a whole called by us 'the universe,' a part limited in time and space. He experiences himself, his thoughts and feelings as something separated from the rest. A kind of optical delusion of his consciousness."[180]

These ideals are synonymous with Transcendentalist individualism as each person is empowered to behold within herself a piece of the divine oversoul. The influence of Eastern religions, including Vedantism, are plainly evident in Emerson's work, but his essays are also influenced by Western tradition: the works of Plato, Plutarch, the Neoplatonists, and the writings of the Christian mystic Emanuel Swedenborg.[181]

Whether he liked it or not, Emerson would become the preeminent face and voice of the young transcendental movement. Its very nature defied precise definition or universality of thought, though it would come to be described as "an influential group of authors, philosophers, poets, and scholars who rejected the primacy of institutions in favor of the individual, intuitive thought, and the role of nature in helping man to understand the divine."[182]

THE "LIKE-MINDED" CLUB

If you really want to know what the Founders thought,
look to the Transcendentalists.

Mitch Horowitz

Despite mainstream religious criticism, Emerson's supporters and contemporaries grew in number and stature. The Transcendental Club, formed by Emerson and others in 1836, became the intellectual salon of its day. Luminaries such as Henry David Thoreau, Margaret Fuller, George Ripley, Theodore Parker, Emily Cady Stanton, Amos Bronson Alcott and his daughter Louisa May Alcott (*Little Women*), and Walt Whitman (*Leaves of Grass*) would, at some point, become associated with the Transcendentalist movement or the "like-minded club." But what brought them together also set them apart. Reverend James Freeman Clarke, a Unitarian clergyman, wittily noted, "They called themselves 'the club of the like-minded' primarily because 'no two . . . thought alike.'"[183]

On a purely philosophical level, there was much to agree upon. The hallmark of American Transcendentalism was spiritual unity with

God, man, and nature, all sharing a universal soul. Unlike their Second Great Awakening counterparts, Transcendentalists believed that man was inherently good. The prime principle of Transcendentalism was "the substantive, independent existence of the soul of man, reality of conscience . . . the inner light . . . his love for beauty and holiness . . . not dependent on education, custom, command or anything beyond man himself."[184]

Transcendentalism taught that every man had the instinctive capacity to know right from wrong, good from bad, God from Satan.[185] Man's ideas and inspiration were not limited to "the five senses, or the powers of reasoning; but are either the result of direct revelation from God, his immediate inspiration or his immanent presence in the spirit world."[186] Man's access to the divine was intuitive, not learned. There was no need of confirmation from holy scriptures, books, or venerated teachers. Rather they had only to listen to "the teachings of [their] own souls, the light that shines within [them]."[187]

TRANSCENDENTALISM: "ANOTHER AMERICAN REVOLUTION"

As the Grandison Finneys and Lyman Beechers moved beyond the George Whitefields and Jonathan Edwards in their version of an American awakening, so too did the Transcendentalists up the ante over their predecessors: Emerson and his cohorts triggered the "second coming" of Unitarianism. They were not content with the sobriety, mildness, and calm rationalism of historic Unitarianism. Instead—not unlike their Second Great Awakening counterparts—they longed for a more intense spiritual experience. Thus, Transcendentalism was not born as a counter-movement to Unitarianism but rather as a parallel movement to the very ideas introduced by the first Unitarians.[188]

Margaret Fuller embodied this new ardor and the activism that would come to define the movement. Arguably the original American feminist battling on behalf of women's rights, she co-founded *The Dial* with her friend Emerson in 1840 and served as its original editor. It became the official publication of the Transcendental Club. "'These brave souls,' Fuller wrote of her compatriots in one of *The Dial*'s first editions, tried to 'quicken the soul, that they may work from within outwards' and thus help their fellow men and women find more meaning in their lives."[189] Unitarian minister and journalist George Ripley maintained that Transcendentalism was but "the assertion of the high powers, dignity and integrity of the soul; its absolute independence and right to interpret the meaning of life, untrammeled by traditions and conventions."[190]

If the revolution of 1776 had fallen short in implementing its essential vision that all are born equal, of protecting the inherent rights of every man and woman, then the Transcendentalists were dedicated to delivering on what the founders themselves could not. J. A. Saxton wrote in *The Dial* that "the very existence of the United States is transcendental[,] for its right to be a nation . . . unequivocally legitimated the instinctive truth of the principle of equality and brotherhood of universal man."[191] They attempted to redirect and reenergize what they increasingly saw as the country's faltering, misguided democratic experiment. Much as the Deists, Freemasons, Rosicrucians, Unitarians, and Quakers did in the previous century, the Transcendentalists raised the consciousness of the nation and served as its conscience to steer it through the crises ahead.

Along with the "expatriate" generation of the 1920s and the Beat Generation of the 1950s, the Transcendentalists remain one of the nation's most compelling and influential intellectual coteries as well as the source of many ideas that have come to define what is "American."[192] Oliver Wendell Homes called Emerson's "The American Scholar" lecture "our intellectual Declaration of Independence."[193] Simply put, Transcendentalism "was another American Revolution, spiritual in nature and remarkably varied in its practical implications."[194]

"BLEEDING KANSAS" AND A BEATING
ON THE FLOOR OF CONGRESS

For all their focus on the inner spiritual journey, the Transcendentalists were the movers and shakers of their age. Though they were channelers of America's mystical core, worthy inheritors of the Enlightenment, they were one of the nation's first coherent activist groups. They would be frontline agitators for the abolition of slavery and at the forefront of educational reform; they'd campaign for the rights of women, laborers, prisoners, the indigent, and the infirm; and they helped initiate the environmental movement.[195] An event in 1856 galvanized the Transcendentalists to act in ways they hadn't before.

Americans rue our country's polarization today. Imagine, in the heat of differences, one congressman so insulted by another that he arises on the Senate floor, approaches the man, and beats him senseless with a cane until the man, bloodied, lies helpless and near death.

This shocking assault in the halls of Congress was another key marker in the country's inexorable slide into civil war. The Fugitive Slave Act of 1850 exacted fines and imprisonment on anyone caught aiding escaped slaves. In effect, this law compelled Northern states to enforce slavery by returning runaway slaves to their owners in the South. The law enraged many, principally the Boston and Concord Transcendentalists. Even the inward-looking Emerson said, "I will not obey it by God," encouraging civil disobedience to oppose the act.[196]

Things got worse. In 1854, the Kansas–Nebraska Act overturned the Missouri Compromise that had outlawed slavery above a certain latitude. Kansas was north of the line, but this bill pushed by Southern Democrats and Northern moderates permitted slavery based on "popular sovereignty"—meaning citizens of the various new territories could now determine whether that region would be slaveholding or free. This "hollow bargain for the North" backfired when slavery supporters and abolitionists alike rushed Kansas to vote on the fate of slavery in that state. Hostilities led to government corruption and widespread violence.[197] The real Civil War, it is said, did not start with the first shot fired over Fort Sumter in 1861 but rather in 1850s "Bleeding Kansas."

On the fateful day of May 20, 1856, Sen. Charles Sumner of Massachusetts delivered an incendiary speech in the Senate against slavery and slaveholders, accusing them of "raping the virgin territories" in the name of an "abominable institution." This raised the ire of Sen. Preston Brooks of South Carolina. At first he contemplated a duel. But then Brooks and his acolytes in the Senate reconsidered, thinking Sumner did not deserve the gentlemanly honor of such, and instead chose to humiliate him with a public caning.

Two days later, as Sumner arose at the end of a session, Brooks bared a gold-leafed handled cane and proceeded to strike the helpless Massachusetts senator before he had time to fully

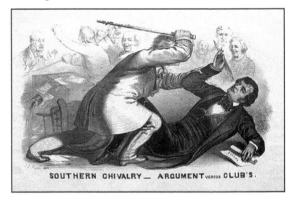

The Caning of Sen. Charles Sumner

rise from his seat. While Brooks's allies cordoned off others who might come to Sumner's defense, the stricken senator was bludgeoned to the point of unconsciousness. He managed to survive.

"WE MUST GET RID OF SLAVERY... OR FREEDOM"

What did not survive was any further compromise the country might have had regarding slavery. Two weeks after the attack, Emerson suggested the incident represented the nation's divide: "I do not see how a barbarous community and a civilized community can constitute one state. I think we must get rid of slavery, or we must get rid of freedom."[198]

The tenor of the moment sent adversaries to their respective corners where they devised even more fractured policies, signifying what was becoming an ultimate, unavoidable split. The *Dred Scott* decision by the US Supreme Court in 1857 cemented the notion that slaves were property, not citizens, and therefore afforded no human rights. After Kansas, *Dred Scott*, and the caning of Sen. Sumner, for many there was no going back.

Members of the "like-minded club" concurred—slavery was a deeply immoral institution and had to be abolished. As early as 1848, in his *Letter to the People of the United States Touching the Matter of Slavery*, Unitarian minister Theodore Parker wrote, "American slavery is the greatest, foulest wrong which man ever did to man; the most hideous and detested sin a nation has ever committed before the just, all-bounteous God—a wrong and sin wholly without excuse."[199]

Further, Parker noted that financial interests propped up and legitimized slavery even as it pricked at the nation's conscience. According to Parker, the United States' historic love of individual liberty was being eroded by inordinate love of wealth. The selfishness, Parker observed, was now the "most obvious and preponderate desire in the consciousness of the people," having grown exponentially in the past half century, particularly among those whom he called the "controlling class." With them, he continued, "everything gives way to money and money gives way to nothing, neither to man nor to God."[200] He asked, "What had the church been doing that slavery was tolerated and war glorified and labor exploited and woman oppressed and the rich suffered to lord it over the poor?"[201] He went on to claim, "The church, the State, the law is not for man, but for money."[202]

Not only did the Transcendentalists' efforts to end slavery help trigger the Civil War, but they raised awareness of equal rights among the sexes, welcoming women to express themselves more freely, advocating for the role women were about to play in the evolution of American spirituality.

SPIRITUALISM: RAPPINGS OF A GENDER SHIFT

Long before the *Long Island Medium*, there were the Fox sisters.

In March 1848 Hydesville, New York, young Maggie and Kate Fox heard rappings in their house. They learned to act as "interpreters" of what they understood to be visitors from the spirit world. Though by no means the first to claim direct contact with their ancestors, they became the first celebrity mediums, quickly growing famous for their public séances in New York's Burned-Over District, the psychic playground that, ironically, had been the site of the evangelical Second Great Awakening movement before it.

The experiences of the Fox sisters sparked a wildfire of public interest in communicating with ancestral spirits. Later they admitted that this "contact" with the spirit was a hoax, though shortly afterward they recanted that admission.[203] On shaky ground, thus began the Spiritualist movement. The term was used to identify a loose set of beliefs and practices involving communication with the dead in the "great beyond." The movement gained widespread and popular attention in the mid-nineteenth century, mentioned in the media of the day and through nontraditional faith communities. While many Spiritualists still identified themselves as Christians, their interest in the occult and their critique of Christianity placed them outside any dominant religious culture.

Regardless of Spiritualism's authenticity, or lack thereof, it sparked a curious development: it grew as a syncretic movement, a blend of varying religious doctrines with no specific church or leader at the helm. With Spiritualism, the wall of male dominance in the pulpit showed signs of fracture: many Spiritualists were women. They supported causes such as the abolition of slavery and women's suffrage.[204]

Despite allegations and instances of fraud, Spiritualism nevertheless elevated women to an unaccustomed level. Although sporadic evidence of women in places of religious leadership had appeared earlier (e.g., African Methodist Jarena Lee and Mother Ann Lee of the Shaker movement), Spiritualism encouraged larger numbers of women to challenge the bounds of traditional religious authority. This independence inspired women across the spiritual spectrum to speak up and stand out, even when they had no connection to Spiritualism.

TO "NOT OBEY":
WOMEN AND HOLY INDIGNATION

Enter Elizabeth Cady (later Elizabeth Cady Stanton). She initially listened intently to the preachings of evangelist Charles Finney as he barnstormed through Upstate New York and the Burned-Over District. Though she attended his performances for six straight weeks in the midst of his Great Revival of the early 1830s, something was not clicking. "I cannot understand what I am to do," she told Finney. "If you should tell me to go to the top of the church steeple and jump off, I would readily do it, but I do not know how to go to Jesus." When she finally accepted Finney's advice to confess her sins and convert, "fear and judgment seized [her] soul."[205]

The evangelical fervor of the Second Great Awakening and organized religion became too limiting for many women. It constrained them not only spiritually but socially as well. Clerics, they believed, were not teaching the "great doctrine" of individual rights but instead used the Bible to justify the subjugation of women.[206] Cady and other "radical women" of the time gravitated towards the liberal spirituality and feminism of a Margaret Fuller. As women became active in mission societies and in temperance or abolition crusades, it became more difficult to sustain the myth of female subordination. Elizabeth Cady and her compatriots in revival and reform circles openly rejected male religious authority.[207]

Cady had shown these tendencies of bucking male superiority early on. In her youth, she had enough of sermons on biblical authority and the natural superiority of men as church leaders. As a young Presbyterian, she exhibited Jeffersonian behavior: taking a pair of scissors to scripture, she isolated all of the passages pertaining to women. She then pasted them onto sheets of paper, offering commentary of each segment.[208]

For her part, Cady did not believe that a just God would arbitrarily limit women to a separate, second-class sphere of existence. When the Bible seemed to contradict her on this point, she responded with appeals to natural law. "The writings of Paul," she wrote in 1855, "like our State Constitutions are susceptible of various interpretations. But when the human soul is roused with holy indignation against injustice and oppression, stops not to translate human parchments, but follows out the law of its inner being written by the finger of God in the first hour of Creation."[209]

Cady married fellow abolitionist and reformer Henry Stanton, though she retained her maiden name within her full name and omitted "to obey" in their vows. She went on to work with Susan B. Anthony in establishing women's rights, including the right to vote (leading the historic Woman's Rights Convention at Seneca Falls, New York, in 1848), divorce, own property, protection from abuse—even to ride a bicycle. She argued that the Bible and organized religion denied women their full rights, co-writing *The Woman's Bible* in the late 1890s with her daughter, Harriot Stanton Blatch. It was a critique of the inherent chauvinism in religion and English-translated scripture.[210] Cady Stanton was roundly criticized by the church, by men of every stripe, even by some of her supporters in the suffragette movement who thought she'd gone too far. Even so, she carried on as a reformer until her death in 1902.

The influences of Spiritualism and the likes of Emily Cady Stanton would open doors for women in positions of spiritual leadership, from Mary Baker Eddy to Myrtle Fillmore, Antoinette Brown Blackwell, Dr.Johnnie Coleman and Terry Cole Whitaker.

"SO THIS IS THE LITTLE WOMAN WHO STARTED OUR BIG WAR!"

Two names well known to American history straddled the line between the influences of the Second Great Awakening and Transcendentalism. What they did forced the United States to face its shadow side, ultimately resulting in civil war.

Harriet Beecher Stowe was the daughter of renowned evangelical preacher Lyman Beecher. She was raised in relative prosperity, at one time living as Mark Twain's neighbor in Hartford, Connecticut. To know Stowe's beginnings is to understand her father's religious views: as part of the growing evangelical movement associated with the Second Great Awakening, Rev. Beecher cast a suspicious eye on religious pluralism. The spiritual liberalism that led to the Transcendentalist movement repulsed him. He often painted Unitarians and Deists, as well as Catholics and Episcopalians, as "'enemies of truth' or 'infidels,' even going further by calling them a 'throng' of 'drunkards' and 'adulterers.'"[211]

Beecher, the fundamental evangelical Calvinist that he was, drove his six sons and two daughters along the straight and narrow path of devotion to God, to duty, and to himself. Much of her father's religious influence would show up in Harriet's writings as an adult.[212]

And yet, this daughter of Lyman Beecher—the man who thought evangelist William Garrison had "gone too far in his radical approach to abolition"—would be the one to light the fuse of America's deadliest war, leading to Black emancipation. As a young woman, Harriet witnessed riots against Blacks in Cincinnati by violent anti-abolitionists. A few years later, upon visiting the South, she observed and came to understand the slave system, and was moved to write based on her experiences. *Uncle Tom's Cabin* (1851) epitomized the plight of the Southern Negro. Her book would raise the awareness of not only the nation but also the world to the stark realities of slavery.

Sharing stories of the cruel lives experienced by slaves, *Uncle Tom's Cabin* was banned in the South. In its condemnation of slaveholding, the book was as "radical" as anything written or professed by the Transcendentalists. The first printing of 5,000 copies quickly ran out, and the book eventually sold over 300,000 copies in its first year. It was the second best-selling book—eclipsed only by the Bible—in the nineteenth century.[213]

Uncle Tom's Cabin had the kind of impact on the start of the Civil War that Thomas Paine's *Common Sense* had on the American Revolution. Both awakened the intellectual elite as well as the common man to the inequities of their time, creating a demand for change that would ultimately lead to conflict. When Stowe met Abraham Lincoln in 1862, he was reported to have said, "So you're the little woman who started our big war!"[214]

Though not an actual member of the Transcendental Club, Stowe's involvement in Boston abolitionist circles intersected with the club's broad progressive agenda. Ralph Waldo Emerson said, "*Uncle Tom's Cabin* encircled the globe, and was the only book that found readers in the parlor, the nursery, and the kitchen in every household."[215]

"THE METEOR OF THE WAR"

You could say he was on fire for Jesus.

By the 1850s, John Brown's evangelical ardor for abolition was popularly known and respected in diverse circles. But his Old Testament demeanor and tendency towards violence put off many, including evangelical preacher and abolitionist William Lloyd Garrison.

Brown initially studied with the intention of entering the ministry. Eventually he took up tanning, the family trade. Raised in a Calvinist household, Brown adopted his parents' strict religious views and staunch abolitionist stance. A twelve-year-old John Brown witnessed a young slave brutally beaten with a shovel at the hands of his owner and was haunted by the gruesome images for the rest of his life.[216] By the late 1840s Brown became deeply entrenched in the growing abolitionist movement, meeting with the likes of Frederick Douglass and sharing his dream of a runaway slave community in the Alleghenies.

Brown was at the center of "Bleeding Kansas," meting out an eye for an eye. When pro-slavery forces destroyed Lawrence, the capital of Kansas, killing an abolitionist newspaper publisher and burning down his business, Brown, his sons, and a group of antislavery loyalists retaliated, killing pro-slavery settlers in a series of incidents. Brown lost a son and returned east. He did not give up the fight; instead he looked for support to continue his crusade.

A strange intersection of John Brown and the Transcendentalists took place in Massachusetts. Brown, on a tour to raise funding for his efforts, came to Concord and was introduced to Emerson, Thoreau, and later to Theodore Parker. Although Emerson and Thoreau admired Brown's ardor, they were skeptical of his means and distanced themselves—as did Frederick Douglass, who early on had lauded Brown as "the Captain."

Theodore Parker was another story. He had been writing his book on *The Historical Development of Religion,* but current events (and later, illness) interrupted its completion. Parker had come to believe that men held against their will had a natural right to kill anyone who sought to prevent their liberty. It was a natural duty for freemen to do for the enslaved all that they had a right to do for themselves.[217] Both Parker and Brown became enraged by the caning of Massachusetts senator Charles Sumner. To them it was the last straw.

In March 1859, in a Boston hotel, Parker and five others (known as the Secret Six) heard directly from John Brown about his plans to attack a federal armory in Harpers Ferry, Virginia, freeing and arming slaves on nearby plantations. The Secret Six aided Brown in raising money. Brown attacked the federal arsenal in October of that year. He met his fate at the hands of US brevet colonel and future Confederate commander Robert E. Lee, who counterattacked and swiftly brought the rebellion to its knees. Brown was captured and hanged weeks later.

Lee called Brown's act the plans of "a fanatic or madman." Future Republican candidate Abraham Lincoln "agreed [with Brown's] thinking slavery is wrong," but even he argued "that cannot excuse violence, bloodshed and treason."[218] Nevertheless, Brown would become a hero and icon of the North. From 1859 until Lincoln's assassination in 1865, no American was more famous. Union soldiers marched to "John Brown's Body," adapting an old camp song and portraying the man as a heroic martyr whose "truth is marching on." Newly freed Blacks walked to the song, many lowering their voices when speaking of Brown, as if he were a saint. The man who posthumously summed up John Brown best was *Moby Dick* author Herman Melville, who called him "the meteor of the war."[219]

"THE MOST AMERICAN OF US ALL"

Parker's support of Brown demonstrated just how far he had gone in his radicalism. Before he could become implicated and indicted as a co-conspirator, Parker set off to Italy as a guest of British poets Robert and Elizabeth Barrett Browning to recuperate from his advancing tuberculosis, but he would die within a year.

Other Transcendentalists, while not endorsing John Brown's violent stance, wholeheartedly supported Brown's dedication to abolishing slavery. After Brown's execution, Emerson, Bronson Alcott, and Henry David Thoreau spoke at a memorial for him. Thoreau's eulogy underscored Brown's ideals, if not his most recent actions. "No man in America," he said, "has ever stood up so persistently and effectively for the dignity of human nature." In that way he was "the most American of us all."[220]

Despite the praise heaped on Brown, Emerson's reticence for supporting Brown's methods was clear in his assessment of Parker, who had gone far beyond the sentiments of his fellow Transcendentalists. From Emerson's private journal he stated, "I can well praise him [Parker] at a spectator's distance, for our minds and methods were unalike— few people more unalike," a tacit admission of the fractures within Transcendentalism itself.[221]

THE "LIGHT" SHADOW

The Transcendentalist influence on the American soul is second to none in the nation's history.

In some ways Emerson's foray into multicultural, interreligious exploration laid the groundwork for ecumenical and comparative spiritual pursuits that would become far more common in the twentieth and twenty-first centuries. Emerson was among the first serious American writers to carefully consider the philosophies of the Persian prophet Zoroaster, the Greek sage Pythagoras, Confucius, Buddha, Hindu mythology, the Vedas, Hermes, the Neoplatonists, and reincarnation.

While Emerson read Eastern texts as essays of spiritual philosophy, his compatriot Thoreau went further, turning them into models of moral action. Thoreau was quick to seize upon the lofty ethical teachings of the *Bhagavad Gita*, the Hindu text whose principles were consistent with his own tenet of nonviolent civil disobedience. Thoreau's impact on future revolutionaries Gandhi and Martin Luther King would become self-evident.

The legacy of Emerson and the Transcendentalists helped spread the teachings of mystical traditions from both the East and West, influencing and making way for such organizations as Madame Blavatsky's Theosophical Society, Manley P. Hall's Philosophical Research Society, Rudolf Steiner's Anthroposophical Society, Charles and Myrtle Fillmore's Unity movement, Ernest Holmes' Religious Science, and Edgar Cayce's Association for Research and Enlightenment.

Leigh Eric Schmidt argues in his book *Restless Souls* that Americans who today identify as "spiritual but not religious" come from a documentable tradition dating to at least the nineteenth century's shift towards religious liberalism—a shift that began ostensibly with the Transcendentalists, whose "non-creedal spirituality espoused religious ecumenism, inclusivity, and individual mystical access to the divine. Whether labeled 'mysticism,' 'metaphysical religion,' or 'spirituality,' this American religious tradition is 'excitedly eclectic, mystically yearning [and] perennially cosmopolitan,' offering a liberal, progressive, left-leaning spiritual counterweight to orthodox religions and the Christian Right."[222]

As the esoteric expressions of eighteenth-century Enlightenment paralleled the emotive overtones of the First Great Awakening, helping foment the American Revolution, so did Transcendentalism play "light shadow" to the evangelical passions of the Second Great Awakening. Together they created a field of resonance that initiated the greatest conflict in American history, leaving seismic social changes in race, gender, labor, and the environment.

Though the nature and approach to spirituality of these two forces were intrinsically different, the nation that grew out of the Civil War, with its ensuing evolution, owes its genesis to these separate yet intertwined "trunks" in the tree of America's evolving soul. The fundamental and the metaphysical, hallmarks of the nation's birth, once again acted as midwives to one of the greatest chapters in the country's history. Together they were prime movers of the ideals and actions that would usher in the American Century.

Will this interactive spirit show itself again and catalyze the nation to move through the crises of the current century?

CHAPTER FOUR

Awakening Catalysts
and "The Other"

*Theodore Roosevelt warned that the rock of democracy will founder
when people in different regions, classes, races and parties regarded one
another as "The Other" rather than the common American citizen.*

Doris Kearns Goodwin

*Throughout evolution, crisis has played a critical role. When things got
stretched that's when major shifts happened.*

Peter Russell, *Waking Up in Time*

THE ARCHITECTS OF FEAR

I remember traveling as a young boy with my father to one of our favorite places, a small summer home on the eastern end of Long Island. It was at the height of the Cold War. After World War II, much of the world saw the US as the savior of democracy. But no sooner had the nation prevailed over the Japanese, German, and Italian Axis than the specter of communism loomed. Former allies, the Soviet Union was now America's archenemy, pushing the world to the edge of nuclear war.

My dad said something to me in the car that day that I will never forget: "The only way Russia and America will ever unite is if we are attacked by a superior force from outer space." Now, first and foremost, my father was an entirely pragmatic man. He was a chemical engineer and US Army veteran who took no nonsense from me or my siblings. But this was the early 1960s, not far removed from the intrigue of the television classic *The Twilight Zone*, movies such as *The Day the Earth*

Stood Still, and the unresolved Roswell UFO mystery. So while my father had no predilection towards science fiction or metaphysics, he was not alone in his thinking that only a common enemy, an attack by an "other," could unify the world. In other words, humanity could never fully cooperate unless facing a common foe.

Numerous literary and visual mediums agreed: Theodore Sturgeon's 1948 science fiction story *Unite and Conquer* (a "false flag" UFO alien invasion where a disunited population comes together to repel an alien invader); the 1951 cartoon story "The Last War on Earth" by Harvey Kurtzman (where a scientist creates a fake threat from another world); Kurt Vonnegut's 1959 novel *The Sirens of Titan* (a fake invasion is carried out to unite Earth and eventually leads to world peace); and a 1963 episode of the *Twilight Zone* knockoff *The Outer Limits*, appropriately entitled "The Architects of Fear," starring Robert Culp. In that program the world has entered a Cold War–like setting in which nuclear holocaust appears imminent. In the hope of staving off an apocalyptic military confrontation between nations, an idealistic group of scientists plans to stage a fake alien invasion of Earth in an effort to unite all humanity against a perceived common enemy.

These concepts weren't limited to the imaginations of 1950s and '60s Hollywood scriptwriters, either.

THE PRESIDENT AND THE ALIENS

Three times Ronald Reagan addressed the UN about alien threats. Perhaps it had something to do with his previous UFO experiences. Or his concern for the role he played in a nuclear world.

On September 16, 1985, the fortieth US president gave a memorable speech before the United Nations: "What if all of us in the world were threatened by an outer power, from outer space, from another planet? We would all of a sudden find out that we didn't have any differences at all." The president asked the nations of the world to imagine how quickly humanity would come together if confronted by an extraterrestrial threat.

He did so again in 1987 while discussing glasnost with the Soviet Union. Referring to Soviet leader Mikhail Gorbachev, he said, "Just think how easy his task and mine in these meetings that we held if suddenly there was a threat to this world from some other species from another planet outside in the universe. We'd forget all of the little local differences that we have between our countries and we would find out that we are really all human beings living on this earth together."[223] At first Gorbachev wasn't sure if Reagan was kidding but then concluded he was serious. While some believed President Reagan was trying to subtly warn the public of the existence of aliens, most people saw this as an attempt to defuse simmering tensions between the US and the Soviet Union.

The story of countries or groups unifying premised on fear of "the other" is millennia old. The posed or real threat by a common enemy has galvanized nations and fostered powerful alliances. Often for very good reasons. But such fears have also served as the excuse for warfare, subjugation, scapegoating, slavery, and humiliation. Fear has been used to demonize those we set apart from our family, tribe, or country. These alliances often form not out of some moral compunction or recognition of similar concerns but out of fear or expediency. Some unions or alliances form simply based on the notion of "the enemy of my enemy is my friend."

Britain and the United States were not particularly fond of the communist Soviet Union (especially after they partitioned Poland with Nazi Germany at the outset of WWII), but they found a way to ally with Stalin once Hitler turned his guns and tanks on the Russians. Chinese communists under Mao Tse-Tung fought Chinese general Chiang Kai-Shek's Kuomintang for years in the 1930s until the Japanese invasion of their country took precedence.

There are countless other examples, but in most every case, once the superior threat subsided, the former enemies went back to fighting. Hence the fallacy of the egoic notion that having a mutual enemy makes a friend. "He isn't your friend. He is your ally out of necessity," says self-described amateur military historian and fiction writer Cem Arslan. "Alliances borne out of mutual enemies are tools of convenience to be discarded whenever it becomes useful for one side to do so."[224]

TEDDY ROOSEVELT, ROBERT KENNEDY, AND "THE OTHER"

As the American Century drew to a close in the 1990s, the US found itself unchallenged by a rival of near equal status. In a way, America had "won." The Berlin Wall fell in 1989 and, for all intents and purposes, so did communism. By the early '90s, the Soviet Union was no more. Even China moved closer to capitalism, if not democracy. Without an overt natural adversary, America's political divide turned inward and sharply antagonistic. The rise of internal anger has grown ever since.

While today's polarization is not (yet) as dire as that of the War Between the States, America's democracy is teetering because of it. As historian Doris Kearns-Goodwin notes, Theodore Roosevelt warned us that "democracy would founder . . . when we regarded one another as 'the other' . . . rather than as citizens marked by fellow feeling, banding together for the best interests of our country."[225] Teddy's nephew-in-law Franklin Delano Roosevelt would later insist that problems created by man can be solved by man, so long as mankind pulls together towards a common end.

During the ill-fated 1968 presidential campaign in which his life was taken, Robert Kennedy said, "When you teach a man to hate and fear his brother, when you teach that he is a lesser man because of his color or his beliefs or the policies he pursues, when you teach that those who differ from you threaten your freedom or your job or your family, then you also learn to confront others not as fellow citizens, but as enemies—to be met not with cooperation but with conquest, to be subjugated and mastered."[226]

In many ways, this is where America finds itself today.

EGO: AN OPTICAL DELUSION OF CONSCIOUSNESS

God is the "Non-Other." God is nearer to me than I am to myself; my existence depends on the nearness and presence of God.
Christian mystic Meister Eckhart

What does the notion of an ego have to do with individual, national, or collective evolution?

Over the years, the term ego has taken on myriad psychological and spiritual interpretations. Sigmund Freud coined the term; according to his model of the psyche, the id is the primitive and instinctual part of the mind that contains sexual and aggressive drives and hidden memories; the super-ego operates as a moral conscience; and the ego is the realistic part that mediates between the desires of the id and the super-ego.[227] Freudian ego refers to "the organized part of the personality structure," which includes conscious awareness, while "ego, in the Buddhist sense, is quite different. . . . The Buddhist ego is a collection of the individual's mental events."[228]

Other Eastern and modern Western metaphysical texts refer to the ego as something more. In the *Bhagavad Gita*, the ego is the perception of oneself as a completely separate or limited being. This notion coincides with Einstein's observation that experiencing ourselves as ultimately separate is "an optical delusion of consciousness." In *A New Earth*, author Eckhart Tolle describes the ego as the individuated "I" holding, containing, and identifying the image of the separate self. He suggests we suffer because of our identification with the ego and its need for separation—in essence, we don't know who and what we really are.

Tolle's perspective appears to be closely aligned with the *Gita* or that of Carl Jung, who said, "The ego represents the conscious mind as it comprises the thoughts, memories, and emotions a person is aware of. The ego is largely responsible for feelings of identity and continuity." Jung pointed out that knowledge of the ego-personality is often confused with self-understanding.[229]

In more recent history, texts such as the psychological-spiritual compendium *A Course in Miracles* (referenced by many, including Tolle, Marianne Williamson, Oprah Winfrey, and Alan Cohen) addresses the role of the ego within the context of our true spiritual nature. *ACIM* teacher David Hoffmeister describes the ego as "an idea in the mind, a false thought system protected by defense mechanisms of which we are largely unaware. Our minds are not separate from each other, nor from God, and so ego's strength is an illusion. The way out is . . . letting go of the beliefs in sin, guilt and fear in our minds which underlie the ego's thought system."[230]

This notion of ego suggests the underlying fear of eternal separation, death, and finite existence within a three-dimensional time and space frame. In other words, it is that sense of self that identifies more wholly and completely with the body and its thoughts.

"The conceptual 'I' cannot survive without the conceptual 'Other' and the others are most 'other' when I see them as my enemy," suggests Tolle.[231] He asserts the ego needs an adversary to identify and vanquish. It cannot sense unity, only duality. In the classic metaphysical sense, it always needs an enemy, an "other," to justify its existence. Yet Tolle also sees the ego as integral to the evolutionary process of the species, a stage in the evolution of humanity. The great masters saw the enigmatic role the ego plays. "The Buddha called it an illusion," says Tolle. "Jesus said deny thyself, which means recognize the unreality of the ego." In this "illusion of duality," without the ego "ultimately there could be no awakening, no enlightenment."[232]

WHO WILL PLAY "THE OTHER"
IN THE CURRENT CENTURY?

Collective associations such as nationality, religion, race, social class, or political allegiance often foster tribalism, an "us or them" mentality. As the twenty-first century dawned, enemies had become more indistinct. Terms such as the war on terror utilized nebulous terminology to dissolve adversaries into an amorphous whole.

For the United States, who would play adversary? Why not your political enemy as bogeyman? "I noticed the shift after the Cold War," says Mark Gerzon, a former congressional mediator and author of *The Reunited States of America: How We Can Bridge the Partisan Divide*, "because all of our hatred was directed against the Soviet Union. What happened was Russia lost their enemy and we lost our enemy. There [arose] a scientific pursuit of destroying one's domestic political enemy. Stop being civil, collegial and respectful, stop being kind and focus on your political enemy as really evil people."[233]

This perpetuates the meme that humanity will always find a way to fight one another. And once the outer enemy has been vanquished, the fighting and squabbling is turned inward. Another split-off, another enemy. History suggests that's just the way it is—that violence and a common enemy have always been and will always be a predominate expression of humanity's collective experience.

Was my father—or Ronald Reagan—right? Is a common foe the only force that can unify humankind?

POGO WISDOM

In the 1940s, long before it became popular in the "funnies," Walt Kelly originated a political satire cartoon strip known as *Pogo*. Kelly disguised his social commentary with a motley assortment of animals possessed of human characteristics living and interacting in a swamp. According to Kelly, any connection to the events in Washington was purely coincidental. Influenced by Will Rogers, Kelly's genius later inspired socially minded cartoon strips like *Doonesbury, Bloom County, Shoe, Candorville,* and *Non-Sequitur.*[234]

©1970 Walt Kelly. Used with permission.

In the late 1960s, Apollo astronauts sent back pictures of Earth from outer space, giving us an entirely new perspective of our planet. People began to awaken to the idea of Earth's singularity, the sense of a planetary home, our "one world." At the same time, encroaching pollution, smog, as well as a diminishing ozone layer raised awareness of the fragility and abuse of our planet. Out of this, the Earth Day movement began.

In honor of the first Earth Day in 1970, Kelly created a poster using his Pogo character that summed up what Jung might have said when musing upon the great collective: *"We have met the enemy and he is us."*

The phrase Kelly used—later placed in a comic strip attributing the comment to Pogo—is a play on words from the War of 1812. After the victory over the British at the Battle of Lake Erie, Commodore Oliver Hazard Perry reported to US general and future president William Henry Harrison, "We have met the enemy and they are ours."[235]

Kelly's use of the phrase addressed two matters facing us then, as they do today. First, that fighting "our enemy" is ultimately an illusion. In Kelly's world, we are edging closer and closer to becoming "the other" we have projected onto our so-called enemy. On the quantum level, the enemy turns out to *be* us. Asserting a similar dynamic, poet-philosopher Maya Angelou, paraphrasing Carl Jung, said, "We must look past complexion and see community. We are more than our brother's keeper—we ARE our brother and our sister."[236] Growing in awareness, Kelly might have suggested, allows people and nations to retain their individuality while simultaneously identifying with an innate interconnectedness.

Secondly, the perfect launching pad for Pogo's sentiment was Earth Day itself. Because Kelly's phrase was a pun on a very familiar quote, it caught the collective imagination of Americans. It is still used in public discourse to describe the potential results of man-made global warming.[237] The degradation of the environment is largely, if not completely, a self-inflicted crisis. Our laxity in dealing with the issue, now fifty-plus years after it arose in the zeitgeist, has made climate change the existential crisis of our age. It looms as an enemy to be "fought," but it is literally of our own doing. Pogo's phrase lives on, not by constant reuse in similar circumstances but by clever rephrasing in new situations. What keeps this phrase from becoming a cliché is that it continues to tell us about ourselves—and the world around us.[238]

SIMULATED ENEMIES

Here's a question all of mankind has likely pondered at one time or another: will humanity forever war with itself? Will we ever evolve beyond the notion of "the other" as the enemy, of incessantly demonizing groups of people to galvanize lesser unions? History and the most practical minded among us would suggest that violence and perpetual division is simply the innate nature of humankind. The best that organized religion seems to offer us is the promise of a heavenly afterlife or that some outside savior will descend upon the earth and bring about a thousand years of peace. Or, as science fiction suggests, maybe alien invaders turn friendly to help save us from ourselves.

In the 1950s film *The Day the Earth Stood Still*, it is an alien who comes to save Earth. Klaatu, a Jesus-like figure, differs from other aliens in that he "comes in peace and goodwill," warning humans that their "unreasoning suspicions and attitudes" will lead to their downfall. In his interaction with earthlings, Klaatu concludes, "Your choice is simple: join us and live in peace, or pursue your present course and face obliteration." *Washington Post* White House correspondent Lou Cannon and then NSA advisor Colin Powell both believed that the film inspired President Reagan to address alien invasion with Gorbachev.

All of these scenarios—whether religious or positive science fiction scenarios—paint the picture of an outside savior saving the day.

But positive human evolution does not necessarily require dreams of whimsical utopias or the cessation of all conflict. In his book *The Promised Land*, former president Barack Obama says it succinctly: the United States seeks "to become a more perfect union," meaning the process is endless. As long as we reside in physical form, conflict will remain, but it can take on many guises, ranging from genocide to armed warfare to a debate.

This may very well point to what Eckhart Tolle refers to when he states that the ego has played a vital role in the evolution of the human species but is outliving its usefulness. Can we move forward without creating an enemy that leads to mutual destruction? In other words, will humankind ever work together as a coordinated, integrated unit for reasons other than to fight a common foe?

Here is where the long-ignored specters of climate crisis and authoritarianism come in: they are the ersatz enemies, the faux foes and perhaps the very catalysts to foster the next integral step in human evolution.

THE CLIMATE CRISIS:
THE SELF-CREATED "OTHER"

In the cabin of a boat traveling across the roiling Atlantic ocean, a girl sits in silence.

Outside, it's a tempest: rain pelts the craft, ice coats its decks, and the sea batters the vessel taking this slight girl, her father, and her companions to the United Nations' Climate Conference. Outside, the entire natural world seems to amplify her small voice, screaming along with her. "We can't just continue living as if there was no tomorrow, because there is a tomorrow," she says, tugging on the sleeve of her blue sweatshirt. "That is all we are saying." Those sentiments are the main reason *Time* magazine honored sixteen-year-old Swede activist Greta Thunberg as 2019's Person of the Year.[239]

The United Nations asserts that climate change is the defining crisis of our time, and the data should be indisputable, even for those who willfully ignore the science. In late 2020 a UN report indicated the pace of climate change has humanity on a "suicidal" path.[240] No spot on the globe appears to be immune. Triple-digit heat recently descended upon Siberia, one of the planet's coldest places, setting a record since such record keeping began in 1885.[241] "To put it simply," UN secretary general António Guterres said, summarizing the findings in unusually stark terms, "the state of the planet is broken."[242] "For every fraction of a degree that temperatures increase," *Time*'s Person of the Year article states, "these problems will worsen. This is not fearmongering; this is science. For decades, researchers and activists have struggled to get world leaders to take the climate threat seriously. But in 2019, an unlikely teenager somehow got the world's attention."[243]

This is where we find ourselves some fifty years after the pure and selfless efforts to create an Earth Day.

While most political discussions surrounding climate change focus on carbon emissions, there are multiple factors: soil erosion, contaminated groundwater, weakened watersheds due to damming of rivers, the decimation of the Amazon rainforest, destruction of animal and fish habitats; a near annihilation of bees, butterflies, insects, and other pollinators from pesticides in industrial agriculture, among others.[244] But rather than overwhelm the reader with bad news—the amygdala, that ancient, reptilian emotional center of the brain where we process fear, shuts down after the initial adrenaline jolt[245]—let's consider alternative perspectives that hearken back to the nation's very roots.

What can climate change teach us? One lesson is something most Native American tribes instinctively understand: the radical interrelatedness of all nature. Nature is a nonlinear flux—not a billiard table of cause and effects but an orchestra playing together. It takes careful observation to understand the natural world because it is composed of so many relationships, and relationships upon relationships, all occurring simultaneously.[246]

We have not only been at war with each other and with other nations; we are at war with the earth. It is our "us versus them" war mentality that most needs to change if humankind, and much of the remaining biodiversity of life, is to survive.[247] Greater humanity will have to recognize, as indigenous cultures seemingly understand, that man is an integral part of nature, not something above it or outside it, or something to be dominated and plundered. The 2021 Intergovernmental Panel on Climate Change (IPCC) states that indigenous knowledge may be the key in addressing climate change.[248] It is due, in part, to indigenous peoples' "methods of managing forests and agro-ecological systems, as well as their traditions passed down through the generations. We must change our values to honor Nature more than money; otherwise, we will not survive. It is a Cree Indian proverb that says: only when the last tree has been cut down, the last fish been caught, and the last stream poisoned, will we realize we cannot eat money."[249]

"WE VOTE NEXT"

While nations and their leaders have dithered, young people have taken to the streets. Anxious about their future on a hotter planet, they are angry at world leaders for failing to arrest the crisis. On September 20, 2019, masses of young people participated in a day of global climate protests and strikes. Organizers estimated the turnout to be around four million in thousands of cities and towns worldwide. It was the first time in this century that young people demonstrated to demand climate action in so many places and in such numbers around the world. "You had a future, and so should we," demonstrators chanted as they marched through New York City. Then, "We vote next."[250] Will Thunberg's generation force a climate of Great Awakening on older generations?

If so, that will call for unprecedented cooperation—among cities and rural areas, among states, nations, cultures, religions, and tribes. Former vice president Al Gore, who won the Nobel Peace Prize for his decades of climate advocacy work, says, "This moment does feel different. Throughout history, many great morally based movements have gained traction at the very moment when young people decided to make that movement their cause."[251]

Paraphrasing Peter Russell from his book *Waking Up in Time*, crisis has the ability to foment evolutionary change on the planet: "When things got stretched," he says, "that's when major shifts happened."[252] If there is a chance to rise beyond previous barriers, then the existential threat of today's current climate poses an opportunity to awaken and rise above those thresholds.

How fast would the world have united if there *had* been an attack from outer space during the Cold War? All the movies, television shows, and books tell us the US and the USSR would have immediately put down their arms, collectively used their ingenuity, and united the world in a coordinated effort. This is the response the climate crisis warrants. "I want you to panic," Thunberg told the annual convention of CEOs and world leaders at the 2020 World Economic Forum in Davos, Switzerland. "I want you to feel the fear I feel every day. And then I want you to act."[253]

AUTHORITARIANISM:
AN URGENT, EXISTENTIAL GLOBAL THREAT

Defending the rule of law . . . is the law's version of climate change—an urgent, existential global threat that affects us all. The rule of law is the foundation that supports the pillars of democracy and freedom.

Marc Cohen, American Bar Association (ABA) Journal

The New Republic ran a series on "The Future of Democracy," arguing that "at no time since the rise of political democracy have its tenets been so seriously challenged as they are today." Only it isn't a quote from a current article. It's from 1937.

Democracy was on the run throughout the world in the 1930s. Right- and left-wing autocrats, prominent leaders in both the East and West, solidified their power by creating faux "others" both without and within. Mussolini was the first noteworthy and notorious fascist dictator in Europe, creating a full right-wing authoritarian regime, although Spain's Francisco Franco could almost lay equal claim. Hitler's Germany would come to epitomize the darkest form of autocracy, but many other nations, including the USSR and Japan, fully embraced authoritarianism as alternatives to Western liberal democracy.

We may never know how close the United States came to a political breakdown of order and the emergence of homegrown fascism in that era. During the Great Depression there were riots, tension between labor and capitalism, and growing threats from the right and left in America. There are credible accounts of several attempted right-wing coups to overthrow FDR, one allegedly derailed by a former military hero.[254]

Though Roosevelt won by a landslide in 1932 over unpopular incumbent Herbert Hoover and handily won reelection in 1936, talk of democracy's demise seemed to be everywhere. Hardly a month went by without the press asking, "Is Democracy Doomed?" "Can Democracy Survive?" In the same time period, *The Christian Science Monitor* published a debate called "Whither Democracy?" addressed "to everyone who has been thinking about the future of democracy—and who hasn't."[255]

In the 1937 article, *The New Republic* editors asked, "Do you think that political democracy is now on the wane?" The series' lead contributor, Italian philosopher Benedetto Croce, took issue with the question. "The trouble," Croce explained, "is that political problems are not external forces beyond our control; they are forces within our control. We need solely to make up our own minds and to act."[256] That epitomized Roosevelt's stance, who, appealing to the common man, maintained the political center and preserved American democracy. His vision and successes came to define the American Century.

The nation, and the world, find themselves in a similar place today.

"FLAWED DEMOCRACY"

In a word, democracy is in trouble.

In its 2021 report, the UK-based company Economist Intelligence Unit (EIU) issued its latest democracy index, which shows that less than 50 percent of the world's population now lives in a democracy, and authoritarian regimes are gaining ground. The report found that democracy had experienced its biggest annual decline since 2010.[257]

The 2021 report revealed another astounding fact: the United States fell to number twenty-six on the list of the world's democracies.[258] Democratic health is based upon five key criteria: electoral process and pluralism, civil liberties, the functioning of government, political participation, and political culture. The United States fell below Costa Rica, Estonia, South Korea, Chile, and Spain. The United Nations posits similar lists and analyzes democratic values among nations. It notices a similar wanting: although there are likely dozens of worldwide threats to global unity and cooperation, the world's shrinking away from democracy and embracing authoritarianism must be at or near the top of that list.

The US was classified as a "flawed democracy" for the second consecutive year, failing to achieve the "full democracy" status earned by twenty other sovereign nations. The US relegation reflects "a sharp fall in popular confidence in the functioning of public institutions."[259] Public faith in government has eroded and so too has government accountability under the law. The checks and balances of our tricameral government have been blurred, and accountability wanes among officials sworn to uphold it. Rules, precedent, and institutional processes have yielded to "alternative facts" and ad hoc, partisan rule-making. "Defending the rule of law is a less concrete but seminal challenge the [profession] must focus on [in the 2020s]," says former American Bar Association president Marc Cohen. "It is the law's version of climate change."[260] US Supreme Court chief justice John G. Roberts Jr. cautioned in the *2019 Year-End Report on the Federal Judiciary*, "We have come to take democracy for granted, and civic education has fallen by the wayside."[261]

RETREAT INTO AUTOCRACY

The rule of law is under siege in the US, and it's no solace that the nation is not alone. There are the usual suspects, of course: Russia and China, once claiming Marxist-Leninist-Mao roots, have embraced oligarchic capitalism. But democracy is nowhere in sight.

Recently, both autocratic regimes doubled down on their policies: Vladimir Putin was to have ended his tenure as Russian president in 2024, but new laws say he can stay well into the 2030s. Russia has a legislative body and courts, and Russian people can purportedly vote. Yet current Russian leadership holds an authoritarian grip on government more closely resembling the totalitarian regimes of the czars and Josef Stalin. Those who disagree with Putin are hunted down, jailed, poisoned, or worse. In addition to journalists who have been murdered for speaking their minds, Russian opposition leader Alexei Navalny has suffered civil and criminal harassment and jailing. Attempts—by Putin, Navalny alleges—to blind, poison, and kill him have not yet taken him down.

In China, the story is similar. President Xi Jinping has tightened his grip on power with new rules for top policymaking bodies. A recent critic of Jinping and Chinese Communist Party has been jailed for eighteen years. China has placed new restrictions on Hong Kong and made its first arrests under its new set of anti-protest laws.[262] But perhaps most disturbing is language in Article 29 of the new law, which outlaws "provoking . . . hatred" of China's central government.[263] China has shut down Hong Kong's democratic newspaper *Apple Daily*, harassing and arresting journalists, representing a startling rollback of media freedom across Asia. Laws ostensibly packaged to protect national security, combat terrorism, or stop misinformation are often used to target journalism and online activism.[264]

Some nation states that had moved towards democracy after the fall of the Berlin Wall and the collapse of the Soviet Union have retreated into authoritarianism with autocratic leaders: Poland's President Andrzej Duda, Hungary's Prime Minister Viktor Orban, Turkey's President Recep Tayyip Erdoğan, the Philippines' President Rodrigo Duterte, and India's Prime Minister Narendra Modi. India has become one of the most dangerous places in the world to be a journalist.[265] What's worse is that the likes of Putin and Jinping represent "a growing network of authoritarian leaders working together."[266]

Combining the worst aspects of authoritarianism while ignoring the dangers of climate change has been Brazil's President Jair Bolsonaro. The threat that Bolsonaro posed is not just to Brazilian democracy but to the entire planet. While other leaders might flirt with fascism, Bolsonaro has proven that he is the real, full-fledged deal.[267] His reticence to cede power of a democratically-elected challenger fomented a January 6-like riot in his country.

After his pledging to "develop the Amazon," the rainforest has seen an 80 percent uptick in the number of fires in one year alone, caused by agribusiness attempting to clear the land for cattle ranching. These fires are ravaging one of the most important and fragile ecosystems on the planet, home to hundreds of thousands of indigenous peoples and countless animal and plant species, thanks in large part to the actions of one man. Given the implications for the planet as a whole, one could easily argue that Bolsonaro has been the single greatest threat to life as we know it.[268]

RELIGION AND AUTHORITARIANISM: A MATCH MADE IN HEAVEN

How prone is the US to authoritarianism? It may depend on the country's degree of "religiousness."

Italy's Benito Mussolini is the classic story of a despot who rose to power on brute authoritarian force. But few may realize what role religion played in his strategy. He had been an unabashed anti-cleric, anti-Catholic atheist, but it became clear to him that in order to ascend politically, he had to do so within the existing social order.

Mussolini adapted by working within the theological hierarchy—marrying in the church, baptizing his children there, and in his first parliamentary speech in 1921 he announced that "the only universal values that radiate from Rome are those of the Vatican." Mussolini knew where he would find sympathy for his fascistic vision: in church.[269] After laying out his for-show philosophical agenda, Mussolini employed the Black Shirts, the paramilitary wing of his National Fascist Party. Swearing an oath of allegiance to *Il Duce*, they used brutal tactics against their domestic opponents. This page from the authoritarian playbook has been repeated by other autocrats around the world.

No country is immune.

Historically, authoritarian leaders on both the right and left are generally not spiritual or religious. More often to the contrary. But intuitively they understand the need to coalesce with prevailing religious institutions and thought. And why not? The elements for authoritarianism alignment are already in place: a centralized power structure, obedience to authority, belief in one set of inerrant teachings, and mistrust of outsiders who are not members of the faith, political party, or culture, among other reasons. Perhaps that is why "authoritarian non-believers who seek public office will profess a belief in gods in which they don't believe and a love of religion which they never demonstrate. Indeed, fascism, the authoritarian extreme, has been dubbed a 'political religion' because of the way it mimics orthodox religion."[270]

The relationship between religiousness and authoritarianism has been a topic of study in the political, psychological, and social sciences at least as far back as the 1950s. Religions may preach peace, tolerance, love, and understanding, but a growing body of evidence shows that those who tend to be dogmatically religious often bend towards authoritarianism.[271]

Research over several decades cited in the *Journal for the Scientific Study of Religion* reveals that fundamentalists seem to have the strongest association with authoritative ideas of deference to law and order, social conventionality, submission to authority, and intolerance for outside groups.[272] A 2007 study[273] published in that same journal and a 2011 meta-analysis study[274] revealed a correlation between strong feelings of religious affiliation and authoritarianism, ethnocentrism, militarism, and prejudice. Although some of this may be due to genetic factors, strong religious traditionalism increases the tendency that one will obey authority and respond positively to symbols of authority.[275]

Authoritarians naturally gravitate towards the more punitive sects within a religion and the more authoritarian practices of that religion. The authoritarian Buddhist reveres strict sitting and loves the idea of hitting squirming meditators with a stick. The authoritarian Catholic will argue for the pope's infallibility or the righteousness of Opus Dei. The authoritarian Jew will argue for a scriptural right to seize land. The authoritarian Hindu will pine for the heyday of the caste system and the banished practice of untouchability.[276] In sum, "whatever door a religion allows for cruelty, authoritarians will flock through that door."[277]

ESCAPE HATCH: SPIRITUAL QUESTING

The one escape hatch researchers found in the authoritarian–religion link depends on the kind of religion one practices. The essential distinction is between traditional church/mosque/synagogue-centered religiosity versus noninstitutionalized spiritual seeking or "spiritual questing." The former is characterized as a fundamental religious belief that is conventional, unquestioned, and unreflective.[278] Religiousness is associated with "rigidity in the processing of information, low cognitive complexity, and a lack of openness to new experiences" and being more likely to fall in line with authoritarian thinking.[279] Those of this mentality are essentially saying, "Tell me what to think, what to believe. I need not figure it out myself; it's done for me and I will follow."[280]

The latter group, those who are "spiritually questing," recognize other faith traditions as valid, including those of the Far East. Those seekers are also more likely to question their own religious tradition and upbringing. Spiritual seekers possess characteristics such as creativity, openness to new experiences, and a willingness to experiment, traits that directly oppose conventionality, submission, and authoritarianism.[281]

Centrally organized, fundamentalist religions see people with other religious beliefs or none at all as "the other." This is the slippery slope that opens the door to authoritarianism, a domain of psychosocial functioning where the polarization between religiousness and spiritual seeking becomes substantial. In twenty-first century United States, this polarization has accentuated political differences along a conservative–liberal axis and promotes the perception that American society is irrevocably split along cultural and spiritual lines.[282]

THE RED PHONE

What the above crises may point to, essentially, is this: evolve or die. In millennia past, there was always room to spread out, to isolate, to cut out ground for one's own fiefdom, more or less. Today we have no illusion of isolated forces. The ends of the physical earth have been met. Our ability to communicate instantly has made this a "virtual" world. It's nonlinear, moving at the speed of thought. That may pose drawbacks—witness the challenge of conspiracy theories and "fake news"—but the benefits, potentially, far outweigh them. Instantaneous communication and travel also lend themselves to instant attention to an issue and the opportunity to rectify it, if the will is present.

The "red phone" is a good example of addressing a crisis instantaneously. When the world was on the precipice of a nuclear war during the October 1962 Missile Crisis, there was no rapid communication between Kennedy and Khrushchev, between the White House and the Kremlin. It seems quaint if not foolhardy that the only powers that had the ability to sink the planet into a nuclear winter did not have direct lines of communication. The US–Soviet Missile Crisis ended that shortcoming, and a red phone was installed in the White House shortly thereafter, allowing the president to immediately communicate with the Russian leader.

We have the science, technology, and data to communicate messages worldwide and at a moment's notice. But our intent and action need to proceed with urgency and immediacy, as if the planet *has* been attacked by an outer force. If we can supplant these awakening crises and notions of alien "others" with unitive thought and action, then there is hope for the planet, the possibility of concerted effort taking a collective leap in conscious awareness. For some that is fantasia and a bridge too far. For others, a new Great Awakening may very well be the "best last hope" for humanity.

"ALL WARS ARE CIVIL WARS"

[We] . . . discover, or invent . . . the stranger, the barbarian,
who is responsible for our confusion and our pain.
Once he is driven out—destroyed—
then we can be at peace: those questions will be gone.
Of course, those questions never go,
but it has always seemed much easier to murder
than to change.

James Baldwin from *Nothing Personal* (1964)

The ego, in the metaphysical if not Freudian sense, insists that we are ultimately separate. That ego, as James Baldwin might have suggested if he employed such language, is always going to find an enemy, a stranger, a barbarian to justify its existence, its fears, and to foist its blame. But finding and vanquishing "the other" never brings lasting peace, though we think it will.

Maybe that paradox is at the root of our toxic politics and polarization today. It may also be the key in helping us awaken to what Pogo knew: the enemy, ultimately, *is* us. That sentiment may seem plain or naive on its face. Or perhaps it is the leap that humankind must take.

Think of the evolution and history of modern warfare: male troops, separate and apart from the citizenry, squaring off against one another on the field of battle, usually in brightly colored uniforms, as warriors for the king or state. There was even some sense of a "gentleman's" rules of engagement that spoke of honor and decorum.

Those lines have become blurred. Even in our own American Revolution, the outmanned and outgunned colonial patriots resorted to hidden snipers picking off British officers well schooled in the art of warfare. This was seen as contrary to the rules. Over time, war has become "total." It is no longer between two designated "teams" with rules of honor. Instead, modern warfare devolves into using virtually any means in order to prevail, even if innocents must die. In fact, as witnessed in Russia's attack on Ukraine, civilians are commonly targeted to break the will of the people, including women and children. Bombs and advanced artillery, particularly drone warfare, are guided on a screen that dehumanizes and depersonalizes the actual murder of human beings.

In a 1966 interview, Ram Dass—formerly Harvard's Richard Alpert, Tim Leary's colleague who progressed from LSD advocate to spiritual guru—concurred with a reporter's hypothesis that "all wars are civil wars because all men are brothers." When the East Indian sage Ramana Maharshi was asked, "How should we treat others ?" he replied, "There are no others." To some, those statements suffer from foolish idealism. But on the deepest level of humanity, this appears to be true. "What we see as other is only a projection of what we have rejected in ourselves," says author Glenn Aparicio Parry. "We may feel repelled by certain ideas and perspectives, but we are unwittingly dancing with them, as shadow dances with light, always remaining connected."[283]

Yet unless there is something resembling a new Great Awakening—*unprecedented* co-operation, even among so-called adversaries, to counterbalance climate change and the erosion of democracy, among other crises—the planet will edge towards collective calamity. Things have gotten stretched, as Peter Russell alluded to in *Waking Up in Time*, perhaps to the point of breaking. But like the individual who gets a wake-up call from a heart attack and finally tends to his health, our planetary culture has the opportunity to choose, almost out of compunction, a collective transformation and healing.

Given where the nation finds itself today, the question may be asked: how did we get here? How have those who occupied the Oval Office shaped America's consciousness as reflected in their religious faith? What does the tapestry of presidential beliefs reveal about America's spiritual evolution today?

CHAPTER FIVE

Born Again:
When the President
Talks to God

Those praying for a revival, a new great awakening,
might be careful what they wish for; for they may get that,
but they might not like what they get.

Mitch Horowitz

PRESIDENTS AND "RELIGIOUS TESTS"

As David McCullough writes in *John Adams*, "If Jefferson was a Jacobin, a shameless southern libertine, and a 'howling' atheist, Adams was a Tory, a vain Yankee scold, and, if truth be known, 'quite mad.'"[284]

This is what kicked off the presidential election of 1800.

During that campaign, Thomas Jefferson's critics argued that he was an "infidel," unfit for office due to his "unorthodox" if not atheistic religious beliefs. The allegations cost him friends and admirers. But not the election.

In a preview of future American presidential contests, the election was a rancid affair with mudslinging and yellow journalism that might shock even the twenty-first century social media mindset. Adams ran against Jefferson's "atheism," making this the first presidential race with a religious "litmus test," despite the Constitution's prohibiting such tests for office. Not that Jefferson was an atheist, but it begs the question:

could an atheist—or something considered close to it—be elected president today? According to Pew Research, it's highly unlikely.[285] It is hard to imagine how a candidate who professes to have *no* religious beliefs could find favor. [286]

What if a presidential candidate in this age announced that he or she was a Unitarian? Or a Deist? Shortly after the turn of the twentieth century, whether a Unitarian—the staple of many of the early founders—was electable was questionable. In 1908, Unitarian William Howard Taft is noted to have said in a letter to a friend, "I am interested in the spread of Christian civilization, but to go into a dogmatic discussion of creed I will not do whether I am defeated or not. . . . If the American electorate is so narrow as not to elect a Unitarian, well and good. I can stand it."[287]

After Jefferson, contentious religious "tests" only occasionally played a role in nineteenth- and early-twentieth-century presidential politics. Religious affiliation and allegations of atheism did arise in the elections of both Lincoln and Taft, and Al Smith's Catholicism was likely the single greatest factor in his loss as the Democratic candidate against Herbert Hoover in 1928.[288] However, as the nation matured and reached a stage of homeostasis, the issue generally lapsed because most presidential candidates were older, White, mainstream Protestant men. Religion was seen as a personal, private matter in presidential elections, generally outside the bounds of fair play.

The 1960 Kennedy–Nixon campaign once again shifted the terrain, and religion came to play a much larger role in American politics. The 1950s Red Scare and McCarthyism had exposed fractures in America's mostly agnostic approach to presidential religious beliefs. John F. Kennedy's Roman Catholicism resurrected shades of fear seen in the Smith–Hoover race of 1928. In a predominantly Protestant nation with conventional Protestant presidents, wide acceptance of Catholicism had been slow and grudging. Aside from old feuds dating back to early Europe, nineteenth- and twentieth-century Catholic immigrants hailed from countries largely considered "inferior"—Ireland, Spain, Poland, Italy, and Hispanic nations—and therefore contrary to the US's predominant Anglo heritage. In the Deep South, the hatred for Catholics by conservative or radical White groups, e.g., the Ku Klux Klan, rivaled their enmity towards Jews and Blacks.

The Kennedy–Nixon contest revealed underlying strains of America's religious divide. Ultraconservative, Southern cleric leadership contended that the pope was "the whore of Babylon" and JFK's first allegiance would be to Rome. Celebrated religious figures such as Norman Vincent Peale and Billy Graham publicly or privately denounced JFK's Catholicism. Peale maintained that it would be impossible for JFK to separate himself from the influence of the Catholic Church.[289] Behind the scenes, Graham tried to tip the scales in favor of Nixon.

Well aware of the "religion issue," Kennedy delivered a convincing public address to the Houston Ministerial Association just two months before the election:

> "I am not the Catholic candidate for president. I am the Democratic Party's candidate for president, who happens also to be a Catholic," he said. "I do not speak for my church on public matters, and the church does not speak for me. . . . But if the time should ever come—and I do not concede any conflict to be even remotely possible—when my office would require me to either violate my conscience or violate the national interest, then I would resign the office; and I hope any conscientious public servant would do the same." [290]

Even Nixon suggested Graham back off of his religious politicking: "I told [Graham] he would undermine his own ability to change people spiritually if he engaged in activities designed to change governments politically."[291] Kennedy's election laid the issue to rest, with Graham eventually supporting him. The contentious issue of a president's religious beliefs would skip a few cycles. But the rise of a more cohesive conservative religious bloc began to emerge. Its political impact would be, and still is, enormous.

POLITICS AND THE RISE
OF THE EVANGELICAL RIGHT

They are the lineage of the heralded Great Awakenings, the great Christian movements integral to the American story. They are also the descendants, or contemporaries, of generally positive mentors: Dwight L. Moody, Billy Graham, Norman Vincent Peale, Rick Warren, and Joel Osteen.

Today's evangelicals remain a prominent force in America, both religiously and politically. But not every modern evangelist has been a Charles Finney. In the twentieth century, fundamentalist Christians Billy Sunday, Father Charles Coughlin, Billy James Hargis, Rev. Gerald B. Winrod, and Jimmy Swaggart mixed their acerbic politics with their religion. After September 11, 2001, the Moral Majority's Jerry Falwell and Pat Robertson condemned liberal groups as being the reason that "God punished us" with the 9/11 attacks.[292] In the opening decades of the twenty-first century, a majority of evangelicals were led to believe that Barack Obama was Muslim and not an American citizen. They overwhelmingly supported Donald Trump in 2016 and 2020, welcoming him into their universities and houses of worship, continuing to support him throughout his presidency, even as he contested the legitimacy of Joe Biden's election and sanctioned, if not instigated, the January 6, 2021, Capitol riot.

The "born again" movement has been ever-present in the American story, in some form, enjoying spikes in popularity over time. The emotional outpourings associated with the movement were accelerated by late-nineteenth-century Pentecostalism, which traces its influences to a Bible school in Topeka, Kansas, where teachers and students concluded that speaking in tongues was a definitive sign of "a baptism of fire by the Holy Spirit."[293] Pentecostals' penchant for glossolalia, as the practice became known, is "fluid vocalizing of speech-like syllables" whose precise meaning are unknown to the speaker. To some its sounds like an ancient language, to others gibberish. To Pentecostalists and evangelicals, it conveys an anointing of the Holy Spirit, a sense of communion with God.

In the early twentieth century, the Azusa Street Revivals of Los Angeles became another evangelical benchmark; ecstatic meetings led by William J. Seymour encouraged participants to experience dramatic worship, miracles, and baptisms of fire. Pentecostalism has adapted well to the evangelicalism of the twentieth and twenty-first centuries, emphasizing the joy of worship, altar calls, and glossolalia, often seen at mega churches.[294]

The "Jesus movement" of the early 1970s helped give birth to the modern born-again movement. The mostly young people in the movement became known as "Jesus freaks" or "Jesus people." Though they associated with aspects of the hippie era, of free love and getting back to nature, they remained faithful to biblical liturgy. At first, traditional Christians were wary of the movement. But they welcomed the shift in the younger generation, who began to speak more openly about their Christian belief. They seemingly had an ally on their side: the young thirty-ninth president, Jimmy Carter, affirmed in the press that he was "born again."

But alarmed by the spread of secular culture—including but not limited to the sexual revolution, *Roe v. Wade*, the nationalization of no-fault divorce laws, and Bob Jones University losing its tax-exempt status over its ban on interracial dating—evangelicals became more politically active, and not on behalf of the Jimmy Carters of the world.[295]

Within the next decade, the Religious Right—including Ralph

Reed's Christian Coalition, James Dobson's Focus on the Family, and Jerry Falwell's Moral Majority, among others—became fundraising and organizing juggernauts for the Republican Party. In 1980, the GOP nominated Ronald Reagan for president, its social platform a facsimile of conservative Christian views on sexuality, abortion, and school prayer.[296]

"YOU CANNOT ENDORSE ME, BUT I ENDORSE YOU"

Ever since the ascension of American Christian evangelicals as a preeminent political power, it has become an absolute must for presidential candidates to comment upon their spirituality. Pragmatically, there is simply no way around it.

Ronald Reagan is the first American president in modern times heartily endorsed by the evangelical movement. Though he never overtly identified as an evangelical while a candidate or president or at least never called himself one until after he left office—he clearly curried favor with evangelicals. And they him.

As quaint a notion as it might seem today, in the 1980 election when Reagan squared off against Carter, it was scandalous to run if one had been divorced. Evangelicals initially felt morally bound not to support a candidate who had broken the New Testament edict "What therefore God hath joined together, let no man put asunder." Reagan craftily rallied the faithful by simply stating, "You cannot endorse me, but I endorse you." This marked the unofficial marriage between the evangelical Christian Right and the Republican party, a relationship that has lasted beyond Donald Trump's presidency.

Though Carter was the first American president to identify as "born again" and claimed he regularly read the Bible, those evangelical bona fides did not suffice for the emerging Religious Right. They preferred Reagan's conservative politics over Carter's faith. The rise of Falwell's Moral Majority, Pat Robertson's *The 700 Club*, and others signaled

Christian thinking was becoming overtly political, a significant shift from the Peales and Grahams of yesteryear. Evangelicals stuck with Reagan long after revelations that he and wife Nancy engaged in esoteric practices such as astrology and numerology. Though this became public knowledge, especially after Reagan appointee Donald Regan's tell-all book *For the Record: From Wall Street to Washington*, it mattered little to Reagan's Christian admirers.

Earlier, Republicans Dwight D. Eisenhower and Barry Goldwater had little use or regard for the evocative Bible-believing core. True, the Eisenhower administration weighed in on religious issues—out of necessity. Due to the atmosphere created by the likes of Senator Joe McCarthy, Ike endorsed the National Prayer Breakfast and the inclusion of "under God" in the Pledge of Allegiance. As a response to atheistic communism, "In God We Trust" became the national motto and was stamped on US coins and paper currency. Eisenhower composed a prayer for his first inauguration, began his cabinet meetings with silent prayer, and met frequently with a wide range of religious leaders while in office.[297]

But Eisenhower did not engage or court evangelicals, who, at the time, were neither decisively political nor unified. Goldwater, the ultraconservative, half-Jewish 1964 Republican nominee, had nothing but disdain for evangelicalism's religious moralism and growing influence. After leaving the Senate, Goldwater revealed his long-held distaste for leaders of the movement, criticizing the "'radical right' . . . [and] moneymaking ventures by fellows like Pat Robertson and others [in the Republican Party] who are trying to . . . make a religious organization out of it."[298] Once Reagan was in office, such sentiments were rarely heard by party leadership.

Republican presidential primaries and often state and local elections have largely become referendums on whether a candidate is born again, supports evangelicalism, or is at least "religious enough." Over the last forty years, every Republican presidential candidate has loudly trumpeted his support of conservative Christianity. Reagan, George H.

W. Bush, Bob Dole, George W. Bush, and Donald Trump all more or less pledged their fealty to evangelicals. In 1988, the televangelist and fundraising powerhouse Pat Robertson ran for president and upended Bush Sr. in the South Carolina primary before finally losing to the future president, showing the strength of the growing evangelical base.

The one exception to aligning with evangelicals, at least at first, was John McCain.

McCain likely lost the 2000 primary due to, among other things, his adamant attempt to dislodge the Republican Party from the clutches of the Moral Majority and evangelicalism by calling Jerry Falwell and Pat Robertson "exponents of fear." Eight years later, he had learned his lesson. Not only did he refrain from any such criticism, but, playing to the base, he also inserted the evangelical-friendly Sarah Palin on his ticket. Four years later, Mormon Mitt Romney became the Republican presidential candidate despite conservative Christianity's historic anti-Mormon sentiment. The base's distrust and dislike of Barack Obama trumped any religious bigotry they may have retained towards Romney or his religion.

DIFFERENT FAITHS—OR NO FAITH AT ALL

The legacy of the modern Democratic party is that it is secular and the party faithful often prefer not to mention religion, to both its credit and detriment. Perhaps it is due to a historic acknowledgement that American presidents do not discuss the intimate details of their faith. Or maybe it is because there is no crystallized spiritual consensus that runs through its base as conservatives have experienced with evangelicalism. Or it may simply be that Democrats represent a dying breed of Americans that simply do not care, one way or the other, about a president's spiritual beliefs. Democrats have their religious traditionalists to be sure— Joe Biden and Nancy Pelosi have often touted their Roman Catholic faith. But the party has a much higher percentage of "nones"—atheists or agnostics or the spiritually inclined without any official religious affiliation—within their ranks than Republicans.

In the 2008 through 2020 presidential election cycles, however, even Democrats Barack Obama, Hillary Clinton, and Joe Biden felt compelled to cite their religious backgrounds and dedication to faith. In 2008 Obama claimed, "I am a devout Christian," telling voters, "I pray to Jesus every night and try to go to church as much as I can."[299] Some within and without his campaign remained doubtful. First there were the conservative media memes that Obama had been raised a Muslim in a madrassa in Asia. Then, months prior the 2008 election, Obama's association with the Reverend Jeremiah Wright (who had been criticized for his comments on terrorism and Zionism) embroiled the Democratic candidate in controversy. Finally, examining Obama's religious upbringing—an avowed atheist father and a mother who didn't attend church—suggested that his faith may not be as strong as he claimed. Yet in his first term as president, Obama said his mother "was one of the most spiritual people [he] knew."[300]

Obama has attended various Protestant churches over his lifetime but credits working with Black churches as awakening him to "the power of the African-American religious tradition to spur social change."[301] Early in his presidency, Obama disturbed the faithful and comforted the unbelieving by claiming that "religion has flourished within our borders precisely because Americans have had the right to worship as they choose—including the right to believe in no religion at all."[302]

AN ELECTION FOR "THE SOUL OF AMERICA"

Just as some of Obama's constituents questioned his religious beliefs, some of Trump's supporters have questioned his religious sincerity even as they politically endorse him without reservation. His awkward misnomer referencing "Two Corinthians" at a Liberty University speech during the 2016 campaign raised eyebrows. But Trump's support by evangelicals is nothing short of historic. Trump's relationship with them shifted the religious/political terrain unlike anything in the country's past four decades.

Famous political evangelist Ralph Reed said, "No one—no one—has done more for evangelicals than Donald J. Trump." American evangelicalism's support for Donald Trump has been unprecedented—80 percent voted for him in 2016 and even more did so in 2020—despite the absence of any genuine Christian leanings by the man himself.[303]

The overt political alignment, some evangelicals contend, is hurting their movement. Evangelicals largely ostracized outgoing *Christianity Today* editor in chief Mark Galli in late 2019 for his suggestion that the impeached President Trump should have been removed from office. His pronouncement was interpreted as an act of betrayal. Michael Gerson and Peter Wehner, two evangelicals who have worked in diverse Republican White House administrations, see ominous trends in evangelicals mixing politics so closely with their religion: "What is most personally painful to me, as a person of the Christian faith," says Wehner, "is the cost to the Christian witness."[304]

One of Wehner's mentors, evangelical Karel Coppock, contends, "We're losing an entire generation [of young evangelical witnesses]. They're just gone. It's one of the worst things to happen to the Church."[305] Diane Winston of the Religious News Service suggests, "It was a realpolitik calculation that drove so many white evangelicals to the Trump-Pence ticket." Regardless of Trump's religious background and failing to adhere to traditional Christian principles, "they wanted an affirmation of their status, and Trump offered one."[306]

Despite some who believed that evangelical association with Trump would diminish their numbers, the opposite appears to be the case: according to Pew Research, there is solid evidence that White Americans who viewed Trump favorably and did *not* identify as evangelicals in 2016 were much more likely to *begin identifying as* born-again or evangelical Protestants by 2020.[307]

Where an American president stands today as a reflection of American spiritual values has become muddied. However, one indication of America's evolution on religious matters since Kennedy's campaign over sixty years ago is that Joe Biden's Roman Catholicism was hardly a factor in the 2020 election. If anything, Biden was frequently shown attending his Catholic church during the campaign as a counterpoint to Trump's spotty and strategic church attendance. Biden often cited a phrase borrowed from historian and author Jon Meacham that the 2020 election was for "the soul of America."

EVANGELICAL MILLENNIAL SHIFT?

One of the unwritten stories behind evangelical support for Trump is that while conservative White evangelicals are a significant voting bloc, millions of evangelicals, notably those who aren't White, did not support Trump.[308] There are also increasing signs of a generational rift: young, White evangelicals do not have the same issue with immigration or racial and ethnic diversity as did their parents and grandparents. They generally don't see Islam, homosexuality, atheism, or even yoga as a threat. Though younger evangelicals didn't completely abandon Trump, they had much less enthusiasm for his administration and its policies than their elders. White evangelical women have viewed Trump far less favorably than their male counterparts.[309] As well, there is evidence of a growing #MeToo backlash against rampant sexism in evangelicalism.[310] While religion is on the decline, especially with millennials, there is a hipster evangelical movement afoot. Young evangelicals are reexamining the way their faith informs their politics. This trend can be seen in Los Angeles, where a latter-day Azusa Street Revival appears to be catching on. Churches such as Zoe, Mosaic, Vous, Radius, and Churchome are expanding with campuses across the country. So is Australian-born Hillsong, even with its financial, sexual abuse, and pastor controversies.

These "new brands" are drawing young celebrities such as Chris Pratt, Justin Bieber, Kendall Jenner, Selena Gomez, Hailey Baldwin, and Kevin Durant. For them, this form of Christianity is accessible, cool, and interesting, offering a new breed of Instagram-friendly, celebrity-surrounded pastors. Modern American evangelicalism has always spread in part by being adjacent to power.[311] However, Pratt's religiosity seems refreshingly free of the politics of past evangelicalism. He doesn't endorse political candidates or go on right-wing talk radio.[312]

These churches are, in some ways, more progressive than their predecessors because they reject politics and have a young, non-judgmental appeal. But some contend otherwise. "[W]hen it comes time to dig beneath the surface," says *Vox* journalist Laura Turner, "their theology is still actually fairly conservative and . . . isn't much more forward-thinking than the churches their parents grew up in. It just looks a little cooler."[313]

A SHRINKING ISLAND

Some fifty years ago, evangelist Jack Chick started a Christian ministry, publishing cartoon pamphlets in an earnest effort to save lost souls worldwide. The pamphlets often depicted remorseful sinners in hell who did not believe that salvation came through Jesus Christ alone. Chick Ministries claims to have sold 900 million copies of their pamphlets over time.

But the publishing company depicts other religions as counterfeit. Go to their website today and the same memes are repeated: Catholics are lovers of the pope, the "whore of Babylon"; Jehovah's Witnesses, Mormons, Seventh Day Adventists, and many other "new" religions are cults; and those born into Islam, Judaism, and other world religions shall never "enter the Kingdom" unless they confess Jesus as their true lord and savior. Today, as in earlier days, Chick Ministries make one thing clear: Christianity is the only way out of hell. Pure and simple.

But by the twenty-first century, even evangelical Christians had crossed the Rubicon: growing from a small percentage in the 1950s, a majority of evangelicals now concur that those of differing religious groups, even non-Christians, can attain a heavenly afterlife.[314]

When one ponders the history of religious certitude in the US, its preternatural decline has occurred in a relative nanosecond. Today, one in three millennials have no religious affiliation whatsoever; Christian millennials are still believers, but they reject the evangelicalism of their parents and grandparents. They acknowledge (if not embrace) other religions that their parents once saw as anathema to Christian belief. They are also dispensing with the hard political turn of their elders, who in a twist of fate entered politics to save religion, only to make their "brand" of Christianity unacceptable to millions of young people, thus accelerating the country's turn against, or at least disregard for, religion.[315]

Some evangelical Christians—high-profile members included—are rejecting various fundamental tenets of their belief system.

NO HELL BELOW US

He was a Black bishop with a huge following. His personal mentor was Oral Roberts, who treated him as a son. He was a spiritual advisor to President George H. W. Bush and spoke beside Billy Graham at the Oklahoma City Bombing Memorial in 1996. Millions watched his sermons in person and on television. He boasted a large, prosperous, multiracial megachurch of Christian believers, unheard of for the time.

Bishop Carlton Pearson led a charmed life. But it turned on a dime. One morning, preaching before thousands of people at his Oklahoma church, he declared, "I believe people go through hell, not ultimately to hell." Carlton wanted the church to stop telling people they were going to hell. "Tell them 'your sins are forgiven,'" he said. "Tell them there's no issue between God and them that hasn't been resolved by Christ Jesus."[316]

But the explanation fell flat. Throwing out hell meant throwing out a core Christian precept. If there's no hell, why would anyone need a savior? Powerful church leaders condemned him. Congregants deserted him. Oral Roberts himself pleaded with Pearson to reconsider, to apologize and make amends. But that "revelation from God" that hit the bishop that morning like a bolt out of the blue—that no soul is forever separated from God—could not be denied or turned back upon. "When I started thinking about the absurdity and the vulgarity [of hell]," he said, "I could not reconcile that with a God of love." Bishop Pearson was branded a heretic. It cost him everything. At least, materially.

Is Pearson a voice in the wind? Or, for all the fear associated with a punishing God, does hell have a "sell-by" date? Is this the generation that sees Jonathan Edwards's "Sinners in the Hands of an Angry God" largely come to an end? In 2015, 58 percent of US adults still believed in hell—a place "where people who have led bad lives and die without being sorry are eternally punished."[317] But that number had fallen from 70 percent a mere decade earlier.[318] As the number of "nones" grows, the percentage of people believing in eternal damnation will likely dwindle as well. Does this suggest the coming end of fundamentalism?

Bishop Pearson's dramatic story about hell is captured in the well-received 2018 movie *Come Sunday.* Today he preaches about a loving God that would not eternally damn any sheep in his flock. But to sermonize that, he had to change his stripes. He founded the Metacostal

Network of Churches and Ministries, "bridging the gap between his Pentecostal roots and embracing a Metaphysical approach to ministry and progressive spirituality." Today he often references Albert Einstein's "cosmic religion of the future"[319] and says "that which is impenetrable does exist. . . . The nature of our being is something subtle, intangible and inexplicable. . . . [A] veneration for this force beyond anything we can comprehend is my religion."[320]

INTEGRAL TO THE
AMERICAN SPIRITUAL STORY

One last word on the evangelical movement. It epitomizes one of the quintessential "poles" in the American soul. Because it has likely been more overtly political than most religious groups in modern America, large segments of the population, especially the young, are rejecting the movement outright. It should not be forgotten, however, that much like the First and Second Great Awakenings, the evangelical movement has been an energizing force, an integral aspect to the American spiritual story. Even when evangelical theology has been rejected outright, it has been a catalyst for others to more closely scrutinize their *own* beliefs. Many may never have taken a personal turn inward or made the affirmative, conscious choice to reject orthodox religion if not for the loud voice of American evangelicalism.

This is not new to the American story. The friction between the two poles of the soul of America sometimes appears as the bane of the country's existence. But it also provides contrasting energy to move the nation forward, ultimately resulting in a more expansive view of America's—and our own—essential nature.

CHAPTER SIX

A Tapestry of Cosmic Awareness

*The religion of the future will be a cosmic religion.
It should transcend a personal God and avoid dogmas and theology . . .
based on a religious sense arising from the experience of all things,
natural and spiritual, as a meaningful unity.*

Albert Einstein

*We have people who consider themselves believers because they accept
their religious metaphors as facts and we have others who classify
themselves as atheists because they think religious metaphors are lies.*

Joseph Campbell (paraphrased)

CONVERGENCE, OR THE DEATH OF FUNDAMENTALISM

How far into the future was Einstein looking?

Was he referring to the erasure of all religious lines? Was he speaking of one great future religion? Based on his comments over time, probably not. He likely envisioned a world where individual religions retain a semblance of identity and boundaries but find greater common ground with other belief systems: each maintaining its respective characteristics and rituals but enjoying a heightened sense of interdependence, integrated thinking, mutual respect, and cooperation. His words suggest a natural integration, a thinning of lines between belief systems.

In a word: ecumenism. Originally a Christian concept, the adjective *ecumenical* was applied to any interdenominational initiative that encouraged greater cooperation among Christians and their churches, whether or not the specific aim of that effort was full, visible unity. Today it has taken on greater meaning beyond unity of Christian faiths. It pertains to a broader religious landscape—in that sense, a nonsectarian, nondenominational unity.

With greater worldwide communication and integration, will the planet's belief systems increasingly converge in ecumenical fashion?

Add to the collision/convergence of world religions the emerging presence of atheism and agnosticism. More prominent than ever, atheism expresses itself more openly, more confidently than in decades past and tears away at the artifice of fundamentalism and doctrinal orthodoxy. Then incorporate into this mix the provocative science opening up new worlds of what constitutes consciousness, its genesis, and likely non-locality. The portal from life to death winnows as well, as near-death (NDE) and out-of-body (OOB) experiences open boundaries to what defines consciousness, what defines life. Does your brain generate consciousness? Or does consciousness exist irrespective of the physical brain?

These are concepts to explore, but for the present, here's a question: will these colliding belief systems radically change the perception of who we are? Given some of the awakening catalysts we are facing, are these worlds destined to converge even more closely in the years ahead?

"I'M RIGHT, YOU'RE WRONG"

Someone once asked Jacob Needleman, author of *The American Soul*, to define fundamentalism: "Basically, it's I'm right and you're wrong."[321] From the start, American ecumenism consistently countered fundamentalism. It deterred the young nation from establishing a singular religious viewpoint. This is why it is easy to marvel at the founders' early religious perspectives. Even if they did not adopt another's spiritual beliefs, even if they rejected them outright, they gave due deference. They seemed to learn simply by listening. Their introduction to numerous belief systems, and the resulting ecumenism, had a direct impact on the government those founders birthed. It was spiritual eclecticism, the exposure to *and respect for* others' unique universal outlooks, that made America not only the most tolerant of nations but also a seedbed for innovative action.

The early leaders of the nation knew that religious diversity benefitted the young republic, inoculating the nation against any one dominant thought form uniting church and state. In some places (e.g., Connecticut and Rhode Island), attempts to create a state religion ultimately failed. The young nation squelched theocracy at every turn.

The universal ecumenism at the heart of the founders' spirituality is a stunning reminder of what made our nation great and how we, in our time, may emulate their openness and approach. This is especially true now as more diverse religions, cultures, and political ideologies collide. We would be reminded how they assimilated divergent viewpoints in service to the greater good. More than any specific belief system, holding this awareness alone set the founders apart in history. Spiritually inclined though they were, they were highly skeptical of organized religion. A fine line to tread, but they did so adroitly, leaving us with an American blueprint for unity and transformation.

Perhaps they would most closely identify with what is the fastest growing spiritual group in America today.

HERE COME THE "NONES"

In the 1990s, the historical tether between American identity and faith snapped.[322] Religious nonaffiliation rose, doubling in one decade. By the 2010s, the "nones," an assortment of atheists, agnostics, and "spiritual dabblers," had tripled in size.[323] That was a staggering rise from just a decade earlier. By 2019, approximately one-fourth of the US adult population and a third of adults under thirty were religiously unaffiliated, the highest percentages ever in Pew Research Center polling.[324] The number of people who identify as Christian dropped 12 percent in one decade. Recent surveys on religion show there are sixty million Americans who classify themselves as "nones."[325] By 2020, church/synagogue/mosque membership fell below 50 percent, and less than half the country said that religion is "very important" to them.[326]

The vast majority of "nones," however, do not consider themselves atheists or even agnostics.[327] Many have moved away from mainstream religions into genres described as "nothing in particular" or "spiritual but not religious." This steadfast shift away from the dominance of any one belief system is consistent with the founding principles of a secular society, discouraging one religious power base from rising over another.[328]

Pew Research has taken it a step further, asking a sample of these "nones" *why* they do not identify with any religion. The most common reason is they question the validity of religious teachings. The second most common reason is opposition to the positions taken by religious institutions on social and political issues.[329] In the past three decades "religion has lost its halo effect . . . not because science drove God from the public square, but rather because politics did."[330]

Christian Smith, a sociology and religion professor at the University of Notre Dame, says America's drastic "nonreligious" shift occurred due to three historic turn of events: (1) more people became disenchanted with evangelicals' uniform endorsement of conservative political issues in the 1970s and '80s and the Republican Party's association with the Christian Right; (2) the end of the Cold War and the fall of atheist-influenced communism, allowing atheism to step forward without fear; and finally (3) the events of September 11, 2001, where religious zealots brought down the World Trade Center towers, suggesting to some that all religions are fundamentally dangerous. [331]

Today, although "nones" as a "religious" group lag far behind the 71 percent of Americans who identify as Christian in the Pew poll, they still comprise a significant bloc, much larger than Jews (4.7 million),

Muslims (2.2 million), and Buddhists (1.7 million) combined (8.6 million). The numbers are comparable to politically powerful Christian sects such as evangelicals (25.4 percent) and Catholics (20.8 percent).[332] Today's "nones," despite their atheistic/agnostic contingent, more closely resemble the more deistic/transcendental side of the American soul, which might auger a resurgence of those historical secular values that are still tethered to the sacred and the spiritual.

The shift is likely not an outlier. "The rise of religious non-affiliation in America," says *The Atlantic*'s Derek Thompson, "looks like one of those rare historical moments that is neither slow, nor subtle, nor cyclical."[333]

A HIGHER POWER

The greatest revolution of our generation is the discovery
that human beings, by changing the inner attitudes of their minds,
can change the outer aspects of their lives.
William James

In 1961 Bill Wilson (a.k.a. "Bill W."), the founder of Alcoholics Anonymous, wrote to famed Swiss psychiatrist Carl Jung. It was Jung and his theories of the collective unconscious that revolutionized psychology, taking on a more spiritual tone than espoused by his mentor Sigmund Freud.

In his letter, Wilson references a thirty-year-old conversation Jung once had with a former patient named Rowland H., wherein Jung stated that he believed his patient was beyond any medical or psychiatric treatment. The only hope for him was a spiritual or religious experience—"in short, a genuine conversion."[334] Wilson told Jung in the letter, "That conversation between you was to become the first link in the chain of events that led to the founding of Alcoholics Anonymous."

Jung's insight proved prophetic. Rowland H. experienced a religious conversion that led to his recovery. When Wilson launched AA, he borrowed heavily from the writings of Carl Jung, who was adept at describing spirituality in nontheological terms. AA often references a "higher power" and a belief "in God as we knew him" without the trappings of a church or religion. Alcoholics Anonymous would become a leading proponent in the spiritual-but-not-religious movement, evolving into the blueprint for twelve-step programs worldwide, which lead people out of addiction by spiritual means.

As much as Bill Wilson leaned on the writings and language of Carl Jung, one man would have an even greater influence on him and his programs.[335]

THE PRAGMATIC MYSTIC
(OR THE THINKER WHO BELIEVED IN DOING)

He was born into intellectual and spiritual American royalty.

Notorious outlaws aside, the James surname belongs to one of the nation's preeminent families. Henry James Sr. hobnobbed with—and challenged—nineteenth-century Transcendentalists and those of the social upper crust, and became patriarch to intellectual, literary, and theological legends. The theologian, author, and wealthy real estate magnate "invited metaphysicians of every stripe into his home to discuss matters of religious philosophy,"[336] introducing his children to cutting-edge concepts. Bored by the teachings of existing churches, Henry instead found inspiration in the teachings of seventeenth-century Christian mystic Emmanuel Swedenborg, as well as those of his friend Ralph Waldo Emerson. In January 1842, Emerson, his only son having just succumbed to scarlet fever, agreed to be godfather to Henry James's newborn son, William, who would become one of the greatest figures in American history, forever changing how the world perceived the mind and spirituality. William James is universally acknowledged as the father of American psychology.

James attended Harvard Medical School during the Civil War and eventually chaired Harvard's nascent psychology department. There, he pioneered the systematic study of the psychology of religion. He was also the first to draw America's attention to the work of Sigmund Freud. His monumental tome *The Varieties of Religious Experience: A Study in Human Nature* (1902) influenced twentieth-century mind-body-and-spirit trailblazers, and it's still considered a classic today. His exploration pushed the bounds of contemporary psychology with "Does Consciousness Exist?" (1904) and "How Two Minds Can Know the Same Thing" (1905).

At an Ingersoll lecture at the Harvard Divinity School in 1898, James questioned the scientific materialist view that the brain produces consciousness, suggesting instead it limits and determines the form of something far greater, "a consciousness elsewhere produced."[337] It's fair to say his work set the stage for generations of explorers of Jung's collective unconscious, the theory of relativity, quantum theory, and theories of non-local consciousness. Some consider William James to be the greatest thinker in American history.[338]

But despite the fervency of his spiritual upbringing, James hit a psychical wall in his late twenties, suffering from malaise and depression. To compensate for morbidness and as an antidote for recurring ill health, he recommended optimism and action. James would likely have endorsed the future words of Theodore Roosevelt, one of his students at Harvard, who would write: "Black care [depression] rarely sits behind a rider whose pace is fast enough."[339]

Long before Roosevelt would journey to the Amazon for his own emotional rehabilitation (after losing the 1912 "Bull Moose" presidential election), William James headed there himself, in his twenties, to pull out of his melancholy. Later, when he felt "the absence of God, he finally had no choice but to rely on himself. . . . He concentrated his energies on improving his own will and capacity for effective worldly action."[340] He ditched conventional religion's focus on God's miraculous intervention and the hereafter, constructing a new framework. James articulated a psychological model describing how each of us is a continuous, eternal being. By looking within, we too can awaken to our higher, spiritual powers.[341] He developed a metaphysics that celebrated the role of human action in determining the final shape of the universe.

James was not only a pioneer in psychology. He founded the American Society for Psychical Research (ASPR), investigating the paranormal and the impact of the spirit world on physical manifestation.[342] A number of biographers have suggested the explanation was personal: James and his wife, Alice, were drawn to psychics in 1885 following the death of their young son Herman.[343] Whatever effect Herman's death might have had, it was far less important than James's longstanding interest in the possibility of the soul's immortality.[344]

Fellow Harvard professor, philosopher, and atheist George Santayana said James's examination of religious experience "gave a sincere and respectful hearing to sentimentalists, mystics, spiritualists, wizards, cranks, quacks and imposters."[345] James believed that any of these might have something to teach him. But trained as he was in physiology, psychology became a laboratory science, representing the new scientific mind.[346] For all his metaphysical insights, James lived like there was no substitute for human action if the world was to make progress towards greater wholeness.[347] Ultimately, each person makes his own truth from what works for him. James summed it up simply in the title to his heralded 1907 publication: *Pragmatism*.[348] In short, he was "the thinker who believed in doing."[349]

THE LAST DETOXIFICATION

In December 1934, Bill Wilson went to a New York City hospital for what was to be his last detoxification. In his autobiography, he describes an associated, dramatic event:

My depression deepened unbearably and finally it seemed to me as though I were at the bottom of the pit. . . . All at once I found myself crying out, "If there is a God, let Him show Himself! I am ready to do anything, anything!"

Suddenly the room lit up with a great white light. I was caught up into an ecstasy which there are no words to describe. It seemed to me, in my mind's eye, that I was on a mountain and that a wind not of air but of spirit was blowing. And then it burst upon me that I was a free man. Slowly the ecstasy subsided. I lay on the bed, but now for a time I was in another world, a new world of consciousness. All about me and through me there was a wonderful feeling of Presence. . . . A great peace stole over me and I thought, "No matter how wrong things seem to be, they are still all right. Things are all right with God and His world."[350]

After Bill Wilson's revelation, his physician and counselor William Silkworth, MD, confirmed that he was not "crazy" but that he'd had just the sort of spiritual experience that sometimes cures alcoholics. The next day, Wilson's old school friend Ebby Thatcher, also a recovering alcoholic, brought Bill a copy of James's *The Varieties of Religious Experience*. Wilson "devoured [the book] from cover to cover."[351]

William James's psychological analysis of religious experience emboldened Bill Wilson to abandon conventional belief in the Bible and church doctrines. Wilson came to epitomize a core James truism: self-reliance is possible only once we have connected ourselves to a higher power. He concurred with James that the "truth" of religion is to be found in personal experience—that "religion of this kind acknowledges diversity and makes allowances for personal differences."[352]

Bill W. called William James a "founder of Alcoholics Anonymous." It wasn't a mere figure of speech. James gave AA "a language and metaphysical rationale for a mode of spirituality that is at once deeply personal, optimistic, progressivist and couched in the essentially therapeutic language of self-actualization."[353] Wilson described AA as a "spiritual rather than a religious program,"[354] a description that resonates to this day throughout all twelve-step programs. AA's mystical, non-scriptural approach to spiritual regeneration may have turned off America's religious establishment, but it attracted both the churched and unchurched.[355] Wilson's psychological approach paired with the notion of surrendering to a higher power became a cornerstone in late-twentieth-century New Age philosophy and is arguably an integral component of America's next Great Awakening.

OUT ON A LIMB

In 1987, actress Shirley MacLaine graced the cover of *Time* magazine. A multi-Oscar-nominated and winning actor—not to mention a tough competitor who had beaten the Hollywood studio system twice in court—she had appeared on the cover of or in national magazines countless times. But this time, it was different.

MacLaine had just produced and appeared in the television mini-series *Out on a Limb*, based on her best-selling book of the same name. In it she explored her strong interest in metaphysics, covering topics on reincarnation, mediumship, trance-channeling, holistic health, crystal healing, and even unidentified flying objects.[356] In one famous scene she is seen standing on a beach, arms outstretched, affirming, "I am God, I am God, I am God."

In the mainstream, MacLaine *was* out on the thin, skinny branches of that limb. Her public pronouncements shocked. Religious traditionalists called it blasphemy. Evangelicals warned of "false prophets" presaging Jesus's second coming. Others just laughed. Once, when David Letterman chided MacLaine and would not let up on the New Age subject, she responded by saying, "Maybe Cher was right; maybe you *are* an assh*le!"[357]

Perhaps the notion of "New Age" would not have been so shocking if the public had been more familiar with its esoteric American roots. The psychology, science, and spirituality espoused by William James is often cited as the main influence on what has loosely been described as New Age. Much of it was considered occult in the strictest sense—that is, "hidden," flying under the mainstream's radar, even well into late-twentieth-century America. But most of the topics had been explored before: Deists and Freemasons had addressed reincarnation, e.g., Ben Franklin wrote of it in his *Poor Richard's Almanac*. Mediumship was native to the nineteenth-century Spiritualist movement. Altered-state channeling was "popularized" in that same century by Anthony Jackson Davis and later by the twentieth-century intuitive Edgar Cayce. In the 1960s, meditation emerged in America, inspired by the East–West nexus of Transcendentalism, the '50s Beat Generation, the Beatles, and Transcendental Meditation's Maharishi Mahesh Yogi.

As for the "I am God" part? If MacLaine was celebrating her integral, inner divinity as opposed to identifying herself as *the* Godhead, then millions were apparently open to the notion.

"MIND CURE" AND NEW THOUGHT

MacLaine and her like-minded associates may not have known it, but their revelations borrowed liberally from a nineteenth-century, uniquely American concept: what William James labeled "the religion of healthy-mindedness" in *The Varieties of Religious Experience.* Its focus was on well-being: mental, physical, and spiritual. James believed the "mind-cure" movement of the latter nineteenth century was "America's only decidedly original contribution to the systematic philosophy of life."[358] Here was an awakening of a different stripe. He believed it the up-and-coming religious persuasion for the age: "For the healthy-minded individual, one's happiness and contentment was regarded as evidence for the truth of their religion."[359] James dubbed the movement "New Thought." The appellation stuck.

In James's estimation, New Thought was an "optimistic scheme of life, with both a speculative and a practical side . . . an intuitive belief in the all-saving power [and] conquering efficacy of courage, hope, and trust, and a correlative contempt for doubt, fear, worry, and all nervously precautionary states of mind."[360] New Thought's brand of mysticism is predicated on an essentially friendly universe in which the individual is infused with divine energy. The human mind is assumed to be the supreme channel for this energy with its powerful healing and creative forces. Implicit in New Thought is the view that religious belief should be pragmatic, in tune with the culture of the age, and consonant with scientific laws. Largely absent is redemption theology and the acceptance of the enduring reality of sin in the world.[361]

Growing out of the early, freethinking, individualistic mindset of Deism, mesmerism, and the latter-day influence of Transcendentalism, New Thought looked to the mind for answers. With it, all things were possible, whether practically they were or not. In some ways this new attitude mirrored the unbridled though somewhat naive confidence of the young nation itself. Much like the Fool in tarot or a youthful teen brimming with blind assurance, it suggested one too innocent to appreciate the task and difficulties ahead—a Manifest Destiny without much in the way of consequences.

Still, innocent confidence was better than none at all.

BOTH PROPHET AND SAVIOR

Years before the coming of William James, that freethinking, confident spirit dwelt in hardy New Englander Phineas Parkhurst Quimby, a man who would not be denied. American clockmaker, mentalist, and mesmerist, he is often cited as the founder of the New Thought movement. Suffering from tuberculosis in the 1830s, he experienced intense excitement when galloping on his horse. He discovered it shifted his thinking about his malady, uplifted his mood, and relieved some of his physical suffering. Bent on getting an answer to his illness where doctors could not, he sought out the sciences of the mind and how they affected physical state.

Quimby was introduced to the hypnotic practices of Franz Mesmer when he attended a lecture in 1838 in his home state of Maine. Putting hypnosis methods into practice, he healed himself and then initiated a practice whereby he could "put people under" who also needed medical or psychological attention.[362]

Quimby toured New England, sharing his concepts of mental and spiritual healing based on the view that illness is a largely a matter of one's mind. One of his earliest followers was religious author and speaker Warren Felt Evans, who had pursued the ideas of the aforementioned mystic-scholar Emmanuel Swedenborg. Evans is believed to be the first American metaphysical writer to use the term *New Age* to herald an era of mystical awareness. In his 1864 book *The New Age and Its Messenger*, the "messenger" is Swedenborg.[363] Evans furthered the work of Quimby with *Mental Cure* (1869), *Mental Medicine* (1872), and *Soul and Body* (1876).

New Thought and mind cure caught on. Mary Baker Eddy, one of Quimby's patients, adopted many of his practices. She would later deny such influences after intense fallouts with both Quimby and Evans. But their inspiration was at the heart of her Christian Science. It may never have rivaled mainstream Protestantism in size or significance, but Christian Science has had an undeniably unique impact on American faith. If only for a season, it was the most popular mind-cure religion of its time.

Eddy was also one of the first women to lead a large-scale American church. Beyond the bounds of theology, she produced the respected and enduring *The Christian Science Monitor*, still in print today. The "mother church" (Church of Christ Science) was founded in Boston in 1866, and nearly 2,000 Science Reading Rooms (both bookshop and place for contemplative prayer) exist in eighty countries today.[364] Controversy still follows the church over its "prayerful healing" practices versus traditional and integrative medicine, particularly during the COVID epidemic.[365]

Even with her shortcomings, Mary Baker Eddy changed the trajectory of American spiritual thought.

Today, there is no mention of Quimby or Evans in Christian Science reading material or on its international website. For posterity, Mary Baker Eddy is both Christian Science's prophet and savior. The metaphorical tablets she retrieved from the mount were all her own, and none would be discovered after her. Mark Twain said, "By 1900 Mrs. Eddy was probably the most famous woman in America, but definitely the most controversial."[366] Her persona and certitude in being a singular messenger wore thin with New Thought advocates. They did not accept her teaching or any other of her formulations as the final revelation. Just as Eddy refuted the influence of New Thought pioneers, New Thought today, as loosely configured as it is, does not consider Eddy or Christian Science as part of its movement.

UNIQUELY AMERICAN

About a decade before *The Varieties of Religious Experience* was published, so-called New Thought churches began to dot the terrain. As diverse a movement as it had become, its beliefs interlocked symbiotically with the likes of James and latter-day Transcendentalists. A variety of like-minded churches and denominations emerged: the Church of Divine Science (established in 1888 by Malinda Cramer and Nona L. Brooks with Quimby and Emma Curtis Hopkins as influencers), Charles and Myrtle Fillmore's Unity Church (1889), and Religious Science, established by Ernest Holmes in 1927, teaching the "science of mind."[367]

None of these expressions, however, would dominate numbers-wise in any way comparable to mainstream religions like Protestantism, Evangelicalism, Catholicism, or Judaism. In size, New Thought spiritual centers have more in common with other uniquely American religions:

Unitarianism (Universalist Church of America founded 1793, American Unitarian Association 1825, joining together 1961), Seventh-day Adventists (1863), Church of Latter-day Saints (Mormonism, 1830), Jehovah's Witnesses (1870), Christian Science (1879), the Rosicrucian Fellowship (1909), Nation of Islam (1930), and Scientology (1952), among others.

But if the contention is that New Thought, like Unitarianism, has had a profound influence on core American spirituality, then why has it not been as popular or had as much influence on national culture and politics as, say, evangelicalism or mainstream religions?

Perhaps it has. Though in a much less direct manner.

CHRISTIANS IN NEW THOUGHT CLOTHING

They were less concerned about sin. They spoke of individual success. You rarely heard them talk of hell. They extolled how the mind creates happiness in our lives.

This isn't a reference to the Transcendentalists or William James or Phineas Quimby or Shirley MacLaine. It points instead to prominent religious figures deeply influenced by New Thought thinkers—even if those figures or their faithful dared not speak the names of their inspirers.

In 1952—at the same time L. Ron Hubbard was establishing Scientology—a Christian pastor from New York City published a book that would influence entire generations of Americans. Spiritual leaders would guide their flocks with his words. Some heard the embracing, divine potential of New Thought. Others heard sin-redemption Christianity. Both impressions were valid.

Norman Vincent Peale's *The Power of Positive Thinking* vaulted onto the *New York Times* best-seller list where it would remain for 186 consecutive weeks. It launched the modern self-help industry, selling more than five million copies in forty-one languages worldwide.[368] Annual reprints and dozens of spinoffs by other authors, including branded Bibles, calendars, inspiration cards, and wall art, expanded the book's reach. The magazine *Guideposts* was founded by Peale, and even decades after his death it has a current paid circulation of more than 2.3 million readers. From 1932 to 1984, Peale's pulpit was located at Marble Collegiate Church in New York City, one of the country's longest standing nondenominational Protestant houses of faith, founded in 1628.[369]

Peale's book and its incumbent philosophy embody the most widely held American spiritual perspective since the twentieth century—that the mind can shape circumstance. He maintained that an affirmative attitude contributes, in a concrete way, to the outer circumstances of one's life, whether in health, jobs, or relationships. That concept is a basic tenet of American belief across the religious spectrum.[370] With Peale, the notion that "attitude is everything" became a staple in evangelical and mainstream religious thinking. "I don't know of anyone who had done more for the kingdom of God than Norman and Ruth Peale," said Billy Graham at the National Council of Churches in 1966, "or have meant any more in my life for the encouragement they have given me."[371]

Yet the genesis of Peale's core themes do not hearken back to a Great Awakening. His "psychological spirituality" did not borrow from Calvin or Finney or any early-twentieth-century theologians in his church's tradition. Instead he leaned on the likes of Emerson and James to make a case that our unconscious minds have continual access to the spiritual power that flows through the universe.[372] If one traces the family tree of Peale's positive thinking movement, it goes back to "occult thinkers" steeped in spiritualism, mesmerism, mental healing, and the positive thinking philosophies of the New Thought movement.[373]

What Peale did was brilliantly articulate and synthesize the philosophies of evangelical Christianity and New Thought. "Affirm it, visualize it, believe it, and it will actualize itself," he often said.[374] But his pronouncements were void of any occult or esoteric language. His genius was translating "psycho-theology into the language of the people."[375] He took these ideas and "recast them in words where the mainstream public, the church-going public, the bible-believing public could find comfort. He succeeded so broadly that it is largely forgotten that 'positive thinking' began its life in this country as an esoteric philosophy."[376]

To some extent, Peale himself is responsible for the amnesia.

Peale did not attribute his popular credo to his New Thought mentors. Nor did he go out of his way to remind his Christian followers that he was a thirty-third-degree Mason. When asked of his influences, he usually defaulted to the line that his messages were "scripture based," that Jesus Christ was his primary teacher, and that turning to the Bible is the ultimate guide to life betterment and successful problem-solving. "There is an answer in the Bible for every mood," he extols in the *Positive Thinking Bible.* "All you need to do is open your Bible. The first statement you see may not be your answer, for God does not work in such a mechanical manner."[377]

MIND SCIENCE AND THE FATHER OF "POSITIVE THINKING"

For some drawn to Peale's philosophy, it seemed as though they had heard it before—perhaps it was Emerson, or Quimby, the Fillmores, or twentieth-century New Thought luminary Emmet Fox. If one bothered to examine the roots of Peale's gospel, they'd have discovered that no one had a greater impact on Norman Vincent Peale than Ernest Holmes.

Although broadly forgotten today, Holmes is nevertheless recognized as one of the leading minds in modern metaphysics and New Thought. He was a prolific writer and lecturer, and believed that people, through their self-awareness and power of choice, can control the health of the body and the conditions of their environment by affirmative meditation, which he called "treatment." [378]Author of *The Science of Mind* (1926), he described his ensuing Religious Science (today known as Centers for Spiritual Living) movement as "a group of trans-denominationalists and Judaic-Christian Practical Transcendentalists." For a time, his United Church of Religious Science held the promise of growing into the great American metaphysical faith for which many yearned.[379] Although there is no mention of Holmes in any of Peale's biographies, the ideas presented by Peale could have been plucked right from the pages of *The Science of Mind*.[380]

Late in his life, Peale opened up. In several interviews, he reminisced about his time at the *Detroit Journal* in 1920, lost and confused as a young reporter. His employer was both a personal friend of Holmes and a student of *Science of Mind*. "Never be afraid of anybody, anything, or any situation," his boss admonished him. "If you're afraid, you are thinking almost entirely of yourself. Stop thinking of self!" He then handed him a book by Holmes that Peale said "influenced [his] entire viewpoint of life."[381]

In 1940, after corresponding for years, Ernest Holmes and Norman Vincent Peale finally met. It took place on the movie set of *One Foot in Heaven*, an Academy Award Best Picture nominee about the life of a minister and his family, starring Fredric March and Martha Scott. Holmes and Peale hit it off and their friendship deepened.[382]

Just years before his death, Peale acknowledged his debt to Holmes as mentor: "I found he talked of religion differently from the orthodox way. . . . Whenever I reread things that Ernest said, I always have the feeling he still lives, a warm personal friend. . . . [383] I believe God was in this man, Ernest Holmes. He was in tune with the infinite."[384]

APOSTASY AND THE PROSPERITY GOSPEL

Despite his popularity, Peale had his detractors in theological, to say nothing of secular, circles. Some conservative religious leaders told their congregants to stop reading *Guideposts*, claiming that visualizing as an aid to healing as encouraged by Peale was "a practice that left one open to demon influences."[385] Christian author, publisher, and critic

David W. Cloud of Way of Life Literature believes Peale was nothing less than an apostate. He blames this on Peale's exposure to the works of Emerson, James, and the *Meditations* of Marcus Aurelius when Peale was a student at Boston University School of Theology. According to Cloud, those influences made Peale's gospel "a mixture of theology, philosophy, and social science of The Mysticism of Personalism . . . nurturing a metaphysical subjectivism."[386]

Peale's claim of salvation was also too watered down for those of deep Christian faith. "I have accepted the Lord Jesus Christ as my personal Savior," Peale said in a 1993 interview with *Christianity Today*. "I mean that I believe my sins are forgiven by the atoning work of grace on the cross . . . but I am absolutely and thoroughly convinced that it is my mission never to use this language in trying to communicate with the audience that God has given me."[387] Perhaps his greatest affront to his evangelical brothers was a 1984 appearance on *Donahue*.

"It's not necessary to be born again," Peale said on live television. "You have your way to God; I have mine. I found eternal peace in a Shinto shrine."

Donahue exclaimed, "But you're a Christian minister. You're supposed to tell me that Christ is the Way and the Truth and the Life, aren't you?"

Peale replied, "Christ is one of the ways! God is everywhere."[388]

If the Pentecostal flock did not tear him to pieces, members of the secular press certainly did. They criticized him for his focus on money, materiality, and conservative politics. Peale's see-it-and-believe-it mantra applied to every facet of the believer's life, but "especially in the sphere of material advancement, which was the surest sign of divine favor in the hermetic social world of Pealeism."[389] The implacably right-wing Peale cheerfully described himself as a "missionary to American business" and made good on that by waging a relentless campaign in the pages of *Guideposts* against the New Deal, unions, and others he considered affronts to true-blue individual achievement.[390]

Though others got there long before him, from Napoleon Hill's *Think and Grow Rich* to William Wattles, Peale is considered the godfather of "the prosperity gospel." It has become popular among charismatic preachers in the evangelical tradition who equate Christian faith with material success. Its critics claim the tradition has come to represent the worst conflation of American-style capitalism, religion, and politics.[391] Although rooted in the positivity of abundance found in American New Thought, it has devolved into the kind of material gospel that Transcendentalists likely would have denounced. Emerson criticized "prayer that craves a particular commodity . . . stemming from self-interests and materialistic desires . . . causing people to lose their tie with nature and thus separating them from the ultimate foundation of peace."[392]

Some contend Peale's inerrant philosophy materialized in the person of Donald Trump. Trump's family members were avid fans of Norman Vincent Peale and attended Marble Collegiate Church. Donald and Ivanka were married there just years before Peale's death. Trump biographer Gwenda Blair said the former president loved the preacher and "weaponized" the power of positive thinking.[393]

To be sure, Peale is not the first "prophet" whose broadly positive message had been contorted to serve individual purposes. In hindsight, it hardly seems fair to judge his career or philosophy based on his influence on a few high-profile individuals. Peale made his errors, "but a great number of people were willing to judge him within the full context of the entirety of his work. When he's seen from that perspective, the scales tip heavily in his favor."[394]

Over the course of his career, as many Christian preachers would later emulate, Peale did not draw a line between his theology and politics. In 1952, in response to Peale's criticism of Adlai Stevenson's bid for president, the democratic nominee highlighted Peale's distancing from the apostle Paul's creed, saying, "I find Paul appealing and Peale appalling!"[395] In the 1960 presidential race, Peale openly supported

Richard Nixon, saying Jack Kennedy was unfit for the presidency. He warned Americans that Kennedy's fealty would be to the Roman Catholic pope. "Faced with the election of a Catholic," Peale declared, "our culture is at stake."[396]

Those statements could have derailed his career but did not. Ultimately, President Reagan awarded him the Medal of Freedom in 1985, and upon hearing of Peale's death on Christmas Day 1993, President Clinton said, "The name of Dr. Norman Vincent Peale will forever be associated with the wondrously American values of optimism and service."[397]

Peale's ultra-successful, philosophically nuanced career would serve as a template for a modern-day clergyman who, without saying so, spans the spiritual spectrum from fundamentalism to New Thought/New Age.

SON OF A NEW THOUGHT PREACHER MAN

He was a high school dropout. A popcorn and insurance salesman. After he divorced he went to ministry school, becoming a small-town pastor in Texas. In 1958, not yet forty, he had an ecstatic religious experience and called it the "baptism of the Holy Ghost." His epiphany led him to start a small charismatic church in a dusty, abandoned feed store in Houston, Texas. An animated preacher with Southern Baptist roots, he peppered his sermons with biblical passages, encouraging congregants to accept Christ as their personal savior. Later, his church would grow to thousands and then millions of followers, his messages broadcast around the world.

Somewhere along the way, John Osteen discovered Norman Vincent Peale and New Thought.[398] Osteen walked in Peale's footsteps, as did many others who followed. Robert Schuller of Crystal Cathedral fame primarily comes to mind, but evangelists Kenneth Hagin, Kenneth Copeland, John Hagee, T. D. Jakes, Rick Warren, and others likely fit in that category as well. Amid the scriptural references to Jesus, heaven and hell, and the "Word of God," Osteen emphasized the power of the mind as the key to a happy and successful life. The mind was the critical mediator between people's notions of themselves and their God—their thinking patterns determined the quality of their lives: "You cannot think negative thoughts and expect to live a positive life. . . . See, the things that keep people from God are their thoughts. Our minds are the battlefields where the devil will win or be defeated. The devil has no entrance into you except through your mind. Win the battle of your mind."[399]

When he passed away in 1999, John Osteen left a legacy in more ways than one. His youngest son was an employee at his Lakewood Church ministry, a quiet, unassuming young man who worked behind the scenes. Six days before his father's death, he reluctantly gave his first sermon. When his dad died, he was thrust into the spotlight. No one knew it at the time, but he would take his father's ministry to heights unforeseen.

Today, Joel Osteen is considered the "most popular preacher on the planet" and is often listed as one of the most influential religious leaders in the world.[400] But like Peale, his messages don't fit conveniently inside the evangelical box. Among modern Christian preachers, no one "embodies the spirit of New Thought more than he does. And on the widest scale. Whether he realizes it or not, Joel Osteen is standing directly on the shoulders of an American esoteric spiritual tradition."[401]

It's a characterization Osteen would likely reject. But his homilies—as his evangelical detractors and New Thought admirers agree—clearly suggest that ancestry.

Osteen's positivistic style derives inspiration directly from the pages of Emerson, Holmes, James, and Peale. His focus is on the goodness of God rather than sin. His simple approach to biblical principles emphasizes the power of love and a positive attitude. In a 2013 interview he said, "When I grew up, the devil was a reason why I had a headache or the devil was the reason I got mad today. We always blamed the devil. I think today when I say the enemy, I like to make it broader. Sometimes the enemy can be our own thoughts. We've trained ourselves the wrong way."[402]

This doesn't sit well with evangelical ministries who claim Osteen's gospel "isn't Christian at all. . . . He merely offers a way to speak about New Age nonsense using Christianese."[403] They find his best-selling *Your Best Life Now* filled with platitudes "that human beings have the life force within them to create whatever kind of life they want."[404] His messages, they contend, smack of "universalism" and are dangerously influenced by the likes of Gnosticism, Theosophy's Madame Blavatsky, and Rhoda Byrne's *The Secret*. They accuse him of merely sprinkling scripture into the mix.

Evangelist pastor John MacArthur attempts to expose Osteen as a "pagan religionist, a quasi-pantheist and an agent of Satan."[405] With a wry smile MacArthur says, "Osteen is right. If you believe him, this *will* be your best life. It will be a whole lot better than the next one. If you want your best life now, go for his theology. If you want your best life forever, avoid it."[406]

"NOT THE GOD OF CALVIN AND LUTHER"

Osteen's 2005 interview with Larry King on CNN is a watershed moment in twenty-first-century religious politics. It upset many evangelicals, forcing Osteen to respond:

KING: "You are not the fire and brimstone type?"

OSTEEN: "No. That's not me. It's never been me. I've always been an encourager at heart."

KING: "But don't you think if people don't believe as you believe, they're somehow condemned?"

OSTEEN: "I try not to do that. You may not agree with me, but to me it's not my job to try to straighten everybody out.

The Gospel's called the good news. My message is a message of hope, that God's for you. I know there is condemnation, but I don't feel that's my place."

KING: "Because we've had ministers on who said . . . if you believe in Christ, you are going to heaven; if you don't, you are going to hell."

OSTEEN: "You know . . . I don't know . . . there's probably a balance . . ."

KING: "What if you're Jewish? What if you're a Muslim and don't accept Christ at all?"

OSTEEN: "You know I am careful saying who would and wouldn't go to heaven. . . . I [don't] believe they're wrong; I believe here's what the Bible teaches and from the Christian faith this is what I believe. But I just think that only God can judge a person's heart."[407]

That portion of the interview set off a firestorm in the Christian world. As a caller to King's show said, how could Osteen not say that Jesus was the only way to heaven? But perhaps his comments should not have been all that shocking. Only four days earlier, an elderly Billy Graham, also on *The Larry King Show*, said more or less the same thing:

KING: "But what about those faiths—the Mormons and the others that you mentioned—believe in Christ. They believe they will meet Christ. What about those like the Jews, the Muslims, who don't believe they . . ."

GRAHAM: That's in God's hands. I can't be the judge."

KING: "You don't judge them?"

GRAHAM: "No."

KING: "How do you feel . . ."

(CROSSTALK)

GRAHAM: " . . . going to hell and all that."

KING: "How do you feel when you see a lot of these strong Christian leaders go on television and say, you are condemned, you will live in hell if you do not accept Jesus Christ, and they are forceful and judgmental?"

GRAHAM: "Well, they have a right to say that, and they are true to a certain extent, but I don't—that's not my calling. My calling is to preach the love of God, the forgiveness of God. . . . In my earlier ministry I did the same . . ."[408]

For those celebrating Osteen's initial show of ecumenism on King's show, they'd eventually be disappointed. Within days of his television appearance, he backed off his comments, apologizing for not making it clear that "having a personal relationship with Jesus is the *only way* to heaven"[409] (emphasis his). There were other mea culpas in his all-inclusive apology letter. Though some evangelicals were not pleased with his explanation, it satisfied Albert Mohler of the conservative Southern Baptist Theological Seminary. It was clear that Osteen learned not to offend the most religiously conservative segment of his Christian base.

Today, as before, Osteen imbues much of his sermon with the adopted "positivism" of New Thought, including that of Unity and Religious Science, only to end his message with "remember to find a good Bible-believing church near you." Hell, sin, and repentance still aren't players in Osteen's repertoire. Neither are abortion, homosexuality, or the contested authenticity of Mormonism and other religions. The lack of spiritual, political, and cultural stances lead some evangelical preachers such as Steven Lawson to censure Osteen, suggesting his God is not the God of "Calvin and Luther, Whitefield and Edwards, [those] who would declare from the housetops that the gospel is the power of God and of salvation."[410]

THE SECOND COMING OF PEALE

As they did with Peale before him, the secular press has taken aim at Joel Osteen, and mainly for the same reason: preaching the prosperity gospel. If Osteen is its current poster child, he still came to the game late. Peale, Reverend Ike, Robert Schuller, Oral Roberts, Kenneth Copeland, Pat Robertson, and dozens of others all put an evangelical spin on New Thought's message of an abundant life long before the young Texan preacher did. Osteen's take on prosperity sounds similar to a New Thought perspective: "I get grouped into the prosperity gospel and I never think it's fair, but it's just what it is. I think prosperity, and I've said it a thousand times, it's being healthy, it's having great children, it's having peace of mind. Money is part of it; and yes, I believe God wants us to excel."[411]

Osteen's evenhanded approach, at least as reflected in his words, comes off sounding more closely aligned to an Emersonian ideal of abundance than the greed often associated with evangelical or New Age hucksterism.

On balance, Joel Osteen and Norman Vincent Peale are unique figures in American spiritual history: they are products of both the Second

Great Awakening and classic New Thought. They cross-pollinated the two, adopting pioneering mind-cure concepts and merging them with a fervent form of Christianity. As Peale did in the '50s and '60s, Osteen arguably represents the current middle point in the American spiritual spectrum, at least the center among believers. How many famous religious figures have sat down with—and been lauded by—both Pat Robertson and Oprah Winfrey as Osteen has? Not to put too much emphasis on his convictions, but Osteen's spiritual trajectory is likely a bellwether for where the nation is moving in consciousness. This role comes with both adulation and demonization. That's a lot of weight for one pair of shoulders. But maybe it is Osteen who, on today's world stage, best exemplifies a "middle way."

SIDE-SWIPED, OR
"A KEG TAPPED AT BOTH ENDS"

Christian Evangelicals largely denounce anything with a New Thought or New Age label. The word *occult* has taken on a raft of definitions and to the evangelical faithful represents everything dark and sinister about the unknown. To say many Christian organizations feel threatened by the erosion of numbers, creeping religious integration, and the possible loss of the "purity" of their message—that Jesus is the only way and the more or less literal interpretation of scripture—is an understatement. But some Christian evangelicals who have been moved by the sermons of a Peale or Osteen have adopted ideas from spiritual sources that cut across all belief systems and religious backgrounds. In many respects, whether they realize it or not, evangelical and mainstream Christianity have co-opted themes of the very practitioners they purport to reject.

Something happened in the 1980s and '90s that upended the American belief spectrum. Emerging polarizing forces side-swiped mainstream religion and churches, from both the left and the right. Those leaving traditional religion have fled to evangelicalism on one end of the spectrum and to the "nones" (mostly atheism, agnosticism, New Age/ New Thought) on the other. To borrow a phrase from Benjamin Franklin (although he was alluding to the state of New Jersey!), mainstream religion has become "a keg tapped at both ends." Traditional religion has been bled by more energized liberal and conservative spiritual expression on either side of the belief spectrum. It's a trend likely to continue.

America *is* losing its religion. That is a fact on its face. But unlike Europe, America remains steadfast in its spiritual inclinations, foiling any notions of secular takeovers.

In the midst of seeming chaos, common ground can seem elusive. But in truth there's been a path towards convergence among religions for centuries — a course set out by mystics long ago.

—✳—

CHAPTER SEVEN

Mystics Out
of Monasteries

*Remain true to yourself but move ever upward towards greater
consciousness and greater love! At the summit you will find yourselves
united with all of those who, from every direction,
have made the same ascent.*

Pierre Teilhard de Chardin

I am a god. I am not the God . . . I don't think . . .
Bill Murray, from the movie *Groundhog Day*

"WE'RE ALL IT"

In 1971, John Lennon released the song "Imagine," his anthem
summoning all dreamers for world peace, often considered one of
the greatest songs of the twentieth century.[412] One verse includes the
controversial lyric "Imagine no religion, it's easy if you try; no hell below
us, above us only sky." To believers, it was an affront to their faith; to
atheists, holy ratification. Yet you have to wonder how many understood
Lennon's "middle path" in the 1970s.

When it came to religion, John Lennon was a complicated man.
He grew up with mainstream British Protestantism, but there was
nothing remarkable in its influence on the young Lennon's life. Nothing
overtly transcendent appears in his early work either, until the Beatles'
1966 "Tomorrow Never Knows," the last song on *Revolver*. Recorded
shortly after the Beatles were introduced to hallucinogens, the song
simultaneously drew attention to consciousness-enhancing drugs and

the ancient religious philosophies of the East. The lyrics are inspired by *The Psychedelic Experience: A Manual Based on the Tibetan Book of the Dead*, a book by Timothy Leary, Richard Alpert (later Ram Dass), and Ralph Metzner.

Around the same time, Lennon proclaimed (quite possibly true) that the Beatles were more popular with their generation than Jesus. With the rest of his bandmates he embraced the Maharishi Mahesh Yogi and Transcendental Meditation. But Lennon also at times refuted any notion of a deity (e.g., "God" from the first Lennon/Plastic Ono Band album). Some think he wrote "Imagine" with that belief in mind, hence the lyric. But his eldest son, Julian, and Lennon's own words leave clues to the contrary.

In the 1990s, more than a decade after John Lennon's death, Julian toured Australia. On one occasion, he was summoned to the hotel lobby where he had been staying. A large group of indigenous peoples from the Mirning Tribe, news cameras in tow, hoped to speak with the young Lennon. The aboriginal tribe's elder said, "You have a voice; can you help us?" extending his hand with a male swan's white feather in it.[413] Julian felt goosebumps wash over him.[414] His father had told him two years before his death that "if [John] passed, if he should just pop off one day, if there was any way of getting through to [Julian] . . . letting [him] know that [John] was going to be all right, or that we were all going to be all right, it would be in the form of a white feather."[415] According to Julian, this was an odd thing for his dad to say, but he was very clear about the white feather showing up.[416]

Decades later, in 2009, Julian—a talented photographer, musician, filmmaker, and author in his own right—founded the White Feather Society, a global environmental and humanitarian organization focusing on education, health, conservation, and the protection of indigenous cultures.[417]

Ostensibly, the lyrics in "Imagine" reject religion and a heaven, at least as they are conjured in the West. But some of John Lennon's (and the Beatles') songs had a metaphysical bent.[418] The man who wrote "imagine no religion" also wrote the lyric "Jai guru deva om" in "Across the Universe" (translated as "Oh hail teacher of God, source of all existence," dedicated to Guru Dev, Maharishi Mahesh Yogi's teacher).[419] "Imagine" hearkens more to Einstein's "cosmic religion of the future" than any individuated dogma or creed whose time was, in Lennon's hopeful view, limited.

For those who still cling to the presumptive notion that the lyric could only mean imagining the absence of any religion or any God, a *Rolling Stone* interview given by Lennon three days before his death puts the idea to rest:

> But still, the concept of imagining no countries, imagining no religion—not imagining no God, although you're entitled to do that, too, you know? Imagine no denominations. Imagining that we revere Jesus Christ, Mohammed, Krishna, Melanippe, equally—we don't have to worship either one that we don't have to, but imagine there's no Catholic/Protestant. No Jew/Christian. That we allow all . . . we allow it all—freedom of religion for real, I mean. For real. Just imagine it? Would it be terrible?[420]

Sounding much like the core values of *A Course in Miracles*, Lennon said, "There are two basic motivating forces: fear and love. When we are afraid, we pull back from life. When we are in love, we open to all that life has to offer with passion, excitement, and acceptance."[421] In what would be his last interview, Lennon posited, "If there is a God, we're all it."[422]

Perhaps in Lennon's mind "Imagine" alludes to a time in planetary evolution where divisions over religious dogma have ended and faiths have finally evolved, converging at the apex where they've been all along: the mystical path of every great religion.

MEET AT THE MOUNTAINTOP

Atheists have no God. The polytheists have many Gods.
The monotheists have one personal God.
The mystic, only God.

Huston Smith

Mysticism is likely "one of the most abused words in the English language."[423] Often it is defined, "in a derogatory sense, as metaphysical obfuscation or belief in ghosts and other occult phenomena."[424] The word has been used as an excuse for "dilute transcendentalism, vapid symbolism, religious or aesthetic sentimentality and bad metaphysics."[425] "Mystic," "myth," and "mysticism" are used as terms of contempt by some, but not by those who diligently studied the world's religions and found common universal themes.

One of the first to venture to apply intellectual parameters to mysticism—to describe the indescribable—was William James. By middle age, he had traveled the world several times. He was one of the first to research many of the world's belief systems, hence the series of lectures that constituted the text for *The Varieties of Religious Experience: A Study in Human Nature*. Published eight years prior to his death, in it James dedicated several lectures to mysticism. Mystical experience, he says, is "ineffable—that is, difficult or impossible to convey in ordinary language. It is noetic, meaning that it seems to reveal deep, profound truth. It is transient, rarely lasting for more than an hour or so. And it is a passive state, in which you feel gripped by a force much greater than yourself."[426] Two qualities that James did not include in his list but mentioned elsewhere are blissfulness and a sense of union with all things.[427]

In his classic work, James observes that "Hinduism, Ilrahmans, Buddhists, Christians, Mohammedans and Jews" all enjoy mystical traditions. These experiences span diverse beliefs, pointing towards the same kind of truth—that is, the existence of a greater, incomprehensible reality, beyond common human experience. The knowledge imparted by mystical experience, he says, is on the whole "optimistic" and "pantheistic."[428] It is "a monistic insight, in which the OTHER in its various forms appears absorbed into the One."[429]

In the "gospel" of William James, mysticism is common to all religions yet transcends religion itself. Within decades of his death, numerous intellectual and spiritual giants would emerge, standing squarely on the shoulders of his insights. Many would alternately confirm or challenge his conclusions. Together they'd set new parameters regarding mysticism's universality and its role in the modern world.

"THE MOST NEEDED BOOK IN THE WORLD"

As a teenager, Aldous Huxley contracted keratitis, an eye disease that left him partially blind. But his brother suggested that his temporary blindness may have been a blessing in disguise. It was as if the condition pushed the young man inward, evoking a metaphysical outlook on life. According to his brother, Aldous frequently contemplated "the strangeness of things." His "uniqueness lay in his universalism. He was able to take all knowledge for his province."[430]

Huxley, much like William James, was born into a family of means, education, and influence, and his siblings rivaled him in accomplishment. His temporary blindness kept him out of the Great War of 1914 and forced him to abandon his hopes of becoming a doctor. But upon recovering much of his sight, teaching and writing filled the void. As a young schoolmaster he taught Erik Blair (the future pen-named George Orwell), who noted Huxley's "great command of language."[431]

By his early thirties he had written five novels and provided social commentary for *Vanity Fair* and Britain's *Vogue*. His first blockbuster was the dystopian *Brave New World* (1932), a topic he would counterbalance with his last book, the utopian *Island* (1962). Along the way he wrote nearly fifty books, hundreds of articles, several Hollywood scripts, edited his friend D. H. Lawrence's letters, and frequently appeared on the lecture circuit. He dedicated some of his immense wealth to bring Jewish and left-wing writers and artists to the United States to escape Nazi persecution in the 1930s.

Moving to Southern California in 1937, Huxley's interest in mysticism and universalism grew. His friend Gerald Heard introduced him to the Vedanta Society of Southern California, founded and led by Swami Prabhavananda, who taught Huxley meditation and other spiritual practices. The neo-Vedanta-inspired Traditionalist School argued for a single metaphysical origin of religions. Inspired, Huxley wrote *The Perennial Philosophy* in 1945, deriving its title from the esoteric theological tradition of the same name. The book highlighted teachings of renowned mystics from around the world.

With the book coming out just as World War II ended, the *New York Times* wrote, "Perhaps Mr. Huxley . . . has, at this time, written the most needed book in the world."[432] *The Perennial Philosophy* affirmed a universal sensibility shared between Western and Eastern mysticism: "Beneath the revelations of all great world religions, the teaching of the wise and holy of all faiths and the mystical experiences of every race and age, there lies a basic unity belief which is the closest approximation man can attain to truth and ultimate reality," wrote Huxley. He called it the "Highest Common Factor."[433]

The Doors of Perception, written in 1954, addressed insights and expansion of awareness provided by his psychedelic experience with mescaline. Throughout Huxley's time in Los Angeles, he and his wives (his first wife predeceasing him in 1955) entertained many notable guests and celebrities at their home in the Hollywood Hills. In his waning years he kept up with the Vedanta Society, maintained friendships with

Krishnamurti and Huston Smith, and died on the same day as JFK and C. S. Lewis. His friend Igor Stravinsky dedicated his last orchestral composition to him. At the time of Huxley's death he was considered one of the greatest intellectuals of his era.[434]

THE HARVARD PSYCHEDELIC CLUB

His friend and mentor Aldous Huxley acquainted him with two of the most innovative—and notorious—explorers of consciousness in the Western world.

Son of American missionaries in China, Huston Smith was exposed to every major religion. His exploration of Hinduism and Buddhism would serve him well. According to Mary Rourke in a *Los Angeles Times* article published upon his death, "He had an early insight into the future of religion in America when he recognized that the country's expanding ethnic diversity would lead to greater curiosity about formerly unfamiliar traditions of various faiths."[435]

Smith was a teacher, pure and simple, a professor of Asian philosophy and religion at numerous universities over the course of his life. In 1955, he turned his popular college lectures into a series of programs on world religions for the National Educational Television network, the forerunner to PBS.[436] The show offended some Christian leaders who rejected Smith's parallels between Christianity and other religious teachings.[437] In 1958 he published his classic, the very James-sounding *The Religions of Man*, revised and given the gender-neutral title *The World's Religions* in 1991. A standard textbook in college-level comparative religion classes for over half a century, the two versions have sold more than a combined three million copies.[438]

A straightlaced character, Smith once confessed to Huxley that he had never had a full-blown mystical experience despite his studies of religious mysticism. Huxley introduced him to "this interesting chap over at Harvard" named Tim Leary. Leary and his colleague Richard Alpert wanted a religious scholar to participate in their Harvard Psilocybin Project, so they invited Smith from nearby MIT to join them.

In his book *The Harvard Psychedelic Club*, author Don Lattin memorializes the convergence of Smith, Leary, Alpert, and Andrew Weill at Harvard in the early 1960s and recounts the infamous Good Friday Experiment. Half of a control test group was administered psilocybin—a hallucinogenic alkaloid found in toadstools—and the other half caffeinated aspirin. It soon became apparent which group had *not* taken the placebo. Ingesting the psychedelic mushroom on the Friday before Easter 1961, Smith got his mystical experience. The event filled him with "such a sense of awe. It was exactly what I was looking for,"[439] exclaimed Smith.

After the revelation of the Harvard experiments exploded in the *New York Times* and the subsequent controversies, Smith distanced himself from Leary and Alpert. For the rest of his life he pursued his own unique path of enlightenment, attending Methodist churches and Zen monasteries, meditating with Tibetan Buddhist monks, practicing yoga with Hindu holy men, whirling with ecstatic Sufi Islamic dervishes, chewing peyote with Mexican Indians, and celebrating the Jewish Sabbath with a daughter who had converted to Judaism.[440]

For all of his seeking of common spiritual ground among religions, Smith did not mince words when it came to going deep within the mystical tradition of one belief. "I never canceled my subscription to Christianity," he told a crowded lecture hall at UCLA in 1999. "Religion gives traction to spirituality. If you are looking for water, it is better to drill one 60-foot well than 10 six-foot wells."[441]

A MYSTIC'S DARK NIGHT OF THE SOUL

The pure soul is like a lens from which all irrelevancies . . .
have been removed.
Evelyn Underhill

In the first half of the twentieth century, she was one of the most widely read writers on mysticism in the English-speaking world.[442]

As a child, Evelyn Underhill experienced "abrupt experiences of the peaceful, undifferentiated plane of reality—like the 'still desert' of the mystic—in which there was no multiplicity nor need of explanation."[443] As a young adult she was agnostic but later investigated Neoplatonism and eventually the Catholic mystics, much to her Protestant husband's dismay. A writer with a romantic heart, she first set off to write fiction. At the same time, she became enamored with "the enormous excitement in those days" that was "mysteriously compounded [with] the psychic, the psychological, the occult . . . the advance of science, the apotheosis of art, the rediscovery of the feminine, the unashamedly sensuous, and the most ethereally 'spiritual.'"[444] The combination of these passions would color her writing for the remainder of her life.

Unlike those of her time who wrote of the ecstatic states of mysticism, Underhill's early novels did not avoid the harsh realities of life. She addressed the pain, tension, and final loss of the ego-centered life for the sake of regaining one's true self. For Underhill, engaging the "dark night of the soul" (a concept extracted from a sixteenth-century Spanish poem by the mystic St. John of the Cross) was an integral part of the mystic's journey. This was, for her, the equivalent of working from within out. She intended her mystical stories to be a metaphor for the life story of Jesus.

After her early years of authorship, Underhill took to writing books on religious experience. Though she focused on Christian mysticism, Underhill wrote more broadly in her most important and popular work,

Mysticism: A Study of the Nature and Development of Man's Spiritual Consciousness (1911). She included a chapter on magic to separate mysticism from its most dubious connections. Realizing that mysticism is often associated with secret rites, fanaticism, and "bad metaphysics," and knowing mystics throughout history to be the world's spiritual pioneers, she felt it necessary to mete out its validity.[445]

In *Mysticism*, Underhill maintained her romantic edge while encompassing the roles of the psychologist, symbolist, and theologian. Although she agreed with William James that "rationalism is not the only path to reality," she brushed past his "four marks of the mystic state" from *The Varieties of Religious Experience*. Underhill's mystic went through five stages to attain this state: the awakening of self, the purgation of self, illumination, the dark night of the soul, and finally the unitive self, the sum of the mystic way. This state of "union" produced a fruitful creativeness: "the mystic who attains this awareness is the most active doer, not the reclusive dreaming lover of God."[446]

To Underhill, mysticism was "the science or art of the spiritual life,"[447] as variously defined in different traditions. Much as the Christian Saint Teresa of Avila believed, such consciousness is aimed at human transformation and is not the terminus of one's efforts.[448] Underhill emphatically believed that mysticism represented the highest form of human consciousness.[449] "We are all the kindred of the mystics," she once said. "Strange and far away from us though they seem, they are not cut off from us by some impassable abyss."[450]

ANARCHIST, SERVANT OF GOD

There is a stereotype of mystics seeking to escape the world, concerned only with the ecstasy of their own experience of union with the Divine; yet in that union is a doorway that opens out into everything and everyone.

Liza J. Rankow

Early on, you wouldn't peg Dorothy Day as a budding mystic.

Day has been called many things: activist, journalist, radical, agnostic, bohemian, mother, convert, prophet, and faithful daughter of the church.[451] Because of her interest in communism, sometimes socialism, and all-the-time anarchism—combined with her Catholicism—FBI director Edgar J. Hoover did not know what to do with her.[452]

In 1906, at the age of nine, Day witnessed the San Francisco earthquake and the subsequent self-sacrifice of neighbors in crisis—a formative experience about individual action and Christian community.[453] A college dropout, she emerged as a writer for several Marxist newspapers. Day became interested in social action and the power of the written word to effect change. She eventually led nonviolent protests advocating for labor rights, women's right to vote, racial integration, and the pro-peace movement. Civil disobedience was the hallmark of her support for the poor and disenfranchised.[454]

Day's turbulent life created a circuitous route to her conversion to Catholicism. After one abortion, Day got pregnant again, this time with an atheist. Something inside the young woman prompted a desire to give her baby girl a spiritual upbringing. Though not a Catholic, she asked a passing nun to baptize her child, but the nun told her she could not because Day was not a Catholic. Day studied the catechism with the nun, converted to Catholicism, and had her baby baptized in the faith.

Now a mother at thirty, but with the same fire to promote social justice as before, she combined her activism with her Christianity. In 1933, she co-founded the Catholic Worker Movement.[455] There she discovered a foundation in the sacraments and the inspiration of the saints that would support and inspire her for the rest of her life. Day considered the beatitudes from Jesus's Sermon on the Mount her mission statement. However, the Great Depression had begun, and she struggled to find Catholic leaders dedicated to putting the gospel message into action.[456] Day took up the banner.

Her desire for reform was anything but orthodox. Under her guidance, the Catholic Worker Movement developed a seemingly contradictory agenda, taking prophetic stands against racial segregation, nuclear warfare, the draft, and armed conflict around the world, while opposing abortion, birth control, and the welfare state.[457] For the many causes she supported, for the downtrodden, the powerless, the "less-thans" and "others" in society, she ended up in jail numerous times (one time beaten unmercifully by prison guards for peaceably demonstrating for women's suffrage).

It was in those situations where Day—who said that every person is "another Christ"—had experiences of empathy so vivid that she often felt like she was no longer "herself":

> All through those weary first days in jail when I was in solitary confinement . . . solitude and hunger and weariness of spirit . . . sharpened my perceptions so that I suffered not only my own sorrow but the sorrows of those about me. I was no longer myself. I was man. . . . I was the mother whose child had been raped and slain. I was the mother who had borne the monster who had done it. I was even that monster, feeling in my own heart every abomination. . . . The sorrows of the world encompassed me.[458]

Author, theologian, and activist priest Matthew Fox says it was in prison where this twentieth-century mystic's consciousness expanded beyond her literal self: "She identified with everyone around her, each sorrowing and in need. The *via negativa* of prison helped to empty her of ego so that she learned compassion in a deep way . . . [and] her sense of self disintegrated such that she became one with every victim and every victimizer. . . . This is where divine compassion ultimately leads, to our identification with all aspects of humanity."[459]

Eventually Day became a Benedictine, and this influence can be seen in the Catholic Worker Movement's values of voluntary simplicity, community, prayer, and hospitality. "We cannot love God unless we love each other," said Dorothy, "and to love we must know each other."[460]

After Day's death in 1980, historian David O'Brien famously called her "the most important, interesting, and influential figure in the history of American Catholicism."[461] In his 2015 address before the US Congress, Pope Francis included her in a short list of exemplary Americans, along with Abraham Lincoln, Martin Luther King Jr., and Thomas Merton. The church has opened the case for Dorothy Day's possible canonization and now refers to her with the title Servant of God.[462]

RATIONAL MYSTICISM

Today the likes of John Horgan, science journalist and director of the Center for Science Writings at Stevens Institute of Technology, tackle the subject of mysticism, integrating a scientific framework. In his book *Rational Mysticism: Dispatches from the Border Between Science and Spirituality*, Horgan interviews Huston Smith, Ken Wilber, Terence McKenna, and others in his study "of the scientific quest to explain the transcendent."[463]

The term *rational mysticism* dates back to at least 1911, appearing in the title of an article published by Henry W. Clark (who earlier had written *The Christ from Without and Within*) for the *Harvard Theological Review*.[464] Rice University professor of religious studies Jeffrey J. Kripal defines rational mysticism as "not a contradiction in terms" but "a mysticism whose limits are set by reason."[465] For Horgan, what started as idealistic curiosity in mysticism turned into scientific passion: "Spiritual tomes ancient and modern promised that mysticism is a route not only to ultimate truth—the secret of life, the ground of being—but also to ultimate consolation."[466]

But Horgan had watched many of his friends and those of his baby boom generation lose their way, struggling to reconcile their mystical predilections with their reason. He noted the upsurge in scientific and scholarly pursuits of the mystical, including scanning the brains of meditators and praying nuns to pinpoint the neural correlates of mystical experience; inducing religious visions in volunteers by electromagnetically stimulating their brains with a device called the God machine; and mapping neural circuitry underlying blissful and horrific psychedelic trips.[467]

These scientific pursuits have still not yielded a consensus. But the mystical continues to lure the seeker and scientist alike. Horgan weighed in on the subject decades ago: "The human-potential priestess Jean Houston warned me early on in this project, [that it] begins in mist, has an I in the middle, and ends in schism."[468] Horgan has found plenty of schisms. He contends what constitutes a mystical experience shifts and changes among people and cultures and that in some instances mystical states may even be of little or no benefit.[469] Yet he maintains these experiences are universal, deserving of further study, and are common to all religions—and sometimes occurring to those with no religious attachment at all.

MYSTICAL DECEPTION FILE?

If mysticism is the highest octave of each religion, is it the great equalizer among religions?

A 1984 issue of *Common Ground* magazine featured an article entitled "Religions of the World, Unite!" The author, Colin Cole, urged followers of the world's religions to network, promoting world peace and harmony. Cole mentioned the divisions among faith groups but added, "However, all is not lost; there is good news. There are numerous people within each of the distinct world faiths, some who have had mystical or unitive experiences. . . . These people are open to new perspectives and attitudes. . . . [They] attest to an inner unity yet unseen, but with birth-pangs beginning to manifest in the world."[470]

For those who find solace in such words, the foregoing statement sounds hopeful.

However, this article by Colin Cole was referenced by Darkness to Light Christian Ministry as a *warning* to its followers. Placing the article on their "Mystical Deception File" page, the ministry alerted believers to the dangers of world religions getting too close, undermining or diluting traditional creeds.

Ecumenism has and will continue to threaten established religion, just as the integration of races and cultures threatens some human institutions. The fear is that it fosters a one-world religion and that religious purity, like racial purity, will somehow be lost or compromised through the sharing and integration of ideals. But the growing awareness of mysticism's universality is both breaking down walls among belief systems and, as Huston Smith discovered, driving people to a deeper place within their own tradition.

"NEITHER BIRTHDAY NOR NATIVE LAND"

There is a golden thread that runs through every religion in the world.
There is a golden thread that runs through the lives and the teachings to
all the prophets, seers, sages and saviors in the world's history.
Ralph Waldo Trine, *In Tune with the Infinite*, 1897

Many Americans born in the twentieth century were raised as Christians or Jews. But how many were exposed to the mystical traditions of their own belief systems? Is pursuit of the mystical path, regardless of creed, the code key for triggering a new Great Awakening?

Virtually every major religion possesses a mystical path. For Christianity it's largely the Christian contemplatives and Catholic mystics; for Judaism it is Kabbalah; for Islam, Sufism; in Hinduism,

Vedanta and the Upanishads; for some in Buddhism, it is Zen. Though these paths differ in their approaches, varying in their description of experiences and efficacy in attaining state, Ralph Waldo Trine's assertion of a "golden thread" at the heart of world religions celebrates universalism. As William James cogently described, "This is the everlasting and triumphant mystical tradition, hardly altered by differences of clime or creed. In Hinduism, in Neoplatonism, in Sufism, in Christian mysticism, in Whitmanism . . . [there is] an eternal unanimity which ought to make a critic stop and think . . .that the mystical classics have . . . neither birthday nor native land."[471]

Franciscan Catholic priest Richard Rohr directs New Mexico's Center for Action and Contemplation, built on the wisdom of the Catholic mystics: Meister Eckhart, Thomas Merton, Hildegard of Bingen, Mary Oliver, Teresa of Avila, Padre Pio, William Law, John of the Cross, and others. Their messages underscore the perennial tradition, which according to Rohr encompasses the recurring themes in all world religions and philosophies: a divine reality underneath and inherent in the world of things; the human soul's natural capacity, similarity, and longing for this divine reality; and union with this divine reality as the final goal of existence.[472] This last point could easily have been spoken by Emerson or James, and echoes the words of Huxley: "The final end and purpose of every human being is the unitive knowledge of God's being . . . and to discover the fact for himself, to find out who he really is."[473]

SAINTS IN WAITING

Thirteenth-century theologian Meister Eckhart (c. 1260–c. 1328), whose doctrines were strictly Christian but shared themes common to Buddhism and Sufism, said, "The seed of God is in us. Pear seeds grow into pear trees, nut seeds into nut trees, and God seeds into God."[474] The ultimate goal of all beings, for Eckhart, was the achievement of complete unity with God, a "transcendent Oneness." Those words reflect the sentiments of twentieth-century Trappist monk, author, and social activist Thomas Merton (1915–1968), who said, "The deepest level of communication is . . . communion. It is beyond words. . . . We are already one."

Carl Jung viewed Meister Eckhart as a Christian Gnostic who influenced his seeing Christ as the symbol of the archetypal self. Matthew Fox suggests,

> [Eckhart saw] each being as a cosmic Christ. Similar to Buddhism which says there is Buddha nature in every being . . . Eckhart had gone so deep in the river of his own journey, as a Christian, he came to the depths of the river where humanity dwells, what Jung would call the Archetypes, that we share common experiences whether we are Buddhist or Hindu or Christian or even Atheist. He was a leader in terms of ecumenism.[475]

Both Eckhart and Thomas Merton may have paid the ultimate price for their progressive approach. Merton was keen on interfaith understanding. According to Jacob Needleman, "One of his last essays, 'The New Consciousness,' begins, 'Christian renewal has meant that Christians are now wide open to Asian religions, ready, in the words of Vatican II,' to 'acknowledge, preserve and promote the spiritual and moral goods found among them.'"[476]

On the last day of his life in Bangkok he said, "I believe that by openness to Buddhism, to Hinduism, and to these great Asian traditions, we stand a wonderful chance of learning more about the potentiality of our own traditions, because they have gone, from the natural point of view, so much deeper into this than we have."[477] Merton died later that afternoon from apparent electrocution by a fan in his room. Suspicious circumstances and absence of an autopsy have led several authors, including Mathew Fox, to contend that Merton was murdered at the hands of the CIA due to his anti–Vietnam War stance.[478]

Meister Eckhart may have met a similar fate. Eckhart's use of Neoplatonist language—encouraging a contemplative way of life pointing to the Godhead beyond the nameable God—opened him up to allegations of pantheism. Like many mystics before and after his time, he incurred the wrath of ecclesiastical authorities seeking to safeguard their power. In the 1300s, during the Inquisition, he was prosecuted by the Vatican. The pope's fear of the growing problem of mystical heresy led him to condemn Eckhart to die, but apparently he passed away while in custody. Many believe Merton and Eckhart were martyrs and should be canonized as saints of the Catholic faith. That's unlikely to happen anytime soon because of their integrative approach to faith, social activism, and the resulting condemnation by Catholic authorities of their day. [479]

KABBALAH: "LIVE YOUR BEST LIFE NOW"

And the earth with be filled with the knowledge of G-d
as water covers the sea bed.
Isaiah 11:9

If the Catholic Church has been tough on its mystics, modern Judaism has been, at best, ambivalent with theirs.

When you enter the website of Kabbalah Centre International, you may think you've landed on a Jewish Joel Osteen platform: "Live Your Best Life with the Ancient Tools of Kabbalah" says the banner. Popularized by Madonna in the early 2000s, the Centre draws celebrities from Ashton Kutcher to Mick Jagger to Demi Moore. Paris Hilton and Britney Spears helped popularize the red-string bracelets associated with the movement. The Centre almost single-handedly opened peoples' eyes across America to Kabbalah. It's possible these inquisitive souls had never before known of Judaism's mystical heritage.

Kabbalah holds an enigmatic place in Judaism; it is simultaneously looked upon as ancient wisdom, a virtually new discovery, and a source of embarrassment. Its name applies to an entire range of Jewish mystical activity. Simply, Kabbalah means "tradition" in Hebrew. It arose in the twelfth century among rabbinic sages in Spain and France as a body of commentary on sacred Hebrew writings, primarily the first five books of the Torah but also early mystical texts. It aims to illuminate hidden meanings within those works.[480]

While codes of Jewish law focus on what God wants from man, Kabbalah tries to penetrate deeper, to God's essence.[481] Most tradition interprets the Torah as a narrative and legal work, but the mystically inclined are as likely to interpret it as "a system of symbols which reveal the secret laws of the universe and even the secrets of God."[482] Kabbalah is best described as the inner part of traditional Jewish religion, the official metaphysics of Judaism that was essential to normative Judaism until the modern era.[483] In essence, "Kabbalah goes beyond religion, beyond Judaism as we in the modern age have known it."[484]

The *Zohar*, a collection of mystical commentaries on the Torah, is considered the essence of Kabbalah. Written in medieval Aramaic and Hebrew, the *Zohar* is intended to guide Kabbalists in their spiritual journey, helping them attain the greater levels of connectedness with God. The *Etz haChayim*, the Tree of Life (found in other mystic traditions), also known as the ten *sephirot* (emanations), is a diagram used by Kabbalists to depict the

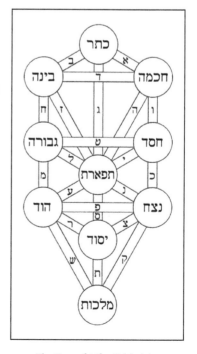

The Tree of Life, Kabbalah

creative forces through which the *Ein Sof* (infinite God) created and rules the universe.[485] The Tree of Life usually consists of ten nodes symbolizing different archetypes and twenty-two lines connecting the nodes. Kabbalah did not so much delineate between God and his creation as view humanity as a continuum of the expression of the energy or force of the Godhead, a notion found in most mystical sects and popularized by Transcendentalist expression in recent centuries.

But Kabbalah—as well as the namesake Centre—has suffered from controversy. With the Jewish entrance into the modern world, a world in which rational thinking was more highly valued than the mystical, Kabbalah tended to be downgraded or ignored.[486] Coming out of World War II, Jewish American families wanted to be taken seriously, fitting into American culture, politics and business. For the larger Jewish community, Kabbalah was not the way. Deemed irrational and superstitious, it was generally considered impracticable and esoteric. For much of the twentieth century, the Jewish Theological Seminary wasn't even allowed to teach Kabbalah because it was not considered part of mainstream Judaism. Additionally, Kabbalah has historically been associated with Hasidism, a conservative, ultra-orthodox sect of Judaism—also not without its controversies—with prominent communities in New York and Israel.

Earlier, at the outset of the twentieth century, a nascent "Jewish Science" emerged, promulgated mainly by Rabbis Alfred Geiger Moses and Louis Witt. In response to Mary Baker Eddy's growing movement, it saw value in Christian Science's metaphysical and therapeutic appeal. Though it did not take conventional Judaism by storm, its impact filtered into the Jewish reform movement, blending the benefits of mind-cure spirituality and the growing popularity of psychological healing. "May it be," wondered Reform Rabbi Maurice Harris, "that we Jews—the rationalists of history—have been rational to a fault and have not realized sufficiently the value of the mystical in life?"[487]

In Europe and other parts of the world, Jewish scholars did not shy away from Kabbalah or Jewish mysticism: Walter Benjamin wrote *Theses on the Philosophy of History* (1940) on the eve of Nazi domination, turning to Jewish mysticism as a model of practice in dark times; Martin Buber published editions of Hasidic, mystical, and mythic texts from Jewish and world sources that influenced generations of scholars; and Gershom Scholem, widely regarded as the founder of the modern study of Kabbalah, called it "the official theology of Judaism."[488]

Scholem wrote *Major Trends in Jewish Mysticism* (1941), *Sabbatai Sevi: The Mystical Messiah* (1957), and a collection of speeches and essays published as *On Kabbalah and Its Symbolism* (1965). Today, Jonathan Garb, the Gershom Scholem Professor of Kabbalah at the Hebrew University in Israel, asserts that Kabbalah has "gone viral" because of its rich variety of contemplation, meditation techniques, and deconstruction of language itself, leading to "dramatic experiences of deep trance, a sense of being absorbed in God, ascending to the higher worlds and communicating with the souls of the dead."[489]

McMYSTICISM?

In the United States, Kabbalah largely flew under the radar until the latter half of the twentieth century. The late Rabbi Philip Berg started the Kabbalah Centre in Queens, New York, in the 1970s, moving to Los Angeles in the 1980s. A quote of his still graces the home page of the Centre's website: "At the core of the world's great religions and spiritual traditions is the wisdom of Kabbalah. Understanding this wisdom and living it has the power to reveal your unique purpose and align you with your best life."

But hints of scandal have also followed the successes of the Kabbalah Centre. Now run by family members, it has been embroiled in several financial controversies. Some traditional Jewish scholars also find Kabbalah as taught by KCI to be anathema to both Judaism and ancient

Kabbalah texts. The phenomenon has been derided on some Jewish websites as "McMysticism."[490] Philip and Karen Berg set out to make secret Jewish mysticism available to the public, but former followers became critics, inviting IRS investigation.

Nevertheless, American interest in Jewish mysticism sparked by the Kabbalah Centre's influence has grown. Synagogues, Jewish community centers, and colleges now offer classes on the topic, as do New Age spirituality centers. For the seeker, there is plenty in common with other mystical traditions: Kabbalah addresses spiritual insights into astrology, intuition, and reincarnation. Some seekers are rediscovering Francis Bacon, a master of Cabala (Christian Cabala based on Jewish Kabbalah), and Carl Jung's *Kabbalistic Visions*, written in 1944. The latter examines Jung's archetypal interpretation of Kabbalistic symbolism and conversely shows Jewish mysticism's impact on Jungian psychology.

Upon his death in 2013, Rabbi Berg's compromised legacy was still widely acknowledged for updating Jewish mysticism. When he passed away, Madonna wrote, "I learned more from him than any human I have ever met."[491]

EVERYTHING ZEN

Integration—or at least interaction—among mystical traditions is now more commonplace. Richard Rohr's Center for Action and Contemplation is founded on principles of Catholicism and the dynamism of that religion's not widely known but rich mystical heritage. The center regularly welcomes those who extol the similarities of mystical traditions, including those of Native American Indians, Black female church leadership, Sufism, and Zen.

The twentieth-century Japanese Zen scholar D. T. Suzuki reveled in the mystical overlap of the world's religious traditions. In 1959 he and Thomas Merton engaged in a dialogue because Merton found so many parallels between the monastic visions of Christian mystics and Zen philosophy, concepts not bound by religious doctrine or culture. Suzuki was one of the first in the Eastern world to write on the noted similarities between Shin and Zen Buddhism and Christian mysticism, especially the writings of Meister Eckhart, juxtaposing cultures that seemed radically opposed yet shared experiences common to all humanity.[492] Suzuki won the 1963 Nobel Peace Prize and later becoming an active Theosophist.

Today, symposiums around the world underscore the commonalties among mystic traditions such as Sufism and Zen Buddhism. Those who are disillusioned with established religious institutions in the West find the esoteric messages of Sufism and Zen not incompatible with other belief systems. As an alternative to conventional religion, Sufism and Zen share a number of teachings and practices that appeal to a similar constituency. Many Sufi and Zen organizations in the West have contributed to creating a peace-loving image by focusing on humanity, love, and the universality of these teachings. This in turn has spurred greater transcultural and trans-spiritual understanding than orthodox or mainstream beliefs in America and Europe.[493]

MYSTICISM IN BLACK AND WHITE

Our loyalties must become ecumenical rather that sectional. . . .
We are all caught in an inescapable network of mutuality,
tied into a single garment of destiny. Whatever affects one directly,
affects all indirectly. . . . We aren't going to have peace on earth until we
recognize this basic fact of the interrelated structure of all reality.
Martin Luther King, "A Christmas Sermon for Peace," 1967

King's words could have been inspired by Francis Bacon's seventeenth-century *New Atlantis*. Or taken from Ralph Waldo Emerson's nineteenth-century "The Over-Soul." Or Einstein's twentieth-century commentary on the "cosmic religion of the future."

To Martin Luther King Jr., these metaphysical truths were timeless and self-evident.

The American Black religious experience, at first blush, is steeped in Christian and evangelical theology. Throughout the torture of 250 years of slavery, another 100 years of lynching under Jim Crow, and twentieth- and twenty-first-century systemic racism, African American families have found refuge under the canopy of the church. This rich heritage, adapted by the first slaves from their White slaveholders, has transmogrified over time into a wholly unique ethnic, cultural, and spiritual genre that has added to the richness and diversity of the American religious quilt. Aside from the solace it has provided Black Americans, it awakened a spark, erupting in African American presence in the arts, music, athletics, science, economics, politics, and social revolution.

But beneath the vibrancy of the Black church experience—its gospel music, altar calls, and emotive preaching—there lie humble, esoteric influences. The story of the soul of Black America includes mystics, Quakers, Theosophists, Transcendentalists, and a universalist social activism. Its inspiration may have originated in Africa, its nature altered in this country, but its full blossoming had to go around the world before finally taking root in America.

SHAKEN AWAKE BY A THUNDERSTORM

One can hardly imagine the plight of a Black, mystically inclined lesbian in mid-nineteenth-century America.

Born a freewoman in Philadelphia, Rebecca Cox Jackson's (1795–1871) ecstatic encounters were well documented. But a woman, especially one of color (not to mention living with a longtime female partner), was deemed not credible. Historically, issues of power and authority loom large for Black women, who are the most marginalized from the centers of power.[494] Legally and socially sanctioned forms of violence, intimidation, and exploitation were designed to silence and control African American women and perpetuate the dehumanization of slavery and oppression of free Black citizens. Religious, social, scientific, and economic institutions collaborated in many ways to objectify African American women as the "other."[495]

Jackson's gift first revealed itself when she was thirty-five years old. She experienced an acute emotional and spiritual crisis when confronted by one of her deepest, darkest fears—a thunderstorm. When lightning struck, she would take to her bed ill. One day in particular, unable to contain her fear and convinced that she would die during the storm, Jackson prayed mightily "for death or redemption."[496] In her journal she describes what happened next: "And in this moment of despair the cloud bursted, the heavens was clear, and the mountain was gone. . . . And I rose from my knees, ran down stairs, opened the door to let the lightning in the house."[497] She writes, "At every clap of thunder I leaped from the floor praising the God of my salvation."[498] The "messenger of death . . . was now the messenger of peace, joy, and consolation."[499]

After this watershed event, Jackson began to experience visions in which "she discovered the presence of a divine inner voice that instructed her in the use of her spiritual gifts."[500] She started to sermonize. When her husband refused to teach her to read and write, she divorced him. She met Rebecca Perot, who would become her companion for life. Both women had visions, even appearing in each other's visions. Perot said that in one of her visions Jackson was "crowned King and me crowned Queen of Africa," while Jackson saw the two of them "unit[ing] in the covenant." The two women were together for thirty-five years until Jackson's death.[501]

As a traveling preacher, Jackson was admonished for her refusal to formally join any church and "aleading the men."[502] A bishop of the African Methodist Episcopal (AME) Church came to one of Jackson's prayer services with the intention of stopping her; but after listening to her, he declared, "If ever the Holy Ghost was in any place, it was in that meeting. Let her alone now."[503]

Jackson interacted with Black female preacher Jarena Lee, also raised in the AME Church. But along the way Jackson was introduced to the White charismatic preacher Anna Lee and her community of Shakers, leading to her departure from the nascent Black Methodist church. It compromised her relationship with Jarena Lee, but the last known documented event in Lee's life was her visit to Jackson's home to repair their relationship on New Year's Day 1857.

Jackson founded the first Black Shaker community in Philadelphia.[504] The Shakers, first established in England, came to life in 1780s America. The ecstatic behavior demonstrated during their worship services gave rise to the name Shaking Quakers. Shakers espoused an egalitarian spirit, allowing women to assume positions of spiritual leadership. This was virtually unheard of in other religious persuasions and remained uncommon until much later in the nineteenth century. Aside from Anna Lee, Quaker women such as Jane Wardley and Mother Lucy Wright often began worship services with silent meditation and then began shaking and rocking, "receiving visions from God."[505] Their beliefs intertwined with the growing Spiritualism of the day, which also included female leadership. They practiced a celibate and communal lifestyle, pacifism, and were role models for the equality of the sexes.[506]

As Jackson grew in her role as a Shaker minister, she "became adamant about acting and speaking according to her inner authority. In rejecting the patriarchal traditions of the churches, Jackson recover[ed] the female aspect of the divine"[507]:

> I received word of understanding how the Spirit of Wisdom was the Mother of children. . . . I was in the spirit speaking these words to the glory of God: I know Thee by revelation, Oh Thou Mother, Thou Spirit of Wisdom, I was begotten in Thee and

brought forth, though I knew Thee not. They that have revelation must live it, that they may see the Father, Son, and Holy Ghost. Oh, how I love thee, my Mother! [508]

Through her myraid experiences and expressions, Jackson "engaged in profound acts of unsaying, a decolonization of mind and spirit."[509]

JESUS AND THE DISINHERITED, MYSTICISM AND SOCIAL ACTION

The mystic's concern with the imperative for social action
is not merely . . . to feed the hungry, not merely to relieve
human suffering and human misery. . . . It's the removal of all
that prevents God from coming to . . . [fullness] in the life
of the individual. Whatever . . . blocks this, calls for action.
Howard Thurman

It seemed innocent at the time, a quirk of fate.

In 1927, a Black preacher rummaging through a secondhand book sale in Oberlin, Ohio, came upon a book by Rufus Jones called *Finding the Trail of Life*. Reading it, he knew he had found his spiritual muse. Then and there the young clergyman, Howard Thurman, resolved to study with the author if he was still alive.

At sixty-six, Rufus Jones was very much alive and teaching. A professor of philosophy at Haverford College near Philadelphia, he had written numerous books, including *Studies in Mystical Religion* (1909), *The Quakers in the American Colonies* (1911), and *The Later Periods of Quakerism* (1921). Considered the world's expert on Quaker mysticism and a leader in the ecumenical Christian world, Jones focused on esoteric spirituality in most of the fifty-plus books he published in his lifetime.[510]

At first, Thurman wasn't even sure if Haverford admitted Black students (they did, the first ones enrolling in 1926). In early 1929, he traveled to Haverford College to study with Jones. Their commitment to a progressive Christianity that included pacifism became a common bond. Welcoming Thurman and praising his plan of study, Jones told him he would not be charged for tuition.[511]

Thurman was drawn to Jones's conviction that the most sound religious orientation is built upon "the transcendence of sects, denominations, races, and creeds . . . the mystical vision of spiritual unity, the superiority of life-embracing, affirmative mysticism . . . and the ethical practices of pacifist peacemaking and nonviolent resistance to injustice."[512] Here, a White Quaker instilled in a Black Baptist minister the pragmatic mysticism of William James—the confidence of knowing the inner light with the empirical experience of man.

In a 1978 lecture to Unitarian Universalists in Berkeley, Thurman said of Jones, "He had a profound mistrust of the powers of the mind and an absolute devotion to the powers of the mind. He felt that always the role of the thinker was to put at the disposal of the motivations of his life the best fruits of learning and the mastery of the external world. But this should be done best if the individuals who were seeking it would be inwardly motivated."[513]

Thurman recounted Jones encouraging him to write about the Christian mystics, "including Meister Eckhart, Madame Guyon and St. Francis of Assisi."[514] Much like his mentor, Thurman pursued a career in academia, becoming dean of Boston University's Marsh Chapel, the first African American dean of chapel at a majority-White university or college in the United States. It was there he taught Rabbi Zalman Schachter-Shalomi, who cited Thurman among the teachers who first compelled him to explore mystical trends beyond Judaism.[515] Thurman's influence drove him to the ecumenical life, where he later worked with the Dalai Lama, Ram Dass and explored the trance "readings" of the famed American intuitive Edgar Cayce.

Long before the term *interfaith dialogue* became common, Thurman worshiped with people of other faiths and warned about the dangers of religious fundamentalism.[516] "Theologies are inventions of the mind [designed to] imprison religious experience," Thurman said in a BBC interview. "Whether I'm Black, White, Presbyterian, Baptist, Buddhist, Hindu, Muslim—in the presence of God, all of these categories by which we relate to each other fade away."[517]

Thurman's lasting legacy is the significant impact of his Quaker-like, nonviolent approach to social change. He focused constantly on the "inward journey" but thought personal transformation should not be preoccupied with self; rather, it should accompany a "burning concern for social justice."[518] In 1936 he traveled abroad, heading Christian missions and meeting with world figures such as Mahatma Gandhi.[519] Because Thurman had been a classmate of Martin Luther King Jr.'s father, "Daddy King," at Morehouse College, MLK adopted him as a father figure while studying for his doctorate at Boston University. King occasionally sat in his mentor's home on Sunday afternoons, watching Jackie Robinson play baseball on television.

Thurman's towering accomplishments in his life include *Jesus and the Disinherited* (1949) and *Mysticism and Social Action* (1978). Martin Luther King studied the former book during the 1955 Montgomery bus boycott. In it, Thurman interprets the teachings of Jesus through the experience of the "disinherited," addressing nonviolent responses to oppression. In doing so, he takes his own religion to task:

> Christianity . . . as it was born in the mind of this Jewish thinker . . . as a technique of survival for the oppressed . . . became . . . a religion of the powerful and the dominant, used sometimes as an instrument of oppression. . . . [This was not] in the mind and life of Jesus. He announced the good news . . . that fear, hypocrisy, and hatred, the three hounds of hell that track the trail of the disinherited, need have no dominion over them.[520]

Life magazine acclaimed Thurman as one of the twentieth century's Great Preachers of America. Others saw him as "a mystic who saw visions" and whose "hard-nosed ideas about social activism . . . changed history."[521] Martin Doblmeier, director of the PBS film *Backs Against the Wall: The Howard Thurman Story*, claims his "voice is needed even more today because of pervasive political and religious tribalism. Thurman constantly sought common ground with people who were different." He called Thurman the "patron saint of those who say I'm spiritual not religious."[522]

Thurman left this world with a well-known mantra of self-discovery: "Don't ask what the world needs; ask what makes you come alive, and go do it. Because what the world needs are people who have come alive."

MLK: AN EXTRAORDINARY THREAD BETWEEN EAST AND WEST

In the quest to end lunch counter and hiring practice segregation, the Rev. Martin Luther King's 1963 protest in Alabama led to his arrest. King's words in his famous "Letter from a Birmingham City Jail" are inspired by his greatest influences: Henry David Thoreau, Mahatma Gandhi, Thomas Jefferson, and Howard Thurman. King cited Thoreau's groundbreaking essay "Civil Disobedience," published in 1846. The Transcendentalist altered American protest and reform, setting a new standard that would influence the entire world. His revolutionary concept of nonviolent resistance guided King. "During my early college days, I read Thoreau's essay on 'Civil Disobedience' for the first time," he remembered, "and I became convinced then that non-cooperation with evil is as much moral obligation as is cooperation with good."[523]

But in order for Thoreau's theory of nonviolence to fully flourish, it literally had to travel the globe before returning to the United States in the person of King. There is an extraordinary thread connecting

Thoreau, Theosophist founder Madame Blavatsky, Mahatma Gandhi, Howard Thurman, and MLK—a fascinating symbiotic relationship between Eastern and Western mystical influences.

Thoreau's spirituality, like that of most of his Transcendentalist colleagues, can best be described as a unique blend of esoteric Unitarianism and the Eastern concepts Transcendentalists came to adopt in the late nineteenth century. As one of the editors of the Transcendentalist publication *The Dial*, Thoreau published translations of several Eastern classics. In 1871, Unitarian minister James Freeman Clarke wrote *Ten Great Religions*, and Walt Whitman sprinkled references to mysticism and Asian religions throughout his works, including *Leaves of Grass* and *Passage to India*.[524]

Around the same time, Madame Helena P. Blavatsky, a Russian immigrant living in the United States, formed the Theosophical Society with American corporate lawyer Henry Steele Olcott. Theosophy sought to uncover the "secret" workings of the divine, tracing current philosophies and religions back to their supposed "common origins" in the ancient East. Theosophists drew their inspiration from the Neoplatonic and Gnostic writings of the first three Christian centuries in the West and from recently published Buddhist, Hindu, and Chinese texts.[525]

Theosophy may have had the greater impact on the way Americans appropriated Eastern religious philosophies. While Transcendentalism was largely a movement of the upper-class literary elite, Theosophy was a middle-class movement that transformed esoteric traditions into a philosophy geared to everyday spiritual concerns.[526]

As Eastern-based Theosophy influenced the West, Transcendentalism returned the favor. For all of her Eastern occult leanings, Blavatsky was greatly inspired by Emerson's "magnanimous eclecticism," lauding his revelations in "The Over-Soul": "It is such men as these who knew of no other Deity but that which dwelt in them as they felt themselves inseparable from it."[527] Religious scholar Alvin Boyd Kuhn in his 1930 study *Theosophy* says, "It may seem ludicrous to suggest that Emerson was the chief forerunner of Madame Blavatsky, her John the Baptist . . . yet seriously, without Emerson, Madame Blavatsky could hardly have launched her gospel when she did with equal hope of success."[528]

Though motivated by American esoteric thinking and becoming a US citizen herself, Blavatsky felt moved to leave the country. She and Olcott set up shop in India where they established the next iteration of the Theosophical Society. There, it would play a critical role in setting civil rights in motion, for both India and America, through the person of Mohandas Karamchand Gandhi.

"I AM A CHRISTIAN AND A HINDU AND A MOSLEM AND A JEW"

The young Gandhi grew up in relatively secular surroundings and was encouraged to study law in England. There he encountered two Theosophists who asked him if he had read the *Bhagavad Gita*. Sheepishly, he replied no. They invited him to read a copy, as it held a central place within Theosophy. Gandhi began to read the *Gita* and attended Theosophical classes. In a biographical essay about Gandhi in *The New Yorker*, Indian writer Ved Mehta relates this story and says, "In time the *Bhagavad Gita* became the most important book in his life." It was in London where he was also introduced to Buddhism and Christianity.

At one point Gandhi met with Madame Blavatsky, and they discussed theosophical doctrine and Hinduism. Gandhi also read theosophical literature such as *The Key to Theosophy*. After his early inter-actions with Theosophists, Gandhi uttered, "I am a Christian and a Hindu and a Moslem and a Jew. . . . Looking at all religions with an equal eye, we would not only not hesitate but would think it our duty to blend into our faith every acceptable feature of other faiths."[529] Gandhi maintained contact with the Theosophical Society throughout much of his life.[530]

What moved the Mahatma, however, was Transcendentalism, not conventional Christianity. Gandhi admitted that "Thoreau's ideas greatly influenced [his] movement in India."[531] When he met with Howard Thurman in 1936, Gandhi was puzzled as to why African Americans adopted the religion of their masters. Thurman said it was not Christianity as it had been practiced that he had fallen in love with but the teachings of Jesus. Thurman did ask Gandhi what message he should take back to the United States. Gandhi said he regretted not having made nonviolence, or "ahimsa," more visible as a practice worldwide and remarked, "It may be through the Negroes that the unadulterated message of nonviolence will be delivered to the world."[532]

In 1959 Dr. King made a long-awaited pilgrimage to India, twenty-three years after Thurman. Although Gandhi had passed away more than a decade earlier, King hoped to learn more about the Mahatma's use of nonviolence in the civil rights battle against the British Empire. After leaving India, King's interest in this kind of revolution became an irrepressible passion. His clear decision to employ "non-violent resistance to oppression" would not only keep him emotionally nurtured during the personal struggles that followed but also lay crystal-clear guidelines for the hundreds of thousands of informal followers he would attract.[533] This ethos became the hallmark of his movement, from Birmingham to Selma to the Lincoln Memorial "I Have a Dream" speech, until his 1968 death in Memphis.

THE "ARC OF THE MORAL UNIVERSE"

The title of this section is perhaps the most memorable and oft-repeated of King's many quotes. It's also a fitting coda for Transcendentalism's impact on the greatest nonviolent revolutionary the United States has ever known.

On two occasions, Martin Luther King uttered the words that

encapsulated his innate optimism. In a 1958 essay in *The Gospel Messenger* periodical he wrote, "Yes, 'the arc of the moral universe is long, but it bends towards justice.' There is something in the universe which justifies William Cullen Bryant in saying, 'Truth crushed to earth will rise again.'"[534] Though he did not name the author of the first idiom, King purposely placed the words in quotes.[535]

In 1964 King delivered the baccalaureate sermon at the commencement exercises for Wesleyan University in Middletown, Connecticut. In closing he said, "The arc of the moral universe is long, but it bends towards justice."[536] In 2009, *Time* magazine published an article by President Barack Obama that included the distinctive subphrase about history, that it "bends towards justice." Obama credited the words to King.[537]

But upon closer examination, the original inspiration stems from another source.

In 1853 Theodore Parker, the prominent abolitionist, American Transcendentalist, and Unitarian minister, wrote a collection of essays called "Ten Sermons of Religion." His third sermon, entitled "Of Justice and the Conscience," includes the familiar words:

> Look at the facts of the world. You see a continual and progressive triumph of the right. I do not pretend to understand the moral universe, the arc is a long one, my eye reaches but little ways. I cannot calculate the curve and complete the figure by the experience of sight; I can divine it by conscience. But from what I see I am sure it bends towards justice. Things refuse to be mismanaged long. Jefferson trembled when he thought of slavery and remembered that God is just. Ere long all America will tremble.[538]

The words from this particular sermon foreshadowed the Civil War.

They were later reprinted in collections of Parker's works[539] and are undeniably the origin of King's inspiration.

Although the fervor and the emotion of Great Awakening Christianity and its biblical influences can be heard in Martin Luther King's voice and sometimes seen in his writings, the prevailing guiding light behind his mission is grounded in an awareness born of the parallels between Eastern and Western mysticism. The beliefs of those who influenced both his soaring rhetoric and strategies—Gandhi, Thoreau, Parker, and Thurman—speak of an ecumenical universalism.

URBAN SHAMAN

In reality, all mystics declare, our True Nature is God, Brahman,
Buddha-Nature, the Tao, or Consciousness Itself.
"The Mystical Core of the Great Traditions,"
Center for Sacred Sciences

"Mystics tell us a different story through the ages—the possibility of being personally connected to divinity," suggests author Cara Herbet. Mystics feel that personal growth towards the universe's ultimate plan must come from within. It cannot be dictated or ordered. Herbert goes on to say, "Mystics value internal growth; rituals and traditions are meant to trigger internal insight and transformation, not to appease a higher power. The mystic values intuition [and is] uncomfortable with religious hierarchies. For mystics, the world is expansive and magical yet also intricately connected, moving every action towards the accomplishment of a greater plan."[540]

The path of the mystic is no longer relegated to the few in isolated settings. There is a movement afoot: some call it becoming the urban shaman. "There was a time," says author and speaker Caroline Myss, "when mystics were shuttered away as shamans, Sufis, Monks and

Sadhus. Today's 'mystics' are not cloistered. They are active in the world, participating in daily activities, and yet take the time to be away from the world—the silent time in contemplation or a walking meditation."[541]

Myss believes more people are now being driven to ask "soul-sized questions because we have entered the age of the soul. The questions we are asking and the deepening of our inner lives combined with the challenges we are confronting as a planetary community indicate that we are evolving into 'mystics out of monasteries.'"[542]

This growing current of mystical awareness, both as an individual experience and as a historical trend, reveals the possibility of personal and collective evolution. This progression appears to be occurring regardless of peoples' religious backgrounds—and in some instances, for those without any religious inclination at all.

CHAPTER EIGHT

— ✳ —

God/Not God:
Atheism, Science, and Consciousness

For a while, I thought of myself as an atheist. Until I realized it
was a belief, too. It's too bad we have to label everything.

George Carlin

Science at its best is an open-minded method of inquiry,
not a belief system.

Rupert Sheldrake

THE MOST HATED WOMAN IN AMERICA

After the US Supreme Court's *Abington School District v. Schempp* (1963) decision, she would mock those of faith, start a controversial magazine, tour the nation debating a God-fearing evangelical, and in the 1990s end up in a bizarre kidnapping caper that would take her life.

Brash and unapologetic, Madeline Murray O'Hair (1919–1995) became the nation's face of atheism in the 1960s. Although some famous Americans had proudly proclaimed their atheism along the way—Mark Twain, Ayn Rand, Margaret Sanger, and Ernest Hemingway among them—for years it was the belief system that dared not speak its name. The rise of twentieth-century communism based, at least in theory, on Karl Marx's credo "Religion is . . . the opiate of the people" made atheism an unwelcome guest in the United States, antithetical to the country's spiritual DNA.

Between the conservative religious expression of the Puritans and Great Awakenings on one end of the belief scale and the esoteric influences of Deism and Transcendentalism on the other, America sported a wide range of spiritual persuasions with literally dozens of mainstream and fringe religions within that spectrum. But atheism was not in the catalogue. Although many atheist organizations have attempted to shoehorn the likes of Jefferson, Franklin, Monroe, or Lincoln—even Chester Arthur—into their brand, no Founding Father or American president has claimed being an atheist. It is possible that some cloaked their atheism, but each executive expressed, at one time or another, a belief in a higher, overarching consciousness, even when describing it as "nature's God" or "Providence."

O'Hair filed a lawsuit in 1959 challenging the policy of mandatory prayers and Bible reading in Baltimore public schools. Her first son, William J. Murray—who would come to revile and disown his mother—served as the designated plaintiff in *Murray v. Curlett*. By the time the case made its way through appeals courts and was granted certiorari, the US Supreme Court had already weighed in on religion in schools. *Engel v. Vitale* (1962) found it unconstitutional for state officials to compose an official prayer and encourage its recitation in public schools.

In 1963, the *Murray* case was consolidated with *Schempp*, another case with similar facts, as it made its way to the high court. The landmark decision ruled eight to one in O'Hair's favor that both state-mandated prayer and Bible readings in public schools were a violation of the Establishment Clause of the First Amendment to the Constitution. In the wake of that victory, O'Hair established *The American Atheist Magazine* and morphed her Society of Separationists into the nonprofit American Atheists. She served as the organization's president until 1986 when her son Jon Garth Murray succeeded her.[543]

O'Hair continued to litigate issues of church and state throughout her life, further angering Southern religious conservatives who were already reeling from Warren Court decisions on racial integration of schools, public housing, and other institutions. Matters of race and religion in the 1950s and 1960s led to cries of impeaching Chief Justice Earl Warren and powered the rise of Southern Dixiecrats, who bolted from the Democratic Party. O'Hair gladly poured fuel on the fire with an adamancy verging on belligerence.

Nevertheless, with its emphasis on reason and the scientific pursuit of understanding consciousness, atheism has come to play a pivotal role in America's spiritual evolution. And with the increasing number of "nones" in the US today, especially those under thirty years of age, atheism's impact is likely to expand.

THE "NEW AGE" OF ATHEISM

Tumult presided over almost every theater of American life in the 1960s. It was not limited to Vietnam War protests, race riots, the women's equality movement, the drug and sexual revolutions, or the generation gap.

In the watershed year of 1968, *Time* magazine published a cover article entitled: "Is God Dead?" The question may have threatened mainstream American religion, but it provided oxygen for self-described agnostics and atheists. Within a decade, atheism's popularity grew, and by the 1990s books on atheism began selling in the millions. Beyond Madeline Murray O'Hair making television appearances on *Donahue* and *The Tonight Show*, atheists spoke openly about their ethics and beliefs (or non-beliefs, as it were).

A number of factors contributed to opening those doors of expression. With the fall of the Berlin Wall in 1989 and the disintegration of the Soviet Union in the early '90s, atheism was no longer implicitly associated with "godless communism." With the wave of historic events and First Amendment protections, atheists spoke out more freely.

The political/religious tenor of the times also stirred atheists. The rise of evangelical influence at the table of conservative power alarmed the Christian Right's political and spiritual adversaries. Jerry Falwell,

Jim Bakker, Pat Robertson, Oral Roberts, Ralph Reed, and Jimmy Swaggert had become household names with overt social agendas. With their aversion to this growing power bloc, atheists found allies within communities who, while they may not have shared their beliefs, also viewed "Big Evangelicalism" with suspicion.

Other factors contributed to atheism's ascension. In the late 1980s, esoteric spirituality reemerged from its American cocoon. Though much of it was grounded in New Thought, Transcendentalism, and psychology, the rise of a New Age philosophy with its fringe characteristics (e.g., channeling, crystals, and other metaphysical esoterica associated with spiritualism and the occult) rankled the atheistic faithful. The Amazing Randi and Carl Sagan were at the forefront, calling out those whom they saw as charlatans of the New Age.

Whatever the impetus, atheism's numbers rose steadily, if not dramatically, through the end of the twentieth century. Today almost 10 percent of American adults identify as atheist or agnostic.[544] Millennials and those of Gen Z are nearly three times more likely than boomers to say they don't believe in God.[545] While the aggregate number of nonbelievers is not yet substantial, the numbers swell to over a quarter of the US adult population when those who claim to be "nothing in particular" or "none" are added to the count.[546]

THE HORSEMEN COMETH

A 2007 viral video of the "Four Horsemen" of atheism—featuring Richard Dawkins, Sam Harris, Christopher Hitchens and Daniel Dennett—is cited as "the conversation that sparked the Atheist revolution."[547] At the dawn of the new atheist movement, these four men were considered the most incisive in their critique of religion. They populated the *New York Times* best-seller list and were frequent speakers on the college circuit, engaging in compelling dialogue and dissecting any God-believing person in their path. Hitchens regularly debated the conservative Catholic Dinesh D'Souza. Richard Dawkins took on New Age metaphysician and author Deepak Chopra. Atheism received a tacit nod from newly elected president Barack Obama, who in his 2009 inauguration referred to the United States as a "nation of Christians and Muslims, Jews and Hindus, and non-believers."[548]

But then atheism faced new confrontation. And not just from the very religious, but from within. Some fellow atheists decried the anger, bellicosity, and dismissive tone employed by the likes of the Four Horsemen. Dawkins called religion "the great evil." Hitchens likened God (if he did exist) to Big Brother, conducting never-ending surveillance of our daily thoughts and actions. New Atheism stood at a crossroad. Up until that time, "it had been spearheaded by the sort of white, male firebrands that led the charge for evangelicalism during the Second Great Awakening of the early 19th century."[549] This prompted author Steve Prothero, writing for the United Coalition of Reason, to suggest that "atheists need a new voice." There is "a new generation of unbelievers emerging, some of them women and most of them far friendlier than Hitchens and his ilk. Although the arguments of angry men gave this movement birth, it could be the stories of women that allow it to grow up."[550]

A KINDER, GENTLER ATHEISM

At about the time of the ascent of the Four Horsemen, comedian, talk-show host, and proud atheist Bill Maher co-produced the film *Religulous*, chiding religious belief. As host of the long-running HBO series *Real Time*, Maher has never shied away from robust discussion of religion. One evening he conducted a memorable conversation with writer Aaron Sorkin, future US senator Cory Booker, and self-described atheist S. E. Cupp:

MAHER: "You're an atheist. So you believe that people who believe in God are deluded. And yet—"

S. E. CUPP: "No I don't. I get the appeal of religion. I don't believe in God, but I'm not mad at him (laughter from the panel). I'm not this militant atheist."

MAHER: "If you're an atheist, you must think that people who believe in God are deluded."

S. E. CUPP: "No I don't . . ."

MAHER: "Why don't you have the courage of your convictions? . . ."

S. E. CUPP: "I do, I am an atheist. Stand up as an atheist."

MAHER: "Then why don't you think that people who believe in God are deluded?

S. E. CUPP: "Because I have met incredibly smart people . . ."

MAHER: ". . . who are deluded . . . (audience laughter). How can you believe in one thing but not the other?"

S. E. CUPP: "There has been study after study . . . that religion is actually very good for you . . . both personally and for society . . . religious people happen to be more optimistic. That helps them heal from diseases faster . . ."

MAHER: "It causes most wars, the Crusades . . ."

S. E. CUPP: "That is patently not true . . ."

CORY BOOKER: "Bill, Bill, humans cause wars. . . . We fight over everything from natural resources, to land . . .

S. E. CUPP: ". . . to colonialism, tribalism . . ."

MAHER: "The justification for that is mostly religion. . . . What gets most people to think it's OK to kill other people is religion, very little else . . ."

S. E. CUPP: "Or colonialism, or land power grabs, or nativism . . ."

BOOKER: "Bill, I am sorry, you are evidencing the zeal of a Baptist preacher in your atheism. . . . You are just as dogmatic and intolerant as you often accuse people on the religious side of things . . ."

MAHER (to CUPP): "You say you are an atheist, but that you are open. . . . Explain that . . ."

S. E. CUPP: "Well, some kind of miraculous event before my eyes might make me change my mind, but I am an atheist . . ."

MAHER: "Do you think Jesus is going to come down and say 'Hey you!'?"

CUPP: "I am sold on atheism. I am an atheist. Unapologetic. But I am not delusional. . . . I could change my mind over the course of the next seventy years that I will be on this earth. . . . It could happen . . ."[551]

In some ways, Cupp's perspective is strikingly reminiscent of the liberal, open-minded stance of the American founders in the Age of Reason, *who reserved the right to change their minds.* Many of the founders demonstrated a spiritual curiosity well into their later years. Standard or orthodox religion was not the main impetus behind their evolution; being exposed to various belief systems enhanced their inquisitiveness.

Perhaps that is why they felt more comfortable in Unitarian, deistic, and Freemason circles than in religious ones.

There was, however, a limit to the founders' open-mindedness: they rejected dogmatic fundamentalism and orthodoxy on one end of the spectrum yet were highly skeptical of eccentric esoterica on the other. For example, both Jefferson and Washington looked askance at their friend the Marquis de Lafayette's endorsement of Mesmer and mesmerism, the basis for modern-day hypnosis. In the end, the notion of a providential creator was at the core of their publicly expressed beliefs, however unorthodox those beliefs may have been.

In a 2010 address at the National Constitution Center, author-historian Jon Meacham asserted that in matters of spiritual belief, Washington, like Jefferson, changed his mind often: "His moving from belief to belief made him cherish liberty even more because he needed it himself as he moved from one position to another."[552] Might it be that one of the greatest gifts our founders afforded us is the freedom to doubt, to question, to change our minds?

ENTERING THE VOID

Recent Pew Foundation studies reveal that more than four in ten Americans have switched their religious affiliation since childhood or dropped out of any formal religious group.[553] Marcus Borg (1942–2015), an influential voice in Progressive Christianity and a fellow in the Jesus Seminar, often asked his audiences how many were still in the same denomination in which they grew up. Approximately 60 percent had changed their denominational affiliation in adulthood. Borg found this to be psychologically healthy.

Borg and others in the New Thought movement discovered that people who change their spiritual outlook have a period or a moment of shifting where they enter a "void," making it possible for new awareness to emerge. Some think atheism represents that void. New Thought author and Bible scholar Laura Barrett Bennett says, "There is a sacred emptiness that we can come to, where we are open to what life and the universe have to teach us. That is a questioning of our beliefs. To be in the state where we *stop* asking questions, to come to the place of 'I know what I believe and I am going to stay in that knowing no matter what,' is shutting down what life continues to teach us." [554] Unity/New Thought minister Rev. Diane Scribner-Clevinger suggests these concepts comprise "a willingness to being empty," and that "to be in that void [is] part of the mystical teachings that underlie every faith. Even in biblical teaching, there is a void that is acknowledged and from that place, light comes." [555]

WOLVES WHO RUN WITH THE CARIBOU PACK

I begin with nothingness. . . . Nothingness is both empty and full. . . .
A thing that is infinite and eternal hath no qualities,
since it hath all qualities.

Carl Jung on Gnosticism, from *The Seven Sermons to the Dead*

Spirituality must be distinguished from religion—
because people of every faith, and of none, have had
the same sorts of spiritual experiences.

Sam Harris

The twenty-first century may be the new dawn of American atheism, but atheism's ultimate impact may spur the growth of nonreligious, nonsectarian seekers, those "nones" who consider themselves to be spiritual but not religious.

For centuries the notions of religion and spirituality have been uniformly fused. Some still see the two as synonymous. More recently we have seen greater differentiation between the two concepts. The rise of atheism may be playing a role in that evolution—not so much because of atheism's refutation of religious beliefs but rather in its role as pruning agent.

At its best, atheism strips religion of its artifice and certitude. The stories of religions are fairly consistent: a brilliant teacher comes along—be it Jesus, Mohammed, Buddha, or any one of dozens of others—and sooner or later priests, imams, monks, bishops, and popes (not to mention politicians) get hold of the message. Doctrines, commandments, and orthodoxy take over. Religion often becomes a force of constraint; gone is much of the path or "the way" of an enlightened master who provided a map for self-discovery, a template for one's own hero's journey.

Over the centuries, spirituality has been held hostage by religion, whereby the initial principles are lost. Something precious and personal becomes mummified. In other words, ecclesiastical hierarchies codify spirituality, and religions begin. Steve Bhaerman, a.k.a. Swami Beyondananda, may have paraphrased it best: "Spirituality is an attempt to access the divine. Religion is crowd control."[556]

Calling the basis for religious doctrines into question, atheism strips away at the swaddling of rigid beliefs and tenets, the "thou shalts" and "thou shalt nots." Of course, for some who call themselves atheists, there's nothing redeemable about any aspect of religion—one should throw away not only the wrappings but the entire corpus as well. Yet at its most effective, atheism tears away at the dogma, orthodox creeds, and the malignant layers that obscure a once shining core of insight.

Atheism also allows for doubt, which may be essential for the mind to grasp evolving spiritual truths. Without doubt, if a person cannot jettison her notion of God at some point, has she really made a meaningful choice? "If you just have 'faith' in something, it anesthetizes your search for the truth," said Vincent Bugliosi, who prosecuted Charles Manson and wrote books on Manson, O. J. Simpson, Lee Harvey Oswald, and JFK. In his final book, *The Divinity of Doubt*, he asserted, "If you have doubt, you are more likely to investigate and search and try to find the truth." Bugliosi found doubt to be critical for the evolution of consciousness.

Father Richard Rohr of the Coalition for Action and Contemplation concurs: "Doubt is a necessary tool for growth. . . . As it turns out, [it] is the passageway from each stage to the next. Without doubt, there can be growth within a stage, but growth from one stage to another usually requires us to doubt the assumptions that gave shape to our current stage."[557]

In the 1960s, Ram Dass wrote his seminal book *Be Here Now*. It became the creed for millions of baby boomers determined to more deeply explore their spirituality rather than accept the religious traditions of their parents. Their interest in meditation, psychedelics, metaphysics, and Eastern religions set them apart from preceding generations. Dass's focus was not on the standard notion of religious hereafters but about being fully present in the now. It has been argued that atheism, in its highest octave, "is a belief in the here and now."[558]

If one really believes that there is no afterlife, does adopting such a belief lend itself to becoming more fully present in the moment? Pew's Religious Landscape Study shows that atheists are more likely than US Christians to say that they often feel a sense of wonder about the universe (54 percent vs. 45 percent).[559] As Sam Harris contends—sounding more like Dass or *The Power of Now*'s Eckhart Tolle than a conventional atheist—'It is always now. Each of us is looking for a path back to the present. How we pay attention to the present moment largely determines the character of our experience and, therefore, the quality of our lives. Mystics and contemplatives have made this claim for ages—but a growing body of scientific research now bears it out."[560]

In the wake of the backlash to the Four Horsemen and so-called militant or fundamental atheism, softer tones have emerged. By 2014, even the Sam Harrises of the world were writing books like *Waking Up: A Guide to Spirituality Without Religion*. "Despite its spooky etymology," he says, "there's no better word than 'spirituality' to describe the personal and intimate exploration of human consciousness . . . and it's inconvenient[,] but I feel like the other words that are available are even spookier, something like mysticism, you know, or more specific like contemplation, the contemplative life."[561]

Harris praises meditation as a positive rational practice informed by neuroscience and psychology. He often taps into Eastern religion and Western mystics when addressing the ethics and values of atheism. He cites "extraordinary men and women" such as Meister Eckhart, Saint John of the Cross, Saint Teresa of Avila, and Saint Seraphim of Sarov as pioneers in consciousness where our individuated sense of "self" may be made to vanish.

Harris may quote mystics but does not admit to any supernatural element in his argument. "Mysticism is a rational enterprise," he contends. "Religion is not. . . . The mystic has reasons for what he believes, and these reasons are empirical."[562] Celebrated atheists such as Bill Maher openly refute God but are open to the notion of "a force" à la *Star Wars.* Even Richard Dawkins said on Maher's program that he did not completely rule out the possibility of a God or higher being ("I'm a 6.9 [atheist] on a scale of 1 to 7").

These trends reflect New Atheism's evolution over the last few decades. Early on, its central notion had been that "religious people are stupid and religion is poison, so the only way forward is to educate the idiots and flush away the poison."[563] The new New Atheism is generally kinder and gentler, less controversial, and possesses a more feminine face. It dares dip its toe in the conversational stream of spirituality and consciousness. From this perspective, "atheism is just another point of view, deserving of constitutional protection and a fair hearing. Its goal is not a world without religion but a world in which believers and nonbelievers coexist peaceably, and atheists are respected, or at least tolerated. . . . [T]he new New Atheism isn't out to convert anyone."[564]

The freedom of atheism to express itself in the late twentieth and early twenty-first centuries may threaten the faithful. However, it not only offers people meaningful choice, but it also forces humanity to face its most existential challenge: the fear of death and the possible end of all existence. Perhaps the fear of atheism is based in one's own underlying fear of the end of existence, a threat to the ego-self which identifies more wholly with the body and its thoughts.

Philosopher and atheist Todd May suggests in a *New York Times* series on dying that confronting death is "one of the most important and difficult tasks that we as humans face. It's . . . inspiring to see the ways different traditions grapple with that task." May rejects the supernatural, but not the people who believe in it: "My particular atheism commits me to thinking that those who believe in the supernatural are mistaken. It does not, however, commit me to thinking any less of them for their belief."[565]

Atheism will likely continue to play a valued role in humanity's spiritual evolution because in its noblest expression it is dedicated to the health of the herd. Like wolves who run alongside the caribou pack and eliminate the diseased, elderly, or weaker reindeer, atheism's attack on the narrow-minded ideas of religion plays, perhaps unwittingly, a similar role to spirituality. Exposing the fears of religious fundamentalism, it contributes to the "healthy mindedness" of the entire pack.

"THERE AIN'T GONNA BE AN ANSWER"

God gave us an opportunity through science to understand the natural world, but there will never be a scientific proof of God's existence.

Francis Collins, Director of the National Institute of Health

He was a man ahead of his time. Apparently, too far ahead.

Giordano Bruno (1548–1600) was a Franciscan friar, astronomer, mathematician, and philosopher who not only endorsed Copernicus's controversial heliocentric theory that the earth revolved around the sun but also contradicted church doctrine by suggesting that the universe is infinite, made up of innumerable solar systems and worlds. A forerunner to fellow Italian astronomer Galileo Galilei, he maintained that the Bible should be followed for its moral teaching, not for its astronomical or scientific implications. He criticized Christian ethics, particularly the Calvinistic principle of salvation by faith alone. His physical theory of the universe denied Aristotelian dualistic physics, instead implying the basic unity of all substances, seen and unseen, and the coincidence of opposites in the infinite unity of being.[566]

For this and more, the Inquisition put Bruno on trial in Rome, demanding he renounce his ideas. He maintained his theories were not theological matters but were scientific and philosophical in nature. When Roman Catholic cardinals pressed him further for a retraction, Bruno expressed that he did not even know what it was he was supposed to retract. Sentenced to death, he addressed his judges by saying, "Perhaps your fear in passing judgment on me is greater than mine in receiving it." Days later, his tongue gagged, he was hanged upside down and then burned alive at the stake.[567]

Today, the likes of evolutionary biologist Richard Dawkins and legendary physicist Stephen Hawking have, conversely, taken religion to the pyre. Long uneasy counterparts, science and religion have each enjoyed the popular "upper hand" at the expense of the other. Often it has been a mutual relationship of cautious skepticism and, at times, enmity.

To some degree the battle continues as we traverse the gamut from *The God Delusion* (Dawkins) to *The Science Delusion* (Rupert Sheldrake). But there appears to be some concurrence in both the religion and science camps: while science will continue to explore the depths of our outer and inner universes, it will never provide substantive proof of a deity. Hawking, a staunch atheist, suggested that "science will never reveal the mind of God. . . . [It] will never give us The Answer, a theory powerful enough to dispel all mystery from the universe forever."[568]

For author-researchers John Horgan (*The End of Science*, et al.) and

Vincent Bugliosi, there has been overt joy in taking on both theists and atheists. "Science aspires, like theology used to, to explain absolutely everything," says Horgan, but "science will never, ever answer what I call 'The Question': Why is there something rather than nothing?"[569] Even as scientists and religionists may try to answer the Question, Bugliosi believes "the existence of God is an impenetrable mystery and beyond human comprehension."[570] He may have been mirroring the philosophy of Gertrude Stein, who once famously summed up her agnostic belief this way: "There ain't no answer. There ain't gonna be any answer. There never has been an answer. That's the answer."[571]

THE "LAST GREAT MYSTERY OF SCIENCE"

Gertrude Stein (1874–1946) is historically noted for her brilliance as a novelist, poet, and playwright. But long before her art and literary achievements, before attending Johns Hopkins Medical School, Gertrude Stein studied psychology at Radcliffe College (an annex of Harvard at the time) under the tutelage of William James. There she worked closely with him on several experimental studies, publishing her own articles in scientific journals.

Though Stein performed the experiments, James was given the credit for coining the term *stream of consciousness*. The questions that plagued James—what is consciousness? how does consciousness relate to the whole personality? is consciousness continuous or discontinuous?—are later explored in the literary works of Gertrude Stein.[572] After working with Stein, James publicly questioned the widely accepted view of scientific materialism: that the brain produces consciousness.[573]

Stein herself, though not a practitioner of metaphysical religion, spent formative years in Cambridge, Massachusetts, at the turn of the twentieth century. It was a hotbed of spiritualism, Theosophy, and alternative healing modalities, and James, in addition to running the psychology lab in which Stein studied, ran a multitude of investigations on extrasensory and paranormal phenomena. Those tests winnowed the gap between science and spirituality. They trace a web of associations connecting Ralph Waldo Emerson, Transcendentalism, and liberal Protestantism to Gertrude Stein, and then on to the avant-garde and countercultural seekers of the 1960s and 1970s.[574] As the twentieth century dawned, the pursuit of religious and scientific common ground had emerged in earnest.

That legacy spurred the likes of John Templeton, John Fetzer, and other wealthy twentieth-century philanthropists to invest their treasure in causes designed to investigate consciousness and further shorten the distance between science and spirituality. Today the terrain is shifting. Dropping the G-word and all of its baggage from the discussion has refreshed the conversation. Instead of fighting over the existence of God, the new frontier focuses largely on the nature of consciousness, its genesis and locality. Once viewed with extreme skepticism and deemed beneath the notice of respectable scientists, consciousness has become a significant area of research, albeit a contentious one. It is widely considered the "last great mystery of science."

THE "HARD PROBLEM"

The nomenclature has changed, but controversy remains.

The prevailing consensus in neuroscience has been that consciousness is an emergent property of the brain and its metabolism. The dominant scientific view is that when the brain dies, the mind and consciousness of the being to whom that brain belonged ceases to exist. In other words, without a brain, there can be no consciousness.[575]

However, there is far less unanimity today about such conclusions, even within the scientific community itself. The failure of science to explain how the brain generates consciousness has been called "the

Hard Problem," a term coined in 1996 by Australian philosopher David Chalmers.[576] There are a growing number of voices who suggest that "some of the deepest assumptions of modern biology need to be reexamined—particularly the unproven belief that consciousness is derived from the brain, is confined to it and perishes with bodily death."[577] Neuroscientist Mario Beauregard suggests, "The brain is not the mind; it is an organ suitable for connecting a mind to the rest of the universe."[578]

The contrast of these opposing views has naturally given rise to animosity as well as an exchange of disparaging epithets—from allegations of "pseudo-scientific quackery" to retorts of "fundamentalist scientific materialism."

One early outlier regarding the genesis of consciousness was Dr. Peter Fenwick, a British neuropsychiatrist and neurophysiologist. Fenwick has been studying the human brain, consciousness, and the phenomenon of the near-death experience (NDE) for more than fifty years. Initially highly skeptical of NDEs and related phenomena, Fenwick began to take the matter more seriously after reading Raymond Moody's *Life After Life*. One of his own patients later described a near-death experience very similar to that of Moody's subjects.[579]

In Fenwick's view, the brain does not create or produce consciousness. Rather, it filters it. As odd as this idea might seem at first, there are some analogies that bring the concept into sharper focus. For example, the eye filters and interprets only a very small sliver of the electromagnetic spectrum, and the ear registers only a narrow range of sonic frequencies. Similarly, according to Fenwick, the brain filters and perceives only a tiny part of the cosmos's intrinsic "consciousness."[580] Deepak Chopra has echoed those sentiments, claiming, "Your visual perception is restricted to less than 1% of the electromagnetic spectrum, and your acoustic access is less than 1% of the sound spectrum—so what we experience through our five senses is less than 1% of what's happening out there."[581]

Fenwick's research led him to suggest that consciousness persists irrespective of death. It exists independently and outside of the brain as an inherent property of the universe itself, like dark matter and dark energy or gravity.[582] Ironically, according to Fenwick, "only in death can we be fully conscious."[583] This is reminiscent of Benjamin Franklin's sentiment that "a man is not completely born until he is dead."

As one might expect, Fenwick's suppositions have been met with choruses of jeers by many in mainstream science. Dr. Susan Blackmore, a psychologist, TED lecturer, and writer who's been researching consciousness for decades, said back in 2004 that Fenwick's "dishonest reporting" presented "a completely unworkable and mysterious theory . . . dress[ing] it up in the trappings of real science with beliefs that are rejected by the majority of scientists."[584] Former Catholic seminarian turned Yogananda student turned atheist Robert Todd Carroll (*The Skeptic's Dictionary*) asserted that Fenwick "made metaphysical assumptions and dismissed possible psychological and physiological explanations for near-death experiences."[585]

But Fenwick is hardly alone in his hypotheses.

TO THE MOON AND BACK

He was the sixth man to walk on the moon.

On his return trip to Earth, while looking out of the window of his space capsule, Apollo 14 astronaut Edgar Mitchell had a full-blown mystical experience. "He described it as a palpable feeling of unity with the universe," says former colleague Dr. Dean Radin, PhD. "That's a little bit unexpected for an MIT-trained scientist, jet pilot, and astronaut. All his training and experience were completely dependent on science and technology. Yet he had a classical mystical experience. Not surprisingly, he became curious about what the experience was, and how we could understand it from a scientific perspective."[586]

In 1973, several years after his lunar journey, Mitchell founded the Institute of Noetic Sciences (IONS) to "explor[e] the frontiers of consciousness" at the intersection of science and profound human experience. Its chief scientist today is Radin, who believes consciousness is the underlying building block of the physical universe. In his view, it is the future of science: "[Scientific] materialism is quite robust . . . and very effective for learning certain objective aspects of reality. But materialism doesn't cover the whole territory. Consciousness will be placed front and center, rather than relegated to the far fringe as a meaningless epiphenomenon, which until recently has been a basic tenet of academic psychology and the neurosciences."[587]

Engaging in such research for decades, Radin has attempted to demonstrate the convergence of what have been called psychic and mystical experiences with the scientific worldview by carefully considering the wisdom of esoteric traditions.[588] "We will begin to view reality in a more comprehensive way," he claims, "one that will more easily accommodate commonly reported experiences that have been dismissed as merely 'anomalous,' or worse, as 'woo-woo.'"[589]

Radin's series of studies at IONS in the late 1990s and early 2000s suggest the existence of what biogeochemist Vladimir Vernadsky and philosopher Pierre Teilhard de Chardin termed a "noosphere"—a planetary "sphere of thought and reason" encompassing the earth that has emerged through evolution, constituted by the interaction of human minds. Radin's tested precognition and intuition studies, using both calming and disconcerting photos in double-blind conditions, suggest we can know something before it happens.[590]

Radin has taken that concept further, citing Princeton University's Global Consciousness Project (GCP) in his work. The GCP's random number generators throughout the world appear to shift well beyond their near fifty-fifty "coin flipping" average in the wake of major worldwide events. Immediately *prior* to the 9/11 terrorist attack on the World Trade Center, random number generator(s) spiked. GCP's after-analyses indicate the possibility that humans not only access a collective unconscious but also possess some degree of precognition. Though the findings have aroused controversy, project director Roger Nelson explains, "We do interconnect, we interact, we're not isolated. My consciousness . . . and yours, extend out into the world, and they intermix. We're a little like neurons, in a giant brain."[591] Supporters and skeptics alike have referred to the GCP's aim as being analogous to detecting "a great disturbance in the force."[592]

Skeptics? There are more than a few. The aforementioned Robert Todd Carroll, *The Skeptic's Report*'s Claus Larsen, and others find problems in GCP's methodology and claim that it is jumping to conclusions.[593] They characterize GCP's findings as "pseudoscience." *Skeptic News*'s Wally Hartshorn says the people behind GCP may mean well, but their assertion of collective consciousness connection is faulty "because they're humans, and humans are very good at seeing connections—even when there is no connection to be seen."[594]

TAKING THE NON-LOCAL

*Mind at Large has to be funneled through the
reducing valve of the brain.*

Aldous Huxley

For years he walked the halls of the hospitals where he worked as a medical doctor, hearing people praying for the recovery of their loved ones. A man with agnostic leanings, it unnerved him: "Frankly it would make me uncomfortable, so I moved on as quickly as possible." He even resisted acknowledging the marvel of a case where a man with terminal lung cancer not only survived but was restored to complete health when the only therapy the patient received was prayer.

When early studies produced data showing prayer's positive impact on healing, Larry Dossey, MD, knew it was time to change how he served his patients.[595] These new findings prompted him to write *Healing Words* and *Prayer Is Good Medicine*, asserting that prayer is a valid and vital healing tool.

That was decades ago. Since then Dossey has done a deep dive into not only the connection between prayer and healing but also the nature of consciousness itself. Dossey's hypothesis is that all individual minds are part of an infinite, collective dimension of consciousness. He calls it the One Mind. This state, one which we can all access, explains phenomena as diverse as epiphanies, creative breakthroughs, premonitions of danger or disaster, near-death experiences, communication with other species and with the dead, reincarnation, the movement of herds, flocks, and schools, and remote healing as well.[596]

Dossey views the brain as a filtering agent or "reducing valve." That notion borrows heavily from William James's transmission model, in which the brain is seen as a limiting organ, and Aldous Huxley's hypothesis in *The Doors of Perception*: "To make biological survival possible, Mind at Large has to be funneled through the reducing valve of the brain and nervous system. What comes out at the other end is a measly trickle of the kind of consciousness which will help us to stay alive on the surface of this particular planet."[597] As astrophysicist David Darling observes in his book *Soul Search*, "We are conscious not because of the brain, but in spite of it."[598]

In the late 1980s, as he was writing his book *Recovery of the Soul*, Dossey coined the term *non-local mind*. The premise is that consciousness is not generated by or relegated to the locality of a physical brain. The non-local mind, Dossey asserts, appears to be infinite in space-time, resembling the age-old concept of the soul, hence the title of the book.[599] Dossey concludes, "If we are to have a ghost of a chance of understanding the One Mind and the relationship between mind and brain, we are going to have to think non-locally, not locally. Otherwise we will be forever chasing problems that simply don't apply in a non-local world."[600]

MORE PRIMARY THAN MATTER

Although he may have generated the phrase that now yields more than 1.5 million links on Google, Dossey realized the foundational concept of the non-local mind is not new. A group of physicists emerging in the twentieth century began looking at energy and matter differently than earlier scientists. By the 1930s, shortly after quantum physics had been introduced to the world of science, these physicists broke from Newton's perspective that matter was separate from energy. Nobel Prize–winning physicist Max Planck was among the first to dissent from the materialistic perspective, saying, "I regard consciousness as fundamental. I regard matter as derivative from consciousness. . . . Everything that we talk about, everything that we regard as existing, postulates consciousness."[601]

Around the same time, physicist, astronomer, and mathematician (not to mention agnostic) Sir James Jeans wrote, "The Universe begins to look like a great thought instead of a great machine. Mind no longer appears to be an accidental intruder into the realm of matter. . . . [W]e ought rather hail it as the creator and governor of the realm of matter."[602]

In the same vein, Sir Arthur Eddington, a man of similar pedigree who explained Einstein's theory of general relativity to the English-speaking world, said, "It is very difficult for the matter-of-fact physicist to accept the view that the substratum of everything is of mental character."[603]

Renowned Austrian physicist Erwin Schrödinger went further: "The total number of minds in the universe is one. In fact, consciousness is a singularity phasing within all beings." The concept suggests that the apparent multiplicity of minds is an illusion—that there is only one mind, or one consciousness, expressing itself in a myriad of ways.

"Consciousness cannot be accounted for in physical terms," Schrödinger said, "for consciousness is absolutely fundamental. It cannot be accounted for in terms of anything else."[604]

Other quantum physicists have more or less concurred: Werner Heisenberg, Wolfgang Pauli, Eugene Wigner, David Bohm, Danah Zohar, and Fred Alan Wolf each in their own way found that consciousness is *not* an epiphenomenon of the brain. Some of them went so far as to say that it is *more primary than matter*. It's worth pointing out that this is what many spiritual traditions have been saying for thousands of years. Today even the likes of Sam Harris—both a neuroscientist and atheist—is saying roughly the same thing: there is "nothing about a brain studied at any scale (spatial or temporal) [that] even suggests that it might harbor consciousness."[605]

RALPH KRAMDEN IS NOT IN THE BOX

The day science begins to study non-physical phenomena,
it will make more progress in one decade than
in all the previous centuries of its existence.

Nikola Tesla

I remember my father and brother laughing uproariously while watching Jackie Gleason as Ralph Kramden in *The Honeymooners* television series in the 1960s. The comedy originally aired in the 1950s as Americans were just settling into the reality of a television screen delivering stories—in black and white, of course—into their living rooms every night.

One can only wonder what the initial response must have been to the phenomenon of television. Here were live human beings whose images, voices, and every nuance were "broadcast" into the homes of millions. Somewhere, remotely, the action was captured in a studio, and then those images were transmitted invisibly across hundreds of miles. Something that we take for granted today, those in the 1950s must have marveled at the miracle of those early transmissions. Young children, the uninitiated, and some in third world countries not familiar with radio or television wondered, upon seeing the images, if the actors were "little people" living inside the television set itself![606]

As amusing as that might sound, the television analogy is finding its way into serious discussions about the nature of consciousness. On one hand, the majority of scientists believe it is self-evident that a physical process within the brain produces consciousness, in much the same way that a generator produces electricity. Therefore, if consciousness is a by-product of brain activity, there can be no genuine out-of-body experiences or conscious survival of death. Both consciousness and experience are confined to the brain and must die when the brain dies.[607]

Yet other scientists, equally credentialed, do not concur. According to British journalist and author Graham Hancock, who writes extensively on altered states of consciousness, these other scientists see the brain as less like a generator and more akin to a television set. The set "tunes into" the signal, a metaphor in this case for consciousness. When the physical television set is destroyed—that is, dead—the signal still continues. "True, if certain areas of the brain [are] damaged, certain areas of consciousness are compromised," says Hancock, "but this does not prove that those areas of the brain generate the relevant areas of consciousness. If one were to damage certain areas of a TV set, the picture would deteriorate or vanish but the TV signal would remain intact. Nothing in the present state of knowledge of neuroscience rules this revolutionary possibility out."[608]

How the mind and brain actually interface with one another remains a mystery. How can the brain make consciousness? What if consciousness isn't stuck inside our heads? If our brains don't produce our consciousness, does it exist independently of our bodies? Could we actually be interconnected at some level? Could our consciousness survive when our body dies? Could we all have psychic or telepathic abilities?[609]

Hancock offers,

What seems obvious and self-evident to one generation may not seem so to the next. For hundreds of years it was obvious and self-evident to the greatest human minds that the sun moved around the earth—one need only look to the sky, they said, to see the truth of this proposition. Indeed those who maintained the revolutionary view that the earth moved around the sun [such as Giordano Bruno], faced the Inquisition and death by burning at the stake. Yet as it turned out the revolutionaries were right and orthodoxy was terribly wrong.[610]

As these theories evolve and become more widely investigated, if not accepted by the mainstream, might science be moving to a place where the mystics have already been? Carl Jung observed, "It is almost an absurd prejudice to suppose that existence can only be physical. As a matter of fact, the only form of existence of which we have immediate knowledge is psychic. We might as well say, on the contrary, that physical existence is a mere inference, since we know of matter only in so far as we perceive psychic images mediated by the senses."[611]

A growing number of serious investigators claim the brain processes sensory stimuli and affects the content of consciousness but does not "make" consciousness any more than a TV set makes the image it displays.[612] Ralph Kramden, Gleason's beloved, blue-collar bus driver, may exclaim that he wants to send his wife Alice "to the moon." But it doesn't mean he's doing so from inside the TV set.

THE MEANING OF LIFE

"I am here for one reason. I am a celebrity, you see."

With those words, John Cleese, longtime member of the British comedic troupe Monty Python and key writer of Python classics *The Life of Brian*, *The Holy Grail*, and others, introduced himself to the Charlottesville, Virginia, crowd. They were attending the 2018

Tom Tom Festival highlighting the University of Virginia's Division of Perceptual Studies' (DOPS) research on whether there is life after death. Cleese, moderating the panel, added, "I'm also here because I'm fascinated by what these guys do and I think they are dealing with the most interesting things you can deal with."

The storied history of the University of Virginia starts with Thomas Jefferson, who considered its founding one of his three greatest accomplishments, more so than being the nation's third president. One reason for its unique legacy has flown largely under the radar: the passionate, scientific, and data-driven pursuit of understanding near-death experiences, out-of-body experiences, and the viability of reincarnation. For over fifty years, psychiatrist Ian Stevenson, MD, worked for UVA's School of Medicine. He chaired its psychiatry department for ten of those years, founding the Department of Personality Studies in 1967, which evolved into the present-day DOPS in 2004. Stevenson passed away in 2007.

In his lifetime, Stevenson engaged in compelling studies as reflected in his publications *Twenty Cases Suggestive of Reincarnation* (1974), *Where Reincarnation and Biology Intersect* (1997), and his 2002 presentation "Scientific Evidence for Reincarnation."[613] Stevenson's exhaustive body of work examines the lives of children who speak of previous lives and families—and who have those stories borne out.[614] He conducted studies of young children with birthmarks or birth defects later discovered to correlate to wounds or death blows of people those children claimed as previous incarnations.[615]

To Stevenson, recognizing the possibility of reincarnation meant considering the persistence of consciousness: "We cannot imagine reincarnation without the corollary belief that minds are associated with bodies during our familiar life, but are also independent of bodies to the extent of being fully separable from them and surviving the death of their associated body [and at some later time becoming associated with another body]."[616] Current director of DOPS Jim

Tucker, MD, opines, "While this may seem to be an astounding statement—that memories, emotions, and physical injuries can carry over from one life to the next—the evidence, I think, leads us to that conclusion."[617]

At the end of his life, Dr. Stevenson said that his biggest regret was not that his critics dismissed his work but that they did so without even bothering to read it. But those skeptics who made the effort to examine his research often admitted that Stevenson's 2,000-plus case studies followed the scientific method rigorously, providing the most compelling evidence of reincarnation ever presented. In 1975, *The Journal of the American Medical Association* acknowledged Stevenson, saying, "In regard to reincarnation he has painstakingly and unemotionally collected a detailed series of cases . . . in which the evidence is difficult to explain on any other grounds. . . . He has placed on record a large amount of data that cannot be ignored."[618]

In that vein, today's DOPS program continues the scientific pursuit of the non-locality of consciousness. "Is it possible that our mind or consciousness survives bodily death?" asks neurobehavioral scientist and former DOPS director Bruce Greyson, MD. "There is a wide range of human experiences that suggest that is exactly the case." The longtime psychiatrist, who has served at three university medical centers, observes that "NDEs occur to us when we are on the threshold of death and therefore they may suggest what happens to us after death."[619]

Greyson describes countless NDE cases that reference "thinking more clearly than ever while your heart is stopped and there is no blood flowing to your brain. Looking down and seeing your body on an operating table and noticing unexpected details that your surgeon later verifies for you. Meeting deceased loved ones, family and friends, that you thought were still alive. And meeting deceased people you do not know, but later recognize from family photos." He concludes that each case is unique, but they all share similar features: "enhanced mental functioning, seeing more vividly, creating more vivid memories when your brain is seriously impaired—suggesting a part of us survives death. Now what part is that? And how is that possible? It seems to defy common sense. And yet it happens."[620]

Even if Stevenson's and DOPS's research and data are not yet dispositive, they have opened a conversation that questions a body of scientific conclusions once thought closed. "I hope whatever comes of this is that people are curious," says Cleese, "because many people in the scientific community don't have a theory, so they simply say it couldn't have happened. Which is not seriously impressive."

At the same Charlottesville conference, an audience member prompted the DOPS panel to go beyond science and wade into the philosophical, asking, "If there is life after death, what is the point of physical life itself?" Demurring, one panelist pointed at Cleese, saying, "Why not ask him? He wrote [and acted in] *The Meaning of Life*!"[621]

WARNING: STUDYING CONSCIOUSNESS
WILL CHANGE YOUR LIFE

Psychologist Susan Jane Blackmore, referenced earlier, has been studying NDEs, OOBEs, and the subject of consciousness for decades. In 2018, with the help of her daughter Emily Troscianko, she published the third edition of her book *Consciousness: An Introduction*. Blackmore experienced a life-changing event in 1970 before terms such as near-death or out-of-body experiences were part of philosophical or scientific lexicons. "At the time I called it astral projection because that was the only name I had for it. Later I realized that I had experienced the tunnel, the wonderful light, an OBE that lasted several hours, a difficult decision to return and, finally, a mystical experience which is very difficult to describe in ordinary words. . . . [T]o dismiss the experience as 'just imagination' would be impossible."[622]

But after a few years of "careful experiments" in an attempt to refute scientific materialism, Blackmore changed her mind. "I found no psychic phenomena—only wishful thinking, self-deception, experimental error and, occasionally, fraud. I became a sceptic."[623] Becoming a member of the Committee for Skeptical Inquiry (formerly the Committee for the Scientific Investigation of Claims of the Paranormal, or CSICOP), Blackmore later wrote *Dying to Live* (1993), *In Search of the Light* (1996), and *The Meme Machine* (1999, with a foreword written by Richard Dawkins).

Blackmore's work is often cited by atheists and some scientists as proof that the near-death experience results from a "dying brain." Skeptics also argue her work disproves the existence of spirit and the afterlife. "It is no wonder that we like to deny death," states Blackmore. "Whole religions are based on that denial. Turn to religion and you may be assured of eternal life. . . . [T]his comforting thought conflicts with science. Science tells us that death is the end and, as so often, finds itself opposing religion."[624]

But if you think Dr. Blackmore is wholly for or against your position, you might be wrong.

After publication of her three aforementioned books, Blackmore later clarified her stance. "I have not claimed that any of my work proves the Dying Brain Hypothesis. In fact no amount of research ever could, [but] we can account for all the major features of the NDE without recourse to such ideas as a spirit, a soul, or life after death."[625] She also backed off her comments on religion, no longer referring to it in Dawkins-like terms as a "virus of the mind" and instead seeing some benefit in religious worship.[626]

Blackmore having been a Zen practitioner for several decades, at the heart of her practice is the idea of letting go, of nonattachment, and of the "no-self": "The idea is not that there is no self at all, but that the self is not what we commonly think it is. . . . [A]s happens with many NDEers, my experiences and my research have taken away the fear of death, not because I am convinced that 'I' will carry on after this body dies, but because I know there is no one to die, and never was."[627] Her most recent edition of *Consciousness: An Introduction* states, "You may find that once-solid boundaries between the real and unreal, or the self and other, or humans and other animals or robots, or you right now and someone in a coma, begin to look less solid."[628] Sounding very much like Benjamin Franklin as he neared death, Blackmore muses, "As for what happens next—each of us will eventually get our own one chance to find out."[629]

Blackmore notes that since she originally wrote her seminal book in 2003, there have been numerous developments in the understanding of self: "Not only are more philosophers learning about neuroscience and bringing these two disciplines closer together, but research in another previously fringe area—meditation—has provided surprising insights. From brain scans of long-term meditators, we can see how attentional mechanisms change after long training and how possibly the claim that [the] self drops out may be grounded in visible brain changes."[630]

Quoting from a wide range of consciousness commentators, from Daniel Dennett to Dean Radin, Blackmore echoes other scientists in the latest iteration of her tome, saying, "Consciousness is . . . perhaps the most exciting mystery we can delve into. . . . [W]e do know that when people really struggle with the topic, they find that their own experience, and their sense of self, change in the process. Warning: studying consciousness will change your life."[631]

MERGING RIVERS

The Kingdom of Heaven is really a metaphor
for a state of consciousness.

Cynthia Bourgeault

Even Dr. Fenwick, who has bucked mainstream science on the study of consciousness, confesses, "The plain fact is that none of us understands these phenomena. As for the soul and life after death, they are still open questions, though I myself suspect that NDEs are part of the same continuum as mystical experiences."[632] He maintains those questions should only spur us on in our scientific investigation.

In the early 1990s, shortly after receiving the Nobel Peace Prize, the Dalai Lama aimed to bridge ancient spiritual practices and modern findings in biology, cognitive science, psychology, and neuroscience in an effort to reveal the human mind's capacity to transcend its own fundamental flaws.[633] "Buddhism and science are not conflicting perspectives on the world," he claimed, "but rather differing approaches to the same end: seeking the truth. In Buddhist training, it is essential to investigate reality, and science offers its own ways to go about this investigation. While the purposes of science may differ from those of Buddhism, both ways of searching for truth expand our knowledge and understanding."[634]

When asked what would happen if his religious views conflicted with valid scientific discovery, the Dalai Lama responded by saying his beliefs would have to change. In his book *The Universe in a Single Atom: The Convergence of Science and Spirituality* he says, "If scientific analysis were conclusively to demonstrate certain claims in Buddhism to be false, then we must accept the findings of science and abandon those claims."[635] His words echo those of Gandhi: "I reject any religious doctrine that does not appeal to reason and is in conflict with morality."

In the aftermath of his infamous debates with Richard Dawkins in the early 2000s, Deepak Chopra claimed,

Without screaming that the sky is falling down, one can say that two broad rivers of human experience have run into each other. One river carries science and objective observation of the world. The other river carries subjective experience and our craving for meaning, beauty, love, and truth. There is no reason why these two rivers need to be separated, and what we are seeing . . . is a merging. Within a generation there will be accepted theories that integrate the world "out there" with the world "in here."[636]

Are we moving to a time where the sacred is open to science . . . and science is open to the sacred? Is this convergence from a future we are remembering?

CHAPTER NINE

Remember the Future

It's a terrible memory that only works in one direction.
The Queen of Hearts, *Alice in Wonderland*

[We view] time as linear, but nature always unfolds in a circle.
Glenn Aparicio Parry, *Original Politics: Making America Sacred Again*

*Determine that the thing can and shall be done
and then . . . find a way.*
Abraham Lincoln

THE MYSTIC CHORDS OF MEMORY

On February 11, 1861, a tall but slightly stooped figure carrying the weight of the nation on his shoulders boarded a train bound for Washington, DC.

Heading to the capital from Springfield, Illinois, to be inaugurated as the nation's sixteenth president, Abraham Lincoln was facing the starkest of realities: seven states had already seceded from the Union since his November election. Four more were thinking of doing the same. Southerners believed a Lincoln presidency meant the end of slavery and their way of life. Talk of civil war was rampant. Northerners rejoiced at the election's outcome yet feared it could lead to the country's dissolution. They looked to Lincoln for reassurance.[637]

Quoting George Washington from the eve of his 1789 inauguration, Lincoln felt like "a culprit who is going to the place of his own execution."[638] He hoped to get to the capital while there was "still a country left to save."[639] Allan Pinkerton, who would later found the Pinkerton National Detective Agency, managed Lincoln's security throughout the journey eastward. While they traveled through cheering crowds in Indiana, Ohio, New York, and Pennsylvania—nearly 100,000 spectators gathered to see Lincoln in Philadelphia—the train had to be diverted several times, skirting hostile territory as the capital was wedged between the proslavery state of Virginia and the neutral state of Maryland with its deep Confederate sympathies.

As the president-elect traveled, Pinkerton and his detectives went undercover, investigating possible threats to the Pennsylvania, Wilmington & Baltimore Railroad. They discovered that police forces, government officials, and many citizens in Baltimore were sympathetic to the secessionists and posed a threat.[640] The trip proved frightening, with, according to Pinkerton, at least two thwarted assassination attempts.[641] The threatening scenario would later become known as the Baltimore Plot.[642]

Baltimore was a figurative and literal lynchpin to the story. Once Lincoln's train made it to the city, he would be carried one mile across town by horse-drawn carriage to board another train south to Washington, further exposing the president-elect to antagonistic forces. Pinkerton suspected several would-be assassins armed with knives would greet Lincoln once he emerged from the car to change trains. Baltimore's reputation as a hotbed of antiwar and proslavery contingents would later prove true. Weeks after Lincoln's passage through the city, Baltimore was the site of the Pratt Street Riots, which involved armed conflict between traveling Union soldiers and Southern sympathizers. More than a dozen would die (both soldiers and civilians), with hundreds wounded.

Rather than having Lincoln travel through Baltimore during daylight hours, Pinkerton snuck the president-elect onto a special train, concealing him as it steamed through the city in the dead of night. Then he cut all telegraph communication lines between Pennsylvania and Maryland. Purportedly in disguise and protected by armed Union soldiers, Lincoln arrived in Washington, DC, the next morning. Though he would later be ridiculed in the press for traveling incognito, the security ruse worked. Pinkerton sent a one-line telegram to the president of the PW&B Railroad company: "Plums delivered nuts safely."[643]

But this was only one phase of a larger drama.

In his fascinating book *Lincoln on the Verge: Thirteen Days to Washington*, author Ted Widmer reveals that shortly before Lincoln's DC arrival, there were reports of "plots to take the city, [to] blow up the public buildings, and prevent the inauguration of Lincoln." The nerve center of government, the Capitol building—home not only to Congress but also at the time to the Supreme Court, the Library of Congress, and the repository for all federal records—"was a tinder box waiting for a match." Two days after Lincoln had embarked for Washington, a pro-Confederate, anti-Union mob gathered outside the Capitol and tried to force its way in to disrupt the counting of the electoral certificates that would confirm Abraham Lincoln's election three months earlier.[644]

It amounted to an uncanny historical premonition: 160 years later another mob would attempt to invade the Capitol to stop the electoral count of a presidential election.

Only, in this instance, the aging General Winfield Scott, a Mexican War veteran originally appointed by Thomas Jefferson, had a plan in place. He warned that any intruder would "be lashed to the muzzle of a twelve-pounder and fired out the window of the Capitol." He added, "I would manure the hills of Arlington with the fragments of his body."[645] When the mob reached the Capitol, Scott's soldiers denied them entry. Only those with a special pass gained access to the seat of government. Pro-Southern delegates who were allowed entry to the floor of Congress angrily expressed their displeasure over confirming the election. When a secessionist senator from Texas, Louis Wigfall, asked General Scott if he would dare arrest a senator for treason, Scott exclaimed: "No! I will blow him to hell!"[646]

Some ten days later, the grounds secured, Lincoln took his place at the top of the Capitol steps for his inaugural address. The intensity of an endangered inauguration and threat of violence may have generated the most high-minded inaugural address in American history—and a road map for our own times. The man known primarily as an intellect, lawyer, debater, and politician turned inward. On this day, as he would do so often throughout his presidency, he summoned his muse:

> Intelligence, patriotism, Christianity, and a firm reliance on Him, who has never yet forsaken this favored land, are still competent to adjust, in the best way, all our present difficulty. . . . In your hands, my dissatisfied fellow countrymen, and not in mine, is the momentous issue of civil war. . . . You have no oath registered in Heaven to destroy the government, while I shall have the most solemn one to "preserve, protect and defend" it.

> We are not enemies, but friends. We must not be enemies. Though passion may have strained, it must not break our bonds of affection. The mystic chords of memory, stretching from every battle-field, and patriot grave, to every living heart and hearthstone, all over this broad land, will yet swell the chorus of the Union, when again touched, as surely they will be, by the better angels of our nature.[647]

Simply put, Lincoln knew how to speak from the nation's soul to the American people.

Historians have suggested there existed "a tension between Lincoln's passionate faith in reason and a political faith that must be sustained by passions that reach beyond reason."[648] The president's referencing the "mystic chords of memory" reminded American citizens of their invisible bond, their common spiritual ancestry. His now oft-quoted transcendental, nonreligious appeal to "the better angels of our nature" exhorted Americans to tap into their highest natural instincts. Lincoln's adept lyricism presages the sentiment referenced earlier by the master of myth Joseph Campbell: "When a poet carries the mind into a context of meanings and then pitches it past those, one knows that marvelous rapture that comes from going past all categories of definition."[649]

Lincoln's skillful use of language and metaphysical phraseology allowed the sentiment to move past the purely rational mind. Though it did not convince the South to throw off slavery's hold on its conscience, it roused Northerners to preserve the Union, to be both united and free. Lincoln's perpetual ability to uplift without sermonizing may well be the hallmark of his oratory gifts.

THE PUZZLING FAITH

The irony should not be lost: the man who some historians have labeled an atheist, who never belonged to any house of worship, may have tapped more deeply into what author Jacob Needleman called the "mystical core" of America than any president.

For well over a century, Lincoln's spirituality has challenged historians and biographers. Baptist minister Rev. Noyes W. Miner, who lived across the street from the Lincolns in Illinois and officiated at the burial of the president, said Lincoln "believed not only in the overwhelming Providence of God, but in the divinity of the Sacred Scriptures."[650] Newspaper editor Josiah Gilbert Holland, who published the earliest full-scale review of the fallen leader, said Lincoln was "eminently a Christian President."[651]

Those who knew Lincoln intimately did not concur. His former law partner (and later, bodyguard) Ward Hill Lamon, in his book *The*

Life of Abraham Lincoln, said Lincoln's beliefs paralleled that of early American great Thomas Paine: "He was a deist . . . and he did not believe in . . . the inspiration of the Scriptures in the sense understood by evangelical Christians."[652] Jesse Fell, another law partner, who was instrumental in bringing forth Lincoln as a candidate for president, said, "If I was called upon to designate an author whose views most nearly represented Mr. Lincoln's on this subject, I would say that author was [the Transcendentalist Unitarian minister and abolitionist] Theodore Parker."[653] Lincoln's wife, Mary Todd Lincoln—with whom he joined in at least one Spiritualist seance in the White House—said posthumously of her husband, "He was a religious man always, I think, but was not a technical Christian."[654]

The title of a book by author Mark Noll best sums up the man's spiritual legacy: *The Puzzling Faith of Abraham Lincoln* (1992). Apparently, early in life Lincoln was considered "the village atheist," reading Paine and Voltaire and writing an essay entitled "Infidelity" that attacked Christianity. He intended to have it printed and distributed. Friends were mortified. Fearing damage to Lincoln's political aspirations, one friend seized the offending document and burned it.[655] Over time his public stance on the subject softened, and he certainly employed Christian rhetoric to suit his aims. But he never endorsed nor became a member of any sect. There was nothing much conventional about the man, religious or otherwise.

One story may sum up Lincoln's "true faith." When pushed to pronounce his belief, much as was demanded of George Washington, he demonstrated the cunning of the "sly fox." Poet Carl Sandburg recounts in *Abraham Lincoln: The Prairie Years* that Lincoln attended one of Peter Cartwright's revival meetings. Cartwright was an evangelical preacher, a prominent figure in the Second Great Awakening, and was running against Lincoln for a seat in the US House of Representatives. At the end of the service, the preacher asked all who intended to go to heaven to rise.

Then, he called for all those who wished to go to hell to stand. Lincoln responded to neither option. Cartwright closed in. "Mr. Lincoln, you have not expressed an interest in going to either heaven or hell. May I enquire as to where you do plan to go?"

Lincoln replied: "I did not come here with the idea of being singled out, but since you ask, I will reply with equal candor. I intend to go to Congress."[656] In the campaign, Cartwright labeled his opponent an "infidel" for his lack of religious belief. Lincoln went on to win the election anyway.

As with many of his great American predecessors, Lincoln's beliefs were a moving target that could not be easily categorized. Sometimes he expressed himself in orthodox religious tones; at others he tread lightly upon esoteric inspiration; and in still other instances he was completely agnostic on the matter of God. His sentiments appeared to shift or adapt based on timing and the context of events in his life and that of the nation. But as with most of the great founding American men and women before him, he had a spiritual bent, apparently open to evolving on such matters. "Lincoln was probably . . . a Universalist," says Noll, "who believed in the eventual salvation of all people."[657]

BEGIN WITH THE END IN MIND

One reason among many that Lincoln is the quintessential American archetype is his embodiment of positive, national myth.

Much like the mythical orator at the time of the American Revolution in Manly P. Hall's story of the unknown speaker, Lincoln was fully committed to what he believed was America's hallowed destiny. In his inaugural address of 1861, he stated that the Union was "perpetual." The question for the nation was whether its inhabitants, a diverse collection of races, creeds, colors and tribes, could continue to govern themselves in relative peace and prosperity, evolving under the protection of a constitutionally limited democratic republic. Lincoln pledged his honor and ultimately his life so that government of, by and for the people would not perish from the earth. His prose summoned the wisdom and courage of the storied orator, inspiring others to act. In emancipating the slaves and preserving the Union, Lincoln upheld the unknown speaker's credo: "God has given America to be free." All men were, indeed, created equal.

Lincoln's words also embody the mythical message of Washington's angelic vision: a warning of grave challenges ahead for America, but with the knowledge that no other nation, ultimately, could subdue her. In his Young Men's Lyceum speech in Springfield, Illinois, decades before the Civil War, Lincoln asserted that the United States would never fall to a foreign foe, but should its demise come, it would be by her own hand to "die by suicide." Lincoln's "prophecy" rivals both the promise and warning of the story of Washington's angel.

Lincoln's forewarning is especially chilling in light of the ugly events at the US Capitol on January 6, 2021. That day was far deadlier than when a mob gathered outside the Capitol in 1861. In present-day America, a Confederate flag was unfurled at the seat of government, something that never occurred at any point during the Civil War. It may be the most telling symbol of the stark division in the country today.

As the hour of the Civil War fell upon the nation, world powers anticipated when, not if, the republic would fail. The question then, as now, is can a republic survive in the modern age? Especially in times of accelerated change and existential crises? Would not a king, dictator, or authoritarian ruler serve best? Get things done? Make the trains run on time?

What those nations did not count on at the time of the American Civil War is what Lincoln intuitively understood—the nation could never forsake its core nature. His mind was that of a timeless visionary: "Determine that the thing can and shall be done and then . . . find a way." His rallying cry epitomizes the positive expectation of American mind-cure philosophy. This is Lincoln working backwards, if you will, in nonlinear fashion. Hold the ideal. Have confidence in an outcome. And work like hell to get there—no matter how difficult or unlikely an outcome may appear. It is as if Lincoln sent a grappling hook out to an optimal future and dared America to pull it into its present.

That inspiration is the one we count on today. The times call for as great a degree of trust. There is no way of knowing what the path to reach that hallowed destination will look like. But "beginning with the end in mind," as twentieth-century author of *The Seven Habits of Highly Effective People* Stephen Covey suggested, may be the very mindset that Lincoln held to in order to transcend the crisis of his age.

AWAKENING: JESUS IS JUST ALRIGHT

His disciples said, "Show us the place where you are, for we must seek it." He said to them, "Whoever has ears should listen! There is light existing within a person of light. And it enlightens the whole world."
Jesus the Christ, from the Gnostic Gospel of Thomas, 24

Flying high on a flagpole outside James Dobson's Focus on the Family building in Colorado is a white flag with a red cross inserted over a blue field in its upper corner. Thousands of schools, homes, organizations, and places of worship in the United States fly the same flag.

It is the Christian flag, designed by Charles Overton, the superintendent of a church school in Brooklyn, New York. Originally it signified ecumenical brotherhood among diverse Christian denominations, the white of the flag "representing purity and peace, the blue field symbolizing faithfulness, truth, and sincerity and the red cross a sign of the blood and sacrifice of Christ."[658] Today its meaning has become muddied.

While some still view this flag as representing the highest ideals of the Christian faith, others display the flag as an adamant sign of defiance— that this was, is now, and shall forever be a Christian nation. On the day of insurrection at the

Christian flag, designed by Charles Overton in 1897

US Capitol in 2021, observers commented on the jarring mixture of Christian, nationalist, and racist symbolism among the insurrectionists: there were Christian flags, Christian crosses, signs saying "Jesus Saves" and "Jesus Trump 2020," as well as Confederate flags and "Don't Tread on Me" Gadsden flags, fascist insignia, and a Camp Auschwitz hoodie. Some saw apples and oranges. But according to former evangelist Frankie Schaeffer Jr., it was really a fruit cocktail of White Christian nationalism.[659]

Rev. Keith Haemmelmann, a United Church of Christ minister from Florida, took note of the symbols under which the violence transpired. "I watched one rioter bludgeon a Capitol police officer with an American flag and I thought, 'People sacrificed their lives for the ideals that flag represents, and beside it, a Christian flag.'"[660]

When some rioters entered the hallowed Senate chamber, they utilized language closely aligned with those who espouse a "biblical worldview."[661] They joined in with the "QAnon shaman," his horned helmet in hand, with their heads bowed, shouting, "Jesus Christ, we invoke your name!" and "Thank you heavenly Father for gracing us with this opportunity!"[662] The insurrectionists not only thought Jesus wanted them to violently storm the Capitol but also believed God empowered their efforts.[663] It's hardly the first time Jesus's name has been paired with a lost cause. As with most conflagrations in the Western world fought with "God on our side," the name of Jesus has ultimately been used in vain.

It has been surmised for years, but perhaps now the time is upon us: American Christianity is at a choice point. Bishop John Shelby Spong summed it up in the title of his book *Why Christianity Must Change or Die*. Although the January 6 insurrectionists hardly represent the majority of Christians in the country, the event demonstrates the increasing radicalization of certain elements of Christianity in the United States. The creeping vines of patriarchal, White Christian nationalism have been wrapping around that religion in America for years, in the same way we have seen fundamentalist factions weigh down Islam, Hinduism, and other religions around the world.

In her book *The Great Emergence*, Phyllis Tickle observes that "about every 500 years, Christianity goes through a groundbreaking paradigm shift."[664] The list so far includes the life of Jesus; the collapse of the Roman Empire, forcing the church to go underground; the separation of Eastern Orthodoxy from Roman Catholicism; and the Protestant Reformation. And now? "It would seem therefore," said Bishop Spong, "that we are due another revolution, perhaps the greatest one of all."[665]

Despite the exodus from Christian churches, the words and the wisdom of Jesus today emerge in a variety of places: not only in the New Testament but also in the Gnostic Gospels; in the Jefferson Bible; in discussions about the religion of Gandhi; in *The Aquarian Gospel of Jesus the Christ*; in *A Course in Miracles*. For Christians. For Jews. For believers in other world religions. For so-called New Agers and followers of New Thought. For the spiritual but not religious. Even for nonbelievers who deny the divinity of Jesus and perhaps even his existence[666] but nevertheless endorse the values he is purported to have taught. In other words, there's a consistent takeaway across the board: Jesus *is* just alright.

This convergence holds a master key to America's next Great Awakening.

"Jesus, as a philosopher, is wonderful," Bill Maher has said, despite his atheism, on more than one occasion. "There's no greater role model, in my view, than Jesus Christ. It's just a shame that most of the people who follow him and call themselves Christians act nothing like him."[667] Years earlier, Gandhi said more or less the same thing, calling Jesus "one of the greatest teachers humanity has ever had," but when asked by Christian missionary E. Stanley Jones, "Mr. Gandhi . . . why is it that you appear to so adamantly reject becoming his follower?" his reply was "Oh, I don't reject your Christ. I love your Christ. It is just that so many of you Christians are so unlike your Christ."[668] When he met with Howard Thurman in 1936, Gandhi told him that the greatest enemy of the message of Jesus in India was Christianity itself.

There appears to be far more agreement over the value of what Jesus taught, as opposed to the stories about him or the religion created after him.

Those who admire Jesus but do not espouse a biblical worldview point almost entirely to his moral teachings as the basis for their praise. Gandhi found that the passages from the Sermon on the Mount in the New Testament "went straight to [his] heart."[669] The font of the beatitudes found there, those eight main, proverb-like blessings in the canonical gospels of Matthew and Luke—blessed are the meek, the merciful, the pure of heart, and the peacemakers, etc.—has been universally accepted as a body of great universal truth, regardless of one's religious background, if any.

Gandhi noted that "Jesus was the most active resister known perhaps to history. His was non-violence par excellence." Jesus inspired Gandhi to unify the teachings of the *Gita*—the Buddhist "Light of Asia"—and the Sermon on the Mount. [670]He claimed, "[If] I was deprived of the *Gita* and forgot all its contents but had a copy of the Sermon on the Mount, I should derive the same joy from it as I do from the *Gita*."[671]

For those—Christian or otherwise—who are turned off by the

shame, guilt, and weight of "sin" as enumerated by early Puritanism and the most fundamental of the Great Awakenings, there are dozens of references in the New Testament where Jesus evidences what the early American Quakers identified as the inner light: that we are to know that we are gods (John 10:34); that the things Jesus did, we shall do and even greater (John 14:12); that we can access the same mind that was in Christ (Philippians 2:5); that if we "let our eye be single," our entire being shall be full of light (Matthew 6:22); and that we *are* the light of the world (Matthew 5:14). Jesus the Way-shower, having the mind of Christ, "thought it not robbery to be equal with God" (Philippians 2:5). "When Christ is revealed, and his life is your life, you will be revealed in all your glory with him" (Colossians 3:4). Cynthia Bourgeault notes in *The Wisdom Jesus: Transforming Heart and Mind*, "The words call us [to] not just admiring Jesus, but acquiring his consciousness." New Thought departs from mainstream Christianity in seeing Jesus as the "great example," not the "great exception."[672]

The next prospective evolutionary stage in America's storied spiritual history, an authentic next Great Awakening, may offer a perspective that is Jesus-centric yet is not often seen or appreciated in mainstream or evangelical Christianity. It may be the most sublime convergence of all belief systems. And it actually hearkens back to one of our earliest presidents.

WWJD–WHAT WOULD JEFFERSON DO?

In 1926 Gandhi wrote that he couldn't subscribe to the Christian belief that Jesus Christ was the only son of God. The great nonviolent leader may have been unaware that he was echoing the view of many deistic founders, most prominently Thomas Jefferson.

Jefferson had a penchant for reading inspiring works, including the Bible, prior to bedtime. But some things in the Bible, to him, were amiss. While finding Jesus to be a great teacher, Jefferson simply could not believe the fanciful passages in the New Testament about the life of Jesus—stories of a virgin birth, turning water into wine, walking on water, multiplying the fishes and the loaves, even the resurrection. The miracles challenged his capacity to reason.

Perhaps his attitude towards those passages explains why during his first term as president he would go to his study late at night, candles lit, spectacles on . . . with knife and glue in hand. There, he fashioned a Bible of his own making. Taking the King James version, he cut out what he found to be the "irrational" portions (the miracles, original sin, predestination, and the Revelation of John, which he called the "ravings of a madman") and then pasted back together the elements of the New Testament that spoke to him. His wholly personal project was called *The Philosophy of Jesus*. No copies of that text exist today.[673]

Jefferson's "cut and paste" of the Canonical Gospels, King James Bible

After leaving the White House, Jefferson refined his personal sacred text, taking the four canonical gospels (Matthew, Mark, Luke and John) and editing them chronologically to his desired ends. He curated his new version in four languages: English, French, Latin, and Greek. Once finished, he shared his work with close friends and confidantes. Not even his family was aware of it until after his death. His great-granddaughter sold it in 1895 to the Smithsonian where it resides today. As a practical matter, Jefferson's Bible as a printed manual was not obtainable until the 1940s.

Jefferson made the first viable attempt in the modern age to create a Bible based on the teachings and utterances of Jesus alone—not a Bible *about* Jesus. Much like the Gnostic Gospel of Thomas, the Jefferson Bible is a text based on what Jesus is purported to have said. Jefferson also echoed the Gnostic Gospel of Philip in suggesting the virgin birth and resurrection were "naive misunderstandings."[674] To Jefferson it was never about the miracles. Or the religion started

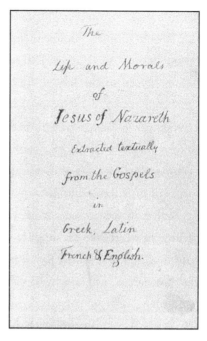

The "Jefferson Bible" in the author's handwriting.

in Jesus's name. Or what Jesus represents to Christians or to other religions. It was about the man's teachings. Do unto others; love one another; you are the light of the world; your life is measured by how you treat the least among you.

Reworking parts of the New Testament was an extension of Jefferson's revolutionary spirit. No tradition was so sacred as to escape reconsideration in the light of the Enlightenment's progress in knowledge.[675] Although Jefferson's intention was to keep his *redivivus* largely private, one has to wonder what impact *The Life and Morals of Jesus of Nazareth Extracted Textually from the Gospels in Greek, Latin, French and English* might have had on the spiritual trajectory of the nation had it been endorsed and widely read shortly after his death. It was, after all, an age of geographical and spiritual expansion for the young nation.

In that era, in utero American religions were nearing their births:

Mormonism, Adventism, Shakerism, a new iteration of Unitarianism that would inspire Transcendentalism, and the nascent roots of the Second Great Awakening. Jefferson finished his Bible some six years before his death on July 4, 1826 (a testament to the nation's most synchronistic simultaneity, the fiftieth anniversary of the signing of the Declaration of Independence and the same day fellow signatory John Adams passed away). One wonders what Jefferson's Bible could have become—perhaps one of the most controversial and influential religious works of early American history.[676]

Jefferson found Jesus to be the greatest moral and ethical teacher of any age. But like an atheist, with which Jefferson has often been confused, it was essential for him to strip away what he believed to be the fantastical, unreasonable, or unimaginable, unveiling "the most benevolent code of morals ever offered." Shortly before his death, Jefferson's self-commentary on his approach to the gospels reveals an unspoken mystic's creed: "I am of a sect by myself, as far as I know."[677]

Where would the United States be today if it had adopted this attitude or had been open to its message? Such a stance strikes at the very heart of fundamentalism. It welcomes seekers everywhere to adopt and devise their own set of universal principles and morals. How the Jefferson Bible came about exhorts the questioning of religious authority, adopting the path of the mystic who seeks the sacred outside of conventional orthodoxies.

There was a time when Jefferson Bibles were passed out to every new senator in the United States Congress (from 1904 to 1957, then again from 1997 to 2005). The conservative turn in our nation's religious path, coupled with the reservation against mixing church with state, would likely not allow for such things today. But would America have been more open to candidates of various religious perspectives (including none at all) if the Jefferson Bible had been more central to the nation's history?[678] Will a nation that is becoming more spiritual but not religious adopt the concepts and attitude of Jefferson's Bible in the future?

THE COSMIC CHRIST OF CONVERGENCE OR A "WONDERFUL DECEPTION"?

I believe that the Messiah whom we await . . . is the universal Christ; that is to say, the Christ of evolution.

Pierre Teilhard de Chardin

While the evangelical world awaits the literal return of Jesus—a notion atheists likely find preposterous if not delusional—those of a more metaphysical bent may see the Second Coming as a convergence of consciousness, a metaphor for a new age of enlightenment. If Bishop John Shelby Spong or Phyllis Tickle are correct in supposing that Christianity must and will undergo dramatic, evolutionary awakening in this century, they are taking a page out of the "book" of a twentieth-century mystic-prophet who thought such an advent, born out of convergence, is not only possible but destined.

Paleontologist, biologist, and philosopher Pierre Teilhard de Chardin (1881–1955) hovers over Christianity as both an angel and menace. The French Jesuit's notions of the "noosphere" and "the Omega Point" are evolutionary concepts, leading all of creation towards greater perfection.[679]

Long before the arrival of personal computers or the internet, Chardin's concept of a noosphere was that of a "planetary thinking network"—an interlinked system of consciousness and information, a global net of self-awareness, with instantaneous feedback and planetary communication. In Chardin's view, the noosphere is analogous on a planetary level to the evolution of the cerebral cortex in humans, moving us closer to conscious awakening. Chardin became absolutely enthralled with both the scientific and spiritual possibilities for humankind. He saw "an exciting convergence of systems, an 'Omega point' where the coalescence of consciousness will lead us to a new state of peace and greater planetary unity."[680]

Many scientists, the church, and evangelical groups took much dimmer views of Chardin's concepts. In the early 1960s, British immunologist and Nobel Prize–winner Peter Medawar wrote a scathing review of Chardin's most popular book, *The Phenomenon of Man*, calling Chardin's scientific conclusions and prognostications "nonsense, tricked out with a variety of metaphysical conceits."[681] Evolutionary biologist, ethnologist, and atheist Richard Dawkins later characterized the book as "the quintessence of bad poetic science."[682]

While the Roman Catholic Church did not specifically condemn Chardin's writings or place them on the Index of Forbidden Books, they did publish a *monitum* or "warning" against Chardin's works in 1962.[683] In 1963 Swiss theologian Karl Barth called Chardin "a giant gnostic snake," and today conservative Christian author and publisher Warren B. Smith of the Lighthouse Trails Research Project calls Chardin the father of the New Age movement (no compliment intended) and "a wonderful deception."

Most of the diatribes aimed at Chardin's works occurred after his death, but they are reminiscent of the antagonism Emerson experienced in the wake of his Harvard Divinity address. Perhaps for the same reasons. Chardin's references to "the Christ" or the "cosmic Christ" cite the metaphysical notion of the consciousness accessed by the man Jesus, and yet, as Emerson also noted, this consciousness is available to all. Chardin's cosmic Christ— not unlike the credo of Emerson's compatriot Thoreau—also emphasizes an "ecotheology." Long before the notion of Gaia emerged, Chardin claimed the earth itself possesses consciousness, which interacts with that of man.

Revered in ecumenical circles, Chardin foresaw "a general convergence of religions upon a universal Christ who fundamentally satisfies them all." He once said, "[It] seems to me the only possible conversion of the world, and the only form in which a religion of the future can be conceived."[684] When Chardin spoke of convergence, it was not merely "our heads or our bodies which we must bring together, but our hearts, without which the ultimate wholeness of its power of unification can never be achieved."[685]

"WE DIDN'T KNOW THAT CHRIST WAS NOT HIS LAST NAME"

Despite resistance to Chardin's notion of the cosmic Christ, the concept has generated long coattails.

Former Catholic (and present-day Episcopal) priest Matthew Fox challenged the Roman Catholic Church on everything from original sin to Native American spirituality, homosexuality, Jungian psychology, feminism, and more. In 1988 he wrote the best-selling *The Coming of the Cosmic Christ: The Healing of Mother Earth and the Birth of a Global Renaissance*. In it Fox borrowed liberally from Chardin's idea of the cosmic Christ and the planet's ecology. It is "time to start paying attention to the cosmic Christ, because we have been ignoring it terribly for centuries," Fox says. "It's one of the reasons we have an ecological crisis and we are no longer aware of the sacredness of nature and the divine, the cosmic Christ in nature. . . . If Christ is the rainforest and the whales and the tigers, the Christ is being crucified all over again."[686]

While still a Catholic priest, Fox underscored the universal truths in all religions, the power of indigenous religions, and each individual's innate Christhood. In 1993 the Dominican Order had enough and expelled him. When asked if he regretted any aspects that led to his removal from the church, Fox responded, "I guess I'd be sorry for the things I've done if I wanted to preserve a male-dominated, anthropocentric, essentially white institution that denies its own mystical tradition."[687]

While Fox was forced out of the church, Father Richard Rohr of the Center for Action and Contemplation (CAC), a Roman Catholic priest and member of the Society of St. Francis, has not suffered a similar fate—yet. His philosophy combines Christianity, Jungian psychology, and a variety of insights gained from Eastern religions. He quotes often from the early church fathers and Thomas Merton, but also the Dalai Lama, Islamic Sufi writers, and Hindus.[688]

Rohr and many of his colleagues at CAC, while not necessarily gaining the trust of the higher echelons of conservative or traditional Christianity have maintained their ecclesiastic appointments while sharing their inspirations from the font of the universal or cosmic Christ. "The first two thousand years of Christianity have largely struggled with Jesus of Nazareth," says Rohr, "not very well I might add . . . because we didn't know that Christ was not his last name. We just lump Jesus and Christ together."[689] Cynthia Bourgeault, an Episcopal priest and fellow CAC member, lauds Rohr's vision of the universal Christ—similar to Chardin's—as "a symbiotic relationship between the infinite (God) and the time-bound (humanity)."[690]

Today, Chardin's legacy is carried on by noteworthy men and women within and outside the bounds of traditional religious institutions. He is positively reviewed in popular press (e.g., *The New York Times*), lauded by some scientists, and even venerated by the Holy See. Four popes (Paul VI, John Paul II, Benedict XVI, Francis I) have made explicit references to his work. There is now a movement in the Catholic Church to remove the *monitum* placed upon Chardin's works from the 1960s.

"BACK TO THE FUTURE": FROM COSMIC CHRIST TO AMERICA'S ORIGINAL SPIRITUALITY

One reason the Dominican Order expelled Fox was his "working too closely with Native Americans." Fox once said, "The power of native religions to regenerate Christianity and to reconnect the old religion with the prophetic Good News of the Gospels has yet to be tapped."[691] Chardin, Fox, and Rohr's Cosmic Christ and its inseparable connection to honoring the earth signals a prospective return to an integral aspect of America's original spirituality.

As Fox's philosophical forbear Thomas Merton had recognized, understanding the philosophy of Native Americans and indigenous peoples could take one deeper within one's own faith. Merton acknowledged that Native American Indians possessed a rich spirituality tied to the planet and the cosmos. In Merton's effort to understand belief systems as they related to and converged with his Catholicism, he explored American Indian culture and its approach to the sacred. He wrote a series of articles on American Indian history and spirituality for *The Catholic Worker*, *The Center Magazine*, *Theoria to Theory*, and *Unicorn Journal*.[692] In *Ishi Means Man*, a book published after his death (with a foreword by Catholic activist-mystic Dorothy Day), Merton explored mystically oriented Native American themes of fasting, vision quests, and other rituals.

Ironically, the original inhabitants of this continent may be the last to be fully included and appreciated for their seminal role in both shaping the country's core spirituality as well as creating the American republic.[693] In truth, the influence of Native America—both the place and the original peoples of this continent—contributed mightily to the consciousness and formation of the United States.[694]

"We have a responsibility to leave a sacred America to coming generations," says Glenn Aparicio Parry in his groundbreaking book *Original Politics: Making America Sacred Again.* But in order to do that, it will be "necessary to piece together the forgotten fragments of history that are currently keeping the country divided. The most significant forgotten piece is the profound effect Native America had on the founding values of this nation."[695]

The concept of inalienable or natural rights, so integral to the Declaration of Independence, was clearly derived from the value that Native Americans placed on life and liberty. They understood these to be natural rights, original blessings given to them by their creator.[696] The notion that the Founding Fathers came up with the idea for America on their own or simply resurrected ancient Greek democratic ideals or were primarily influenced by British philosopher John Locke is erroneous.[697] Many European social reformers, including Locke, were greatly influenced by Native Americans.[698]

The seeds of egalitarianism, inclusivity, and democracy were originally planted by Native American Indians, all while acknowledging and connecting to the sacred nature of the land.[699] This healthy relationship with the natural world meant including nature in their decision-making processes. This inspired Jefferson, Paine, and their peers to create a system of government that would mirror natural law, making government as unobtrusive as possible.[700]

American Indian values focusing on the profound interconnectedness of life still inspire a holistic vision that may hold the key to both healing a polarized American culture as well as safeguarding the planet's survival.[701] For the United States, it means embracing the Native American ethos in its present; that will require a shift from thinking of humans as superior and transcendent to nature and instead seeing humans as an integral part of the whole—interdependent and ultimately inseparable from nature.

It is these seed ideas which the nation yearns to see fully realized, "effectively completing a circle back to our origins" and going "back to the future."[702] This may sound confusing if viewing time as linear, but Native Americans observed that nature always unfolds in a circle: from seed to root, bud, fruit, and back to seed again in preparation for the next cycle. Our country is unfolding in the same way.[703]

THE ORIGINAL ORIGINAL SIN

Prior to the American colonies rebelling against the mother country, the British Crown sent emissaries such as Benjamin Franklin to negotiate a military alliance with the Six Nations of the Iroquois Confederacy. The Crown was ignorant that this could give Franklin and other colonists a taste of a free and egalitarian society. This taste of liberty, coupled with the Iroquois urging the colonists to unite among themselves, contributed to the start of the American Revolution.[704] Yet until late in the twentieth century, few historians considered the impact this cultural exchange had on the founding of the nation.[705]

In 1987, Congress finally addressed the matter:

> Whereas the original Founders of the Constitution, including most notably, George Washington and Benjamin Franklin, are known to have greatly admired the concepts, principles and governmental practices of the Six Nations of the Iroquois Confederacy; and whereas the Confederation of the original thirteen colonies into one Republic was explicitly modeled upon the Iroquois Confederacy, as were many of the democratic principles which are incorporated into the Constitution. . . . Be it resolved by the Senate (The House of Representatives concurring) that the Congress on the occasion of the 200th anniversary of the signing of the US Constitution, acknowledges the historical debt which the Republic of the USA owes to the Iroquois Confederacy and other Indian Nations for their demonstrations of enlightened, democratic principles of government and their example of a free association of Independent Indian Nations.[706]

This rethinking of American origins casts, according to Jacob Needleman, an "astonishing light on the meaning of the democracy created by the Iroquois Confederacy" and "all the mystical pragmatism that lives at the root of our own American democracy."[707] The Iroquois Confederacy was rooted in a deeper knowing and hope, no less than our American Constitution.

As several key writers on Native American contributions to the ideals and founding of the nation are quick to point out, not everything the American Indian did was noble, absent of violence or crimes.[708] They did not live in utopian, warless societies,[709] and they sometimes displayed little ecological sensitivity.[710] The greater sin, of course, is the American Indian story itself: their near extermination, first by the technologically superior White Europeans, and then by the American government. In a sense, it is the nation's *original* original sin. The genocide of the Trail of Tears, the brutal Indian Wars, and the inhumanity of forcing disparate tribes onto endlessly shrinking lands and reservations is held in the memory of the land. It demands acknowledgment and healing.

The greater realization of the Native American contribution to the soul of America "may serve as a catalyst in speeding things up, uncovering the shadow side of America that has previously remained concealed. The manifestation of the national shadow enables us to see what needs to change."[711] As modern-day Native American Red Hawk states, "*They thought they killed us all off, but we are still here. And now, you need us again because you have lost your way.*"[712]

A PROPHECY OF CONVERGENCE

In *The American Soul*, Needleman suggests that William Penn, George Washington, Thomas Jefferson, Benjamin Franklin, and others, especially Abraham Lincoln, embodied a faith in the unifying, peacemaking power latent in the human heart and mind. So too the American Indian seems to have largely understood the power of this inner light. They realized how important it was to "put ones hope in just *this* kind of power, as opposed to the power of an imagined external god or, here on earth, what our Founding Fathers referred to by the term 'monarchy.'"[713]

It is this belief in the ultimate peacemaking power latent in the human heart and mind that makes a new Great American Awakening possible.

An ancient Hopi prophecy once told their people to look to the east and await the return of their lost white brother.[714] They were told that once they "migrated to their permanent home, the time would come when they would be overcome by strange people. They would be forced to develop their land and lives according to the dictates of a new ruler, or else they would be treated as criminals and punished. But they were not to resist. They were to wait for the person who would deliver them."[715] This person was their True White Brother Pahana, who would "return to them with the missing corner piece of the ancient tablet, deliver them from their persecutors, and work out with them a new and universal brotherhood of man."[716]

Like a puzzle piece begging to be inserted, the convergence of these elements may yet hold a key to America's future.

THE GREAT MIDDLE WAY: A NEW KIND OF SPIRITUAL AWAKENING

We need the middle. We just have to remember the very soil we stand on is common ground. So, we can get there. We can make it to the mountaintop. Through the desert. And we will cross this divide. Our light has always found its way through the darkness. And there's hope on the road up ahead.

Bruce Springsteen

"Many of our churches, synagogues and mosques are freaking out when they hear [our] young people are no longer interested in the sacred," says contemplative Episcopal priest Adam Bucko. "But many of them spend more time [in spiritual practices] than regular churchgoers. . . . [I]t is for this reason and many others that I don't think of the rise of the 'spiritual but not religious' among our youth as a sign of spiritual decline but rather a new kind of spiritual awakening."[717]

Some still see the spiritual-but-not-religious moniker as simply not religious. "Not religious has become a specific American identity," says

Derek Thompson, staff writer at *The Atlantic*, "one that distinguishes secular, liberal whites from the conservative, evangelical right."[718] The *Secular Surge*, a book by John Green, Geoffrey Layman, and David Campbell, identifies the boom in Americans who are decidedly secular in their outlook, not just unaffiliated. These are the people "guided by their understanding of the observable, natural world" and committed to "science and objective evidence."[719]

Is it that simple? Are the only meaningful choices of an evolving society secular atheism or religion? Or is there a "middle way"?

For Christians such as publisher Warren B. Smith, it is Jesus or nothing. And not just any Jesus. The biblical-worldview Jesus. For some secularist nonbelievers, the only sign of enlightenment appears to be grounded in a nineteenth-century kind of atheism. Late in that century, "an array of celebrity philosophers—e.g., Friedrich Nietzsche, Karl Marx, and Sigmund Freud—proclaimed the death of God, and predicted that atheism would follow scientific discovery and modernity in the West, sure as smoke follows fire."[720]

But the growing spiritual-but-not-religious class shows every sign of not only being the largest contingent of "nones" but also becoming the largest group among belief systems, cutting into both evangelical and mainstream religion on its right and atheism/agnosticism on its left. Ecumenism and scientific inquiry are pushing people from the further ends of the spectrum to something reminiscent of Francis Bacon's "great middle way."

This age of great uncertainty appears to be accelerating peoples' desire for both an inner and ecumenical awakening—but not in a specifically religious or irreligious sense. Sam Harris is an atheist and Father Richard Rohr is a Catholic priest, yet in their writings and pronouncements they seem to have moved to that great middle way, leaning heavily on the missions of ancient and modern mystics. More and more, it seems, an authentic pursuit of the sacred signals an awakening that traverses between orthodox religion and fundamentalist atheism.

Perhaps the spiritual-but-not-religious path most closely resembles

Jung's or Campbell's individual hero's journey—the way of the pragmatic mystic.

THE WORLD AS MONASTERY

...[T]he most beautiful and most profound religious emotion
that we can experience is the sensation of the mystical.
And this mysticality is the power of all true science.
If there is any such concept as a God, it is a subtle spirit,
not an image of a man that so many have fixed in their minds.

Albert Einstein

Many think mysticism will withdraw one from the world—and from the front lines of changing our society. While there may be a degree of truth to that belief, many of history's great prophets of justice and catalysts for change have emerged from deeply mystical experiences; and without that mystical depth and devotional current they accessed, they would have left far less of an imprint.

Now that we have thousands of years of recorded history and instant access to the stories and biographies of so many people we call "mystics," the jury is in.

These men and women may have spent time away from the world—as Jesus, Mohammed, and the Buddha did—but ultimately, almost to a person, the mystic from the East or West, Christian or otherwise, has emerged from periods of intrinsic insight with courage, purpose, and action. Perhaps the term I have referenced within this text—"pragmatic mystic"—is in fact largely redundant.

The mystic ultimately becomes more, not less, active in the world. Of course, there are those who cloister themselves in literal monasteries or ashrams, raising their own consciousness for the larger benefit of humankind. But the ones we read of, the ones we have come to know and revere, became active participants in their world.

According to Matthew Fox, the scale of our current challenges requires those of us on the planet at this time—not merely those behind monastery walls—to expand the reach of our potential, to truly claim the mystic within us. "You become a spiritually infused agent for change and evolution whose life is dedicated to speaking truth, carrying the message of love, and serving the greater good . . . for everyone alive today AND for future generations," says Fox. "In a world rife with division, now is the time for equipping, empowering, and building your capacity as a modern mystic and prophet . . . a lover and warrior . . . a 'disruptor' and catalyst for profound change."[721]

We are leaving centuries of traditional religions behind and entering into "an age of organic divinity," offers author-speaker Caroline Myss. "All life breathes together and we are one living bio-spiritual ecology, living within the energetic of the Divine. All is God. . . . The world needs to become our living, breathing monastery."[722]

HISTORY RHYMES: THE FOURTH TURNING?

America will pass through a great gate in history, commensurate with the American Revolution, Civil War, and twin emergencies of the Great Depression and World War II . . . involv[ing] questions of class, race, nation, and empire. Yet this time of trouble will bring seeds of social rebirth.

Strauss and Howe, *The Fourth Turning*

Whether or not Mark Twain actually said, "History doesn't repeat itself but it often rhymes," the notion offers an intriguing perspective.

At this time in the country's evolution—where some historians place it on par with the three or four greatest crises to ever face the republic—will America pursue its "better angels" as it has done before, shepherding the nation, and indeed the world, through existential crises? "Without a willingness as a nation to become more self-aware, we will not be spiritually awakened," says Marianne Williamson, "and we will not be able to summon up the emotional and psychological strength to take us to a better place."[723]

If indeed America is poised for a new Great Awakening, it will likely rhyme with historical precedent—perhaps landing, as I said in the preface, in the same place on the circle, but a step or two up the helix. Maybe that place on the circle rhymes with the crises of the American Revolution or Civil War; or facing down the specters of the Depression and fascism in the 1930s and 1940s; or the time of the Vietnam War with its concurrent race riots and the assassinations of three progressive heroes: John F. Kennedy, Martin Luther King, and Robert Kennedy.

One such "rhyming" is posited in the 1997 book *The Fourth Turning: What the Cycles of History Tell Us About America's Next Rendezvous with Destiny* by William Strauss and Neil Howe. In it the authors suggest that every fourth generation—that is, every eighty years—a generation comes into the world that is confronted by massive crises caused by preceding generations. Rising to those crises, that generation leads a "turning" of society and politics for the better.[724] After the Revolutionary War, we became a democratic republic; eighty years thereafter, we ended slavery and defeated the Confederacy to win the Civil War; and eighty years after the Civil War, we ended the Great Depression and fought fascism at home and abroad, winning World War II, building the great American middle class, the first in world history. Each of these turnings transformed America and the world.[725]

At each juncture or "turning," the influences of the Enlightenment and the Great Awakenings, the strongest twin forces within the American soul—often pitted against one another—have cooperated, sometimes *just enough* to move the nation forward. At the time of the American Revolution, the Whitefield-influenced evangelicalism of the First Great Awakening joined forces with the Deism, Unitarianism, and Freemasonry of the Enlightenment to help forge a new nation; as the Civil War emerged, the passion of Second Great Awakening Christianity found ways to partner with Transcendentalism—

evangelical William Lloyd Garrison was as passionate about ending slavery as Unitarian Transcendentalist Theodore Parker—thereby lighting the fires of abolition, women's rights, suffrage, progress for the mentally infirm, labor, and education while safeguarding animal rights, the environment, and more; Catholic priests and mainstream Protestant preachers who rode with the Freedom Riders for racial justice in the 1960s were as progressive as the African-, Eastern-, and Quaker-influenced Howard Thurman and MLK.

When common ground was found among the ideological differences of varying sects, religions, and belief systems, even among these two great strands of American spiritual thought, transformation occurred.

Author Glenn Aparicio Parry offers this both hopeful and sobering assessment of the nation's current predicament:

> I have said that America is on an inexorable path towards realizing its original sacred purpose of unity in diversity. I believe America—the place and nation—will return to that sacred purpose again. I admit to another possibility, however: one in which America rejects its destiny and devolves in the opposite direction so far it cannot right the ship. The devolved state of unitive consciousness is uniformity. America could become a fascist state. In truth, both possibilities have been in play ever since we broke away from monarchy and began our experimental path forward. Today, a fascist America seems more possible than ever before; yet, at the same time, the seeds of a sacred America are still present.[726]

Parry's present appraisal parallels the sentiments uttered by Strauss and Howe in *The Fourth Turning*. More than a quarter century ago, those authors surmised that sometime before the year 2025, America will pass through a great gate of history where the very survival of the nation will feel at stake. The nation could erupt into insurrection or civil violence. Democracy could be destroyed, and millions of people scattered or killed. Or America could enter a new golden age, triumphantly applying shared values to improve the human condition. According to Strauss and Howe, the rhythms of history do not reveal the outcome of the coming crisis; all they suggest is the timing and dimension.[727]

END TIMES

Today, the exigencies fostered by the rise of authoritarianism as well as the perils of climate change only seem to speed up the clock. The "end times" that evangelicals speak of may not be an era of outside savior–like relief, saving us from our own ignorance and greed, but is instead a self-imposed deadline to act due to our choking out both liberty and the life of a self-sustaining planet. The solutions likely will not come from someone or something outside ourselves but from an internal evolution in human consciousness.

The trajectory of transformation and growth, as the great religious and philosophical traditions allude, comprises many metaphors. We could point to the classic hero's journey charted by Joseph Campbell; the four seasons or four directions of most Native religions; the epic accounts of exodus, exile, and promised land of the Jewish people, followed by the cross, death, and resurrection narrative of Christianity. Each of these deeply rooted "myths" shows that growth happens in this full sequence. To grow towards love, union, salvation, or enlightenment, we must be moved from order to disorder and then ultimately to reorder.[728]

If our national and planetary urgencies call us to something greater, then perhaps America is ripe for an awakening. In our own lives we often experience transformation and shifts at times and places where there are no seemingly good options, and yet the exigencies of life compel us to step forward or sink into the abyss. We move forward in faith from a consciousness that is greater than our individual selves. Quoting Churchill, "Sometimes it is not enough that we do our best; sometimes we must do what is required."

OUT OF MANY, ONE

The ideals, the purposes that called the nation into being are well.
It might be answered by saying that there needs to be on the part of
each man, each woman, the adhering to those principles that
caused the formulating of the American thought.
Edgar Cayce Reading 3976-24

The "American Prophet" Edgar Cayce was a nineteenth- and twentieth-century intuitive who utilized his considerable talents to channel messages of healing, hope, and mystical inspiration. In the 14,000 altered-state "readings" that Cayce shared, some 9,000 dealt specifically with individual health issues, but in others he addressed the nature of God and man, karma, reincarnation, common ground among religions, free choice, dreams, nutrition, Atlantis, and future events. He was a devout Christian and Sunday school teacher and yet, through his readings, demonstrated a predilection towards the esoteric, believing minds were timelessly connected. Some have called him the founder for the New Age and the "Father of Holistic Medicine."[729]

Cayce gave several readings on "the mass thought of the American nation, its ideals, principles and purposes."[730] Not all of Cayce's "prophecies" about the United States have come to pass, but he did correctly predict the World Wars, the Great Depression, even religious and racial division that we are seeing today. Ultimately he foresaw that America, through "universal thought, that is expressed and manifested in the brotherhood of man,"[731] was the great hope of the world and that the "democracy of America will not fail."[732]

He believed that "the purposes upon which this land was founded[,] . . . freedom of speech, freedom of purpose for worshipfulness of Creative forces according to the dictates of one's own conscience, shall never perish from the earth."[733]

Those principles that Cayce alluded to may best be summed up by Jacob Needleman, who asserts that the founders bestowed upon this nation a mix of mysticism and pragmatism. "The purpose of America is a place where people can search to become fully human in themselves," he says. "America is the guardian of the possibility of human beings to search for conscience."[734] Conscience, he asserted, "is an absolute power within the human psyche to intuit real values of good and evil, right and wrong . . . [and] we are born with that capacity. It is not just a product of social conditioning. This is what the great traditions teach."[735]

Today the wisdom of the founders may be seen in a newly illumined light that places greater emphasis on the esoteric roots of those early philosophies later expanded upon by the American Transcendentalists. Were they really founding mystics? A mystic recognizes the oneness of life. In that regard, especially when it came to diverse religious expressions, the founders played no favorites. For that very reason alone, a mystic-like view of the world appears to be integral to their thinking. If America's sacred purpose is to demonstrate unity in diversity to the world, is it so surprising that the national motto they chose, the one that graces the Great Seal of the United States, is *E Pluribus Unum*? Out of many, one?

THE SHADOW KNOWS

For millions of years, mankind lived just like the animals.
Then something happened which unleashed the power
of our imagination. We learned to talk and we learned to listen. . . .
With the technology at our disposal, the possibilities are unbounded.
All we need to do is make sure we keep talking.

Stephen Hawking

If "our politics is our spirituality expressed outwardly," as *Conversations with God's* Neale Donald Walsch has suggested, it should come as no surprise that much of our politics has taken on the tone of religious belief. That works and it doesn't. Strongly sectarian, dogmatic religious beliefs tend to divide, while an open-minded spirituality, ideally, should represent one's most ethical, loving, and deeply humanitarian beliefs.

As America sits mired in a seeming irreconcilable, polarizing paradox, one path to awakening is engaging the shadow self. We don't have far to look. It is often in the face of "the other," the judgments we place on our so-called enemy or adversary, that reveal our hidden selves.

EVANGELICAL SHADOW

While many scoff at evangelicals and the lineage of the Puritans and the Great Awakenings, it is worth reminding those critics that passionate Christianity has played an essential role in developing this nation; the can-do attitude and belief in something larger than our physical, human selves has arguably helped build and sustain the nation. As a group, they have been doers and actors.

When evangelicals were on the outside of power looking in, they took action. When the Eisenhowers, Goldwaters, even the Nixons denied them, they did not sit still. They became politically active. They ran for city council, mayor, and school boards. They ran to become the proverbial "dog catcher" in town. Their critics may have found them loud and pugnacious, but they broke through and influenced the likes of Ronald Reagan—in whom they found a political if not spiritual savior. Evangelicalism's influence may have crested, especially in the aftermath of their near universal support of Donald Trump, but it would be a grave mistake to underestimate their influence, political and otherwise.

The shadow side of evangelicalism has been its own racism, its White nationalism and "superiority"—that is, the inability to acknowledge the validity of other religious perspectives. While on one hand sin/redemption Christianity expresses tolerance and acceptance of everyone's own unique path to God, the deeply held evangelical belief remains: Jesus is the only way; fallen humans are innately sinful and in need of an external savior, and salvation can be found in a biblical worldview of Christianity and there alone.

NEW THOUGHT/NEW AGE SHADOW

Thomas Jefferson and William James suggested that Unitarianism or a New Thought–type belief would eventually become the dominant spiritual expression of the United States. The nation is still waiting, though it's possible that the emerging spiritual-but-not-religious contingent is what Jefferson and James foresaw. While today's New Thought/New Age proponents may castigate the fundamentalism of evangelicalism or atheism, they are falling short of their deistic or Transcendentalist influencers, who were both inwardly inspired and outwardly directed in their activism.

In the twentieth century, New Thought became less socially active than its Transcendentalist roots, influenced by the metaphysically driven New Age movement, which placed greater emphasis on "going within" and using the mind primarily to improve one's own lot in life (for spiritual growth, general health, and the fruits of abundant living). It is in its shadow side, reflected back in evangelicalism's political activism, that New Thought/New Age may see its own shortcomings. Jefferson and James were seekers who were doers—prime examples of pragmatic mysticism. That enlightened inner awareness demands the courage to act, even while maintaining spiritual equanimity. This is a shadow lesson that today's New Thought/New Age movement must bear in mind if it is to become a dominant expressive force in the twenty-first century.

ATHEISM'S SHADOW

As for atheism, it has come a long way in a short period of time. First in its ability to express itself—the reins of restriction brought about by cultural negativity and its historical association with communist totalitarianism have been lifted. Now one can freely and proudly express one's atheism with intelligence, grace, and persuasive candor. But its shadow has been revealed in the very fundamentalist certitude it criticizes in evangelicalism. According to Sir Isaac Newton's biographer Richard Westfall, Newton asserted, "The ultimate cause of atheism is 'this notion of bodies having, as it were, a complete, absolute and independent reality in themselves.'"[736] Atheism's historical reticence to explore the nature and genesis of consciousness, psi phenomenon, and parapsychology that it has chided in the New Thought/New Age movement is, in the words of actor-moderator John Cleese, "not terribly impressive." The death of the Amazing Randi brought commentators to the fore who likened Randi's pursuit of fraudulent psychics to Sen. Joseph McCarthy's chasing of communists: he may have nailed a few guilty charlatans along the way but in the end did far worse damage to our pursuit of understanding consciousness. Randi's legacy is one of inhibiting the prospective scientific study of metaphysics with his pseudo-skepticism and demagoguing of people with whom he did not agree.[737]

But atheism is turning a corner, too, giving others with differing beliefs wider berth and finding common ground on which to at least conduct a civil exchange of ideas. The discussion of the locality/non-locality of consciousness is on the table. Some within the pantheon of New Atheism dare to quote mystics and speak in terms of spiritual awakening. A kinder, gentler, more feminine face associated with atheism has certainly helped the cause.

As Stephen Hawking once suggested, "Keep talking"—that process may reveal our shadow selves *to ourselves.* If the answers to greater unity and addressing the existential crises of our age lies in an awakening of consciousness, every thought and action invested in our individual awakening ultimately contributes to that of the collective. Perhaps this is how Chardin suggested that convergence occurs—even among seemingly different political, religious, spiritual, or cultural belief systems.

A LEAP ACROSS THE GREAT DIVIDE

I am in my father and you are in me and I in you.
John 14:20

I am he as you are he as you are me and we are all together.
Lennon/McCartney, "I Am the Walrus"

With growth in radical ecumenism, convergence, and scientific discovery, we may ultimately discover that it is only our egos that separate us, that our consciousness is intimately connected to the same font or source.

Chardin in fact argues that such a realization must be so, that "what we are aware of is only the nucleus which is ourselves. The interaction of souls would be incomprehensible if some 'aura' did not extend from one to the other, something proper to each one and common to all."[738] Chardin believed, too, that this consciousness is not only psychological but also of the greatest spiritual importance. "Nothing is precious," he says, "except that part of you which is in other people, and that part of others which is in you. Up there, on high, everything is one."[739]

There are those, like Chardin, who posit that we are either going to make it as a unified, transformed society or we shall perish. As our existential crises of autocracy and climate push us in the direction of either mutual destruction or recognizing our unity, will humanity finally make this leap, not based on the "illusion" of separateness but rather on our sometimes barely perceptible interconnectedness?

The naivete here may be off-putting—yet it was not so off-putting for the great idealist-doers among us. Whether it was Jesus, Gandhi, King, Chardin, or Lennon—or the Lincoln-like determiners who set an intention and then set out to "find a way"—they dared to be dreamers: "and the world shall live as one," "on earth as it is in heaven."

The rational mind and human ego cannot make sense of this. But now, in addition to the mystics, science is coming scintillatingly close to suggesting the timeless realm of our soul, recognizing that solid objects are largely if not entirely made up of energy. Atoms, we have come to learn in the last century, are essentially composed of space. Quantum physics suggests that even that slight amount of material in and of itself may or may not exist depending upon who observes it. Is it material . . . or a wave? Consciousness, as Planck and Radin and others have said, is the foundation for everything.

Perhaps that unseen, essential self is what our "founding mystics" knew or appreciated all along. The Freemason symbol adopted as the reverse of the Great Seal—the immaterial all-seeing eye, transcending materiality as represented by the physical pyramid—epitomizes the core of this nation. The United States is still likely the best and brightest hope for the world. Not in a national egotistical sense, but based upon the role and logistical placement we have been given in this world: the land of integration of all colors, creeds, and tribes; built upon both can-do religions of action and the esoteric wisdom, conscience, and enlightenment that founded this nation, and the freedom to reject any notion of god if we so choose. America has always been as much, if not more, an idea than a place, founded upon principles of freedom and egalitarianism rather than based purely on inherited tribal notions. This light *cannot* be extinguished for it is the gist of hope for the world.

The core of this nation, its very soul, represents the possibility of transcending these illusions of difference, of separation, and the possibility that humankind can and will take an expanded view of itself and recognize its essential nature. This will take a Great Awakening that combines and transcends all of those seen and unseen awakenings of our past and meets the challenges on an elevated circle of evolution.

There is no doubt it will take a revolution in consciousness. But thankfully, as a nation, we seem to be good at that. The moral arc of the universe does indeed bend towards justice, and we are forever in the process of becoming a more perfect union.

ENDNOTES

PREFACE

1 Eckhart Tolle, quote from his podcast "Inner Peace," Eckhart Tolle Essential Teachings, July 22, 2021, audio 21:50, https://podcasts.apple.com/us/podcast/inner-peace/id1458654443?i=1000529659445.

2 Mitch Horowitz, "Occult America," interview by Christopher Naughton, *New World Radio*, WTAR-850 AM Norfolk, VA., Unity Online Radio, Nov. 11, 2010, audio 22:10.

3 "Doris Kearns Goodwin on whether we are living in 'the worst of times,'" CBS Sunday Morning, Oct. 7, 2018, video 00:42, https://www.cbsnews.com/news/historian-doris-kearns-goodwin-on-whether-we-are-living-in-the-worst-of-times/.

4 Jon Meacham, "Why Religion Is the Best Hope Against Trump," *New York Times*, Opinion, Feb. 25, 2020, https://www.nytimes.com/2020/02/25/opinion/christianity-trump.html.

CHAPTER 1

5 "Exploring the World's Creation Myth," Weekend Edition, NPR, Nov.13, 2005, https://www.npr.org/templates/story/story.php?storyId=5010951.

6 Gregg Braden, "The Silent Battle for Our Story," *Technology, Consciousness & Evolution*, March 31, 2022, 1, https://stream.humanitysteam.org/technology-consciousness-and-evolution/videos/tce-mod-01-greg-braden-1080p.

7 Volume: Hellas, Article: "Greek Mythology," *Encyclopaedia The Helios*, 1952.

8 Steve Connor, "How Did Our Legends Really Begin?" *The Independent* (UK), Jul. 29, 2014, https://www.independent.co.uk/arts-entertainment/books/features/how-did-our-legends-really-begin-9634148.html.

9 Robert A. Segal, "Introduction," *Jung on Mythology* (Princeton: Princeton University Press, 1998), 4.

10 Joseph Campbell, *The Inner Reaches of Outer Space: Metaphor as Myth and as Religion* (Novato, CA: New World Library, 2002), 28.

11 Joseph Campbell, *The Power of Myth*, Episode 2: "The Message of the Myth," PBS, Jun. 30, 1988.

12 Manvir Singh, "The Sympathetic Plot, Its Psychological Origins, and Implications for the Evolution of Fiction," Emotion Review, 13(3): July 2021, 183–198, https://www.researchgate.net/publication/351634281_The_Sympathetic_Plot_Its_Psychological_Origins_and_Implications_for_the_Evolution_of_Fiction.

13 Campbell, *The Power of Myth*, Episode 2.

14 Robert A. Segal, "Introduction," *In Quest of the Hero* (Princeton: Princeton University Press, 1990), vii-xli.

15 Connor, "How Did Our Legends Really Begin?"

16 Manly Palmer Hall, *The Secret Destiny of America* (Los Angeles: Philosophical Research Society, 1944), 44.

17 Mitch Horowitz, "Ronald Reagan and the Occultist," *Salon Magazine*, January 5, 2014, https://www.salon.com/2014/01/05/ronald_reagan_and_the_occultist_the_amazing_story_of_the_thinker_behind_his_sunny_optimism/.

18 "Ronald Reagan Was Absolutely Certain UFOs Existed," *Civilian Military Intelligence Group*, November 17, 2014, https://civilianmilitaryintelligencegroup.com/ronald-reagan-was-absolutely-certain-ufos-existed/; "Ronald Reagan Sees a UFO," *Science/How Stuff Works*, https://science.howstuffworks.com/space/aliens-ufos/ronald-reagan-ufo.htm, https://www.thinkaboutitdocs.com/ronald-reagan-sees-a-ufo/; "Reagan's UFO Sightings," *The Night Sky*, August 15, 2020, https://www.thenightskyii.org/reagan.html.

19 Allen McDuffee, "Ronald Reagan actually used this San Francisco astrologist to make presidential decisions," *Medium Magazine*, May 30, 2017, https://timeline.com/ronald-reagan-astrology-quigley-aa81632662d9.

20 James C. Humes, *The Wit & Wisdom of Ronald Reagan* (Washington, D.C.: Regewery Publishing Inc., 2007), 128.

21 Andrea Mitchell, "The President and the Astrologer," *NBC News*, April 10, 1989.

22 "Reagan's Astrologer," *Discovery Science*, April 2011, https://www.youtube.com/watch?v=VP8ocuNQMJA.

23 Mitchell, "The President and the Astrologer," *NBC News*.

24 McDuffee, "Ronald Reagan actually used this San Francisco astrologist to make presidential decisions."

25 Ibid.

26 Manly Palmer Hall, 1904-1990, from *Lohve - The Wise Alternative* quoting Sahagun, Louis, *Master of the Mysteries: The Life of Manly Palmer Hall* (Port Townsend, Washington: Process Media, 2008), 15, https://lohve.com/manly-p-hall.

27 Steffie Nelson, "Charting the Man Behind a Mystical City," *The Los Angeles Times*, June 21, 2008, https://www.latimes.com/archives/la-xpm-2008-jun-21-et-hall21-story.html.

28 Horowitz, *New World Radio*, Nov. 10, 2010, 25:13.

29 Ibid.

30 Louis Sahagun, *Master of the Mysteries: The Life of Manly Palmer Hall* (Port Townsend, Washington: Process Media, 2008), 52.

31 Horowitz, *New World Radio*, Nov. 10, 2010, 24:18.
32 Ibid.
33 Anna Berkes, "The Unknown Patriot," from *Th. Jefferson Monticello*, Aug. 7, 2008 quoting George Lippard, *Washington and His Generals; Or, Legends of the Revolution* (Philadelphia: T.B. Peterson, 1847), 394-96, https://www.monticello.org/research-education/thomas-jefferson-encyclopedia/unknown-patriot/.
34 Horowitz, "Ronald Reagan and the Occultist."
35 Nelson, "Charting the Man Behind a Mystical City," *The Los Angeles Times,* June 21, 2008.
36 Horowitz, "Ronald Reagan and the Occultist."
37 "Washington's Vision," *The Theosophist Magazine,* Vol. LIX, No. 8, May 1938, 122-125, originally published by Wesley Bradshaw in *The National Tribune,* Vol. 4, No. 12 (Dec. 1880).
38 Edward G. Lengel, *Inventing George Washington* (New York: HarperCollins, 2011), 93-100.
39 Walter F. Prince, "Incidents," *Journal of the American Society for Psychical Research,* Vol XI. (1917).
40 David Mikkelson, "George Washington's Vision," *Snopes,* May 14, 2002, https://www.snopes.com/fact-check/george-washingtons-vision/.
41 "The American Spiritual Vision," *New World Television* (New York), PBS Virginia, March 23, 1999.
42 J.L. Bell, "The Truth About Washington's Vision," *Boston1775,* Dec. 30, 2006, https://boston1775.blogspot.com/2006/12/truth-of-washingtons-vision.html.
43 John Burt, "Lincoln's Address to the Young Men's Lyceum: A Speculative Essay," *Brandeis.Edu.*, Dec. 7, 2001, https://people.brandeis.edu/~burt/lyceumtalk.pdf.
44 Ibid.
45 Eli Merritt, "The Constitution Must Be Our Political Religion: Remembering Lincoln's Words," *Seattle Times*, March 8, 2019, https://www.seattletimes.com/opinion/the-constitution-must-be-our-political- religion-remembering-lincolns-words/.
46 Ibid.

CHAPTER 2
47 Mark A. Noll, *America's God: From Jonathan Edwards to Abraham Lincoln* (New York: Oxford University Press, 2002), 45.
48 "Great Awakening and the Enlightenment," *Univ. of Central Florida Edu.*, Chapter 4: Rule Britannia! The English Empire, 1660–1763, https://pressbooks.online.ucf.edu/osushistory/chapter/great-awakening-and-enlightenment/.
49 Ibid.
50 "George Whitefield, Sensational Evangelist of Britain and America," Christian History, *Christianity Today*, https://www.christianitytoday.com/history/people/evangelistsandapologists/george-whitefield.html.
51 "John and Charles Wesley," *US History.com*, https://www.u-s-history.com/pages/h3853.html.
52 "Benjamin Franklin on George Whitefield, 1739," *Becoming American: The British Atlantic Colonies*, National Humanities Center, as published in 2009, *Benjamin Franklin's Autobiography: An Authoritative Text*, eds. J. A. Leo Lemay & P. M. Zall (New York: W. W. Norton & Co., 1986), http://nationalhumanitiescenter.org/pds/becomingamer/ideas/text2/franklinwhitefield.pdf.
53 H.W. Brands, *The First American: The Life and Times of Benjamin Franklin* (New York: Anchor Books, a Div. of Random House, 2000), 138.
54 "Franklin on Whitefield, 1739," National Humanities Center.
55 Ibid.
56 "George Whitefield, Sensational Evangelist of Britain and America," *Christianity Today*, https://www.christianitytoday.com/history/people/evangelistsandapologists/george-whitefield.html.
57 Ibid.
58 "Sinners in the Hands of an Angry God," verse 16, *Voices of Democracy, The US Oratory Project*, https://voicesofdemocracy.umd.edu/edwards-sinners-in-the-hands-speech-text/.
59 "Jonathan Edwards and the Great Awakening in Colonial America," *The Constitutional Rights Foundation*, https://www.crf-usa.org/bill-of-rights-in-action/bria-20-4-a-jonathan-edwards-and-the-great-awakening-in-colonial-america
60 Daniel Julich and Jenna Clayton, "Sinners In The Hands Of An Angry God by Edwards: Summary, Analysis & Metaphors," *Study.com*, Updated August 28, 2021, https://study.com/academy/lesson/sinners-in-the-hands-of-an-angry-god-by-edwards-summary-analysis-metaphors.html.
61 "George Whitefield, Sensational Evangelist of Britain and America," *Christianity Today*.
62 George M. Marsden, *Jonathan Edwards: A Life* (New Haven and London: Yale University Press, 2003), 218.
63 "Benjamin Franklin on George Whitefield, 1739," *Becoming American: The British Atlantic Colonies*.
64 Ibid.
65 Brands, *The First American*, 149.
66 W. Dugdale, "Voltaire," *A Philosophical Dictionary*, version 2, 1843, p. 473, sec 1, Retrieved January 10, 2021.
67 Don Closson, "Deism and America's Founders," *Probe*, July 3, 2016, https://probe.org/deism-and-americas-founders/; "Faith of Our Founding Fathers," *Unitarian Universalist Fellowship of Tuolumne County*, https://www.uuftc.org/minister/sermons/2008-sermons/faith-of-our-founding-fathers/.
68 Professor Paul Brians, "Voltaire: A Treatise on Toleration (1763)," *Washington State University,* http://www.wsu.edu:8080/~wldciv/world_civ_reader/world_civ_reader_2/voltaire.html.

69 "The Founders Faith," *The Lehrman Institute,* https://lehrmaninstitute.org/history/the-founders-faith.html.

70 Steven Waldman, "Religious Freedom Is America's Greatest Export—and It's Under Attack," *Newsweek Magazine,* May 9, 2019, https://www.newsweek.com/2019/05/17/religious-freedom-americas-greatest-export-under-attack-1418121.html.

71 Mitch Horowitz, "The New Great American Awakening?" interview by Christopher Naughton, *New World Radio,* WTAR-850 AM Norfolk, VA., Unity Online Radio, audio 36:15, February 5, 2010.

72 Jacob Needleman, *The American Soul: Rediscovering the Wisdom of the Founders* (New York: Tarcher/ Putnam, 2002), 42.

73 Ibid., 43

74 Ibid.

75 Caroline Myss, *The Sacred Contract of America: Fulfilling the Vision of Our Mystic Founders* (Chicago: Sounds True, 2007), 4 CD program, CD 1.

76 *The Correspondence of Roger Williams in Two Volumes,* edited by Glenn W. LaFantasie (Hanover, NH: University Press of New England, 1988), Vol. 1, 23.

77 John M. Barry, "God, Government and Roger Williams' Big Idea," *Smithsonian Magazine,* January 2012, https://www.smithsonianmag.com/history/god-government-and-roger-williams-big-idea-6291280/.

78 Glenn Aparicio Parry, *Original Politics: Making America Sacred Again* (New York: Select Books, 2020), 45.

79 Ibid., 58

80 Ibid., 56

81 Ibid., 55.

82 Ibid., 56.

83 Tapper, Alan, "Joseph Priestley," *Dictionary of Literary Biography 252: British Philosophers 1500–1799,* Editors Philip B. Dematteis and Peter S. Fosl (Detroit: Gale Group, 2002),10.

84 Brannon Deibert, "What is Unitarianism?" *Christianity.com,* December 1, 2018, https://www.christianity.com/church/denominations/what-is-unitarianism-discover-the-history-and-beliefs-of-the-unitarian-church.html.

85 Clay Jenkinson, "Priestly," *The Thomas Jefferson Hour,* WHRV 89.5FM, April, 2009.

86 Stuart Andrews, "Priestly and Liberty," *Libertarianism*.org, May 1, 1980, https://www.libertarianism.org/publications/essays/priestly-liberty.

87 Catherine L. Albanese, *A Republic of Mind and Spirit* (New Haven: Yale University Press, 2007), 160-163.

88 Michael Corbett and Julia Mitchell Corbett, *Politics and Religion in the United States* (New York and London: Garland Publishing, 1999), 68.

89 Thomas Jefferson Letter to Benjamin Waterhouse, 13 October 1815, *National Archives,* Founders Online, https://founders.archives.gov/documents/Jefferson/03-09-02-0063.

90 "Jefferson's Religious Beliefs," *Th. Jefferson Monticello,* https://www.monticello.org/site/research-and-collections/jeffersons-religious-beliefs.

91 Ibid.

92 Ibid., quoting The Papers of Thomas Jefferson, *PTJ,* 36:258. Transcription available at Founders Online, https://founders.archives.gov/documents/Jefferson/01-36-02-0152-0006

93 "Jefferson and Religion," from *Th. Jefferson Monticello,* https://www.monticello.org/thomas-jefferson/jefferson-s-three-greatest-achievements/religious-freedom/.

94 Denise Spellberg, "Jefferson, the Constitution and the Quran: Why the Founding Father's Defense of Muslims Is Really Important Today," *Newsweek Magazine,* June 3, 2017, https://www.newsweek.com/jefferson-constitution-and-quran-why-founding-fathers-defense-muslims-matters-619541.

95 "The Barbary Treaties 1786-1816 : Treaty of Peace and Friendship, Signed at Tripoli November 4, 1796." *The Avalon Project, Yale Law School.* Retrieved February 29, 2020, https://avalon.law.yale.edu/18th_century/bar1796t.asp; by James H. Hutson, Article 11 from the Library of Congress.

96 Yair Rosenberg, "The Complicated History of Thomas Jefferson's Koran," *The Washington Post,* January 2, 2019, https://www.washingtonpost.com/outlook/2019/01/02/complicated-history-thomas-jeffersons-koran/.

97 Annette Gordon-Reed and Peter S. Onuf, "Thomas Jefferson's Bible Teaching," *New York Times,* July 4, 2017, https://www.nytimes.com/2017/07/04/opinion/thomas-jeffersons-bible-teaching.html.

98 Letter, Thomas Jefferson to John Adams, 22 August 1813, *National Archives,* Founders Online, https://founders.archives.gov/documents/Jefferson/03-06-02-0351.

99 "Jefferson's Religious Beliefs," from *Th. Jefferson Monticello,* https://www.monticello.org/site/research-and-collections/jeffersons-religious-beliefs#footnote23_udijtyg.

100 Holmes, "Was Jefferson a Unitarian?" from *Th. Jefferson Monticello,* June 25, 2005.

101 Corinne McLaughlin and Gordon Davidson, *Spiritual Politics* (New York: Ballantine Books, 1994), 88; "The American Spiritual Vision," *New World Television,* PBS Virginia, March 23, 1999.

102 Jon Meacham, *American Gospel* (New York: Random House Publishing Group, Kindle edition, 2006), 4.

103 Michael Lipka and Claire Gecewicz, "More Americans now say they're spiritual but not religious," *Pew Research Center,* September 6, 2017, https://www.pewresearch.org/fact-tank/2017/09/06/more-americans-now-say-theyre-spiritual-but-not-religious/.

104 Meacham, *American Gospel,* 12.

105 Benjamin Franklin, *The Autobiography of Benjamin Franklin* (New York: MacMillan Publishing & Co., 1962; A Touchstone Book published by Simon and Schuster, 2004), 89.

106 Brands, *The First American,* 113.

107 Needleman, *The American Soul*, 92. .

108 Franklin, *The Autobiography of Benjamin Franklin*, 1382, quoted in Needleman, *The American Soul*, 92.

109 Thomas S. Kidd, "Reconciling Deism and Puritanism in Benjamin Franklin," *Yale University Press*, May 12, 2017, https://yalebooks.yale.edu/2017/05/12/reconciling-deism-and-puritanism-in-benjamin-franklin/; Franklin, *The Autobiography of Benjamin Franklin*.

110 Christopher Finch, Ph.D., *Was Einstein a Deist?* https://www.quora.com/Was-Einstein-a-deist.

111 Brands, *The First American,* 113.

112 Julius F. Sache, *The German Sectarians of Pennsylvania: a Critical and Legendary History of the Ephrata Cloister and the Dunkers*, (New Haven: Yale University Press, 1966), 323-325; Needleman, *The American Soul*, 91; Peter Dawkins, Director of the Francis Bacon Research Trust and Saira Salmon,"Freemasonry and the Rosicrucian Order," posted February 16, 2016, video, 1:48, https://www.youtube.com/watch?v=aCezov90Hjo.

113 Corinne Heline, *America's Invisible Guidance*, (Los Angeles, CA: New Age Press, 1949), 16.

114 "Faith of Our Founding Fathers," *Unitarian Universalist.*

115 Franklin, *The Autobiography of Benjamin Franklin*, cited in https://www.ushistory.org/franklin/autobiography/page37.htm.

116 "Faith of Our Founding Fathers," *Unitarian Universalist.*

117 Milton V. Blackman, "The Rise of Freedom in America," *BYU Religious Studies Center,* citing Carl Van Doren, *The Great Rehearsal: The Story of the Making and Ratifying of the Constitution of the United States* (New York:Viking Press, 1948), 101, https://rsc.byu.edu/window-faith/rise-freedom-america#_edn1.

118 Dawkins and Salmon,"Freemasonry and the Rosicrucian Order," video, https://www.rosicrucian.org/history.

119 Brands, *The First American*, 657-658.

120 Benjamin Franklin epitaph 1728, *National Archives, Founders Online*, https://founders.archives.gov/documents/Franklin/01-01-02-0033.

121 Brands, T*he First American*, 657.

122 Ibid., 444.

123 Horowitz, *New World Radio*, November 10, 2010, audio 36:10.

124 Mary V. Thompson, "George Washington and Religion: Interview with Mary V. Thompson," Interview by *George Washington's Mount Vernon*, https://www.mountvernon.org/george-washington/religion/george-washington-and-religion/; Mary V. Thompson, *In the Hands of Providence* (Charlottesville: University of Virginia Press, 2008,) Chapter 7, "Evidence of Belief," 101-123.

125 Peter Rodriguez, "Washington: Devout or Deist?" Panel Discussion, *The National Constitution Center*, Philadelphia, PA., December 9, 2009; Horowitz, *New World Radio*, February 5, 2010, audio 19:01.

126 John Meacham, "Washington: Devout or Deist?" Panel Discussion, *The National Constitution Center*, Philadelphia, PA., December 9, 2009.

127 Rodriquez, *"Washington: Devout or Deist?"*

128 "Faith of Our Founding Fathers," *Unitarian Universalist.*

129 "Washington and Catholicism," *George Washington's Mount Vernon*, https://www.mountvernon.org/george-washington/religion/george-washington-and-catholicism/.

130 Ronald E. Heaton, *The Masonic Membership of the Founding Fathers* (Silver Spring, MD: Masonic Service Association, 1965), 18.

131 "Faith of Our Founding Fathers," *Unitarian Universalist.*

132 Letter from George Washington to the Hebrew Congregation in Newport, Rhode Island, 18 August 1790, *National Archives*, Founders Online, https://founders.archives.gov/documents/Washington/05-06-02-0135.

133 Richard Samuelson, "The Theory and Practice of Toleration," *Law & Liberty*, August 23, 2012, https://lawliberty.org/the-theory-and-practice-of-toleration/; "Letter to the Jews of Newport," 18 August 1790, Wash-ington Papers, 6:284-85, taken from George Washington and His Letters to the Jews of Newport, https://www.tourosynagogue.org/history-learning/gw-letter.

134 Hugh Whelchel, "The Surprising Link between James Madison, Baptists, and True Religious Liberty," *Institute for Faith, Works & Economics*, April 18, 2016, https://tifwe.org/madison-baptists-religious-liberty/.

135 Ibid.

136 Joseph Loconte, "James Madison and Religious Liberty," *The Heritage Foundation*, March 16, 2011, https://www.heritage.org/political-process/report/james-madison-and-religious-liberty.

137 "Faith of Our Founding Fathers," *Unitarian Universalist.*

138 Ibid.

139 Ibid.

140 Ibid.

141 Steve Waldman, *Founding Faith: Providence, Politics, and the Birth of Religious Freedom in America* (New York: Random House, 2008), 35; from The Adams Papers, Diary and Autobiography of John Adams, August 1756, *National Archives*, Founders Online, (http://founders.archives.gov/documents/Adams/01-01-02-0002-0008.

142 "Faith of Our Founding Fathers," *Unitarian Universalist.*

143 David L. Holmes, "The Religion of James Monroe," *VQR: A National Journal of Literature and Discussion*, Autumn 2003, https://www.vqronline.org/essay/religion-james-monroe.

144 Heaton, *The Masonic Membership*, 10.

145 C. Clausen, *Masons Who Helped Shape the Nation* (Washington, DC: The Supreme Council 33', 1976), 82.

146 Peter Feuerherd, "The Strange History of Masons in America," *JStor Daily*, August 3, 2017, https://daily.jstor.org/the-strange-history-of-masons-in-america/.

147 Thom Hartmann, *The Prophet's Way: A Guide to Living in the Now* (New York: Simon and Schuster, 2004), 122.

148 Corinne McLaughlin, panel discussion from "The American Spiritual Vision," *PBS Virginia*, 17:35.

149 Feuerherd, "The Strange History of Masons in America."

150 Ibid.

151 "Memorial and Remonstrance Against Religious Assessments (1785)," James Madison, *The National Constitution Center*, https://constitutioncenter.org/the-constitution/historic-document-library/detail/james-madison-memorial-and-remonstrance-against-religious-assessments-1785.

152 [Washington's] General Orders, 2 July 1776, *National Archives*, Founders Online, https://founders.archives.gov/documents/Washington/03-05-02-0117.

CHAPTER 3

153 The Editors, "Charles Grandison Finney & the Second Phase of the Second Great Awakening," *Christian History Institute*, Issue #23, 1989, https://christianhistoryinstitute.org/magazine/article/charles-grandison-finney-and-second-great-awakening.

154 Ralph Waldo Emerson, "Emerson Divinity School Address," Delivered before the Senior class in Divinity College, Sunday, July 15, 1838, *Ralph Waldo Emerson* (1803-1882), updated July 2022, https://emersoncentral.com/texts/nature-addresses-lectures/addresses/divinity-school-address/#complete-essay.

155 Michel Horton, "The Disturbing Legacy of Charles Finney," *Monergism Theological Library*, https://www.monergism.com/disturbing-legacy-charles-finney.

156 "Religious Revival," Chapter 26a., *USHistory.org*, http://www.ushistory.org/us/26a.asp.

157 Charles Grandison Finney," *New World Encyclopedia*, https://www.newworldencyclopedia.org/entry/Charles_Grandison_Finney.

158 "Religious Revival," *USHistory.org*.

159 Horton, "The Disturbing Legacy of Charles Finney."

160 "Religious Transformation and the Second Great Awakening," Chapter 22c., *US History*, http://www.ushistory.org/us/22c.asp.

161 "Jarena Lee, First Woman Preacher," *History of American Women*, https://www.womenhistoryblog.com/2012/02/jarena-lee.html.

162 Clayborne Carson and Emma J. Lapansky-Werner and Gary B. Nash, *The Struggle for Freedom: A History of African Americans* (Boston: Prentice Hall, 2011), 156–157.

163 "Jarena Lee, First Woman Preacher," *History of American Women*.

164 Paul Harvey, *Through the Storm, Through the Night: a History of African American Christianity*, (Landham, MD: Rowman and Littlefield Publishers, 2011), 43.

165 Bertram Wyatt-Brown, "American Abolitionism and Religion," Divining America, TeacherServe®, *National Humanities Center*, http://nationalhumanitiescenter.org/tserve/nineteen/nkeyinfo/amabrel.htm.

166 Geoffrey R. Stone, "The Second Great Awakening: A Christian Nation?" 26 Georgia State University Law Review 1305 (2010), 1323.

167 Ibid., 1312.

168 Ibid., 1323.

169 Robert Jones, "White Too Long," interview by Terry Gross, *Fresh Air*, WHYY Philadelphia, July 30, 2020, audio 30:28.

170 Stone, "The Second Great Awakening: A Christian Nation?" 131.

171 The Editors, "Charles Grandison Finney & the Second Phase of the Second Great Awakening."

172 Nancy Cott, "Young Women in the Second Great Awakening in New England," *JStor Daily*, Feminist Studies, Vol. 3, (1): 15, https://www.jstor.org/stable/3518952?origin=crossref&seq=1#page_scan_tab_contents.

173 Charles Finney, "Why I Left Freemasonry," reprinted from "Memoirs" by President Finney formerly of Oberlin College, http://www.darknessisfalling.com/uploads/2/3/7/0/23701544/__why_i_left_freemasonry_-_charles_finney.pdf.

174 Colleen Walsh, "When Religion Turned Inward," *The Harvard Gazette*, February 16, 2012, https://news.harvard.edu/gazette/story/2012/02/when-religion-turned-inward/.

175 Ibid.

176 Philip Gura, *American Transcendentalism: A History* (New York: Hill and Wang, 2007), 103.

177 Walsh, "When Religion Turned Inward," quote by David Lamberth, professor of philosophy and theology Harvard Divinity School.

178 Lawrence, Buell, *Emerson* (Cambridge, Massachusetts: Belknap Press of Harvard University Press, 2003), 161.

179 Ralph Waldo Emerson, "The Over-Soul," from Essays: First Series (1841), *Emerson Central 1996-2019*, https://emersoncentral.com/ebook/The-Over-Soul.pdf.

180 Robert B. Charles, "The Einstein Few Knew," quoting Albert Einstein in a letter to Robert S. Marcus (1950), *Association of Mature American Citizens*, July 13, 2022, https://amac.us/the-einstein-few-knew/.

181 Robert D. Richardson Jr., *Emerson: The Mind on Fire* (Berkeley: University of California Press, 1995), 65-66.
182 Walsh, "When Religion Turned Inward."
183 Gura, *American Transcendentalism, 5.*
184 Ibid., 10.
185 Ibid., 11.
186 Ibid.
187 Ibid., 13
188 Ian Frederick Finseth, "The Emergence of Transcendentalism," *American Studies at The University of Virginia,* https://www.xroads.virginia.edu/~CLASS/MA95/finseth/trans.htm.
189 Gura, *American Transcendentalism,* 17.
190 Ibid., 24.
191 Ibid., i.
192 Ibid.
193 Ibid.,102.
194 Ibid., 14.
195 Ibid., iv.
196 "The Transcendentalists in Action," *Constitutional Rights Foundation,* Winter 2005 (22:1), https://www.crf-usa.org/bill-of-rights-in-action/bria-22-1-a-the-transcendentalists-in-action.
197 "William Lloyd Garrison 1805-1879," *Biography,* November 21, 2014, https://www.biography.com/writer/william-lloyd-garrison.
198 Stephen Puleo, *The Caning: The Assault That Drove America to Civil War* (Yardley, PA: Westholme Publishing, 2013), 36-37.
199 Gura, *American Transcendentalism,* 249.
200 Ibid., 250.
201 Paula Mekdeci, "When Transcendentalism Gave Way to New Thought," Lecture at Unity Renaissance, Chesapeake, VA., December 14, 2015, unityrenaissance.org.
202 Gura, *American Transcendentalism,* 250, quoting T. Parker *The Chief Sins of the People,* (1851), 7:262, 267.
203 Ann Braude, *Radical Spirits: Spiritualism and Women's Rights in Nineteenth-Century America,* Second Edition (Bloomington and Indianapolis: Indiana University Press, 2001), 296.
204 Ibid.
205 Michael A. Lawrence, *Radicals in their Own Time: Four Hundred Years of Struggle for Liberty and Equal Justice in America* (New York: Cambridge University Press, 2012), 168.
206 Ibid., 169.
207 Ibid., quoting Stanton's biographer Elisabeth Griffith, 169.
208 Jeanne Stevenson-Moessner, "Elizabeth Cady Stanton: Reformer to Revolutionary," *Journal of the American Academy of Religion,* Vol. 62, No. 3, Oxford University Press (1994): 675-676, https://www.jstor.org/stable/1465209?seq=1.
209 Lawrence, *Radicals in Their Own Time,* 170.
210 "Elizabeth Cady Stanton 1815-1902," *Biography,* https://www.biography.com/activist/elizabeth-cady-stanton.
211 Matthew Backes, "Lyman Beecher and the Problem with Religious Pluralism in the Early American Republic," *The American Religious Experience.* The quotation comes from "The Toleration Dream," a satirical pamphlet Beecher published. It is reprinted in *The Autobiography of Lyman Beecher,* vol. 1, Barbara M. Cross, ed. (New York: Cambridge University Press, 1961), 290-300, http://are.as.wvu.edu/backes.htm.
212 "Harriet Beecher Stowe Biography," *The Encyclopedia of World Biography,* https://www.notablebiographies.com/St-Tr/Stowe-Harriet-Beecher.html.
213 Kenneth DiMaggio, "Uncle Tom's Cabin: Global Best Seller, Anti-slave Narrative, Imperialist Agenda," *Global Studies Journal,* 2014, 15.
214 David B. Sachsman, S. Kittrell Rushing and Roy Morris, *Memory and Myth: The Civil War in Fiction and Film* from *Uncle Tom's Cabin to Cold Mountain* (West Lafayette, Indiana, Purdue University Press, 2007), 8.
215 David Herbert Donald, "On the Heels of Eliza," *New York Times,* September 7, 1985, https://www.nytimes.com/1985/09/08/books/on-the-heels-of-eliza.html.
216 "John Brown," *New World Encyclopedia,* https://www.newworldencyclopedia.org/entry/John_Brown; https://www.albany.edu/history/digital/johnbrown/.
217 Gura, *American Transcendentalism,* 209.
218 Thomas Fleming, "The Trial of John Brown," *American Heritage,* vol. 18, Issue 5, August 1967, https://www.americanheritage.com/trial-john-brown.
219 Kent Ljungquist, "'Meteor of the War': Melville, Thoreau and Whitman Respond to John Brown," *American Literature,* vol. 61, No. 4 (December 1989), https://doi.org/10.2307/2927002.
220 Gura, *American Transcendentalism,* 261.
221 Ibid., 263.

222 Dana Tanner-Kennedy, "Gertrude Stein and the Metaphysical Avant-Garde," Religions 2020, Vol. 11, No. 4, March 25, 2020, quoting Leigh Eric Schmidt, *Restless Souls: The Making of American Spirituality* (New York: HarperCollins, 2005), 1–23,152; https://doi.org/10.3390/rel11040152.

CHAPTER 4

223 Sean Martin, "Alien shock: President Reagan attempted to warn the world about alien species," *The Express* (UK), April 30, 2020, https://www.express.co.uk/news/weird/1274940/alien-news-president-ronald-reagan-cold-war-aliens-ufo.

224 Cem Arslan, "The Enemy of My Enemy," *Quora*, https://www.quora.com/profile/Cem-Arslan-2.

225 "Doris Kearns Goodwin on whether we are living in 'the worst of times,'" *CBS Sunday Morning*, video 1:23.

226 Robert F. Kennedy's "Mindless Menace of Violence Speech," excerpts of the speech delivered at the City Club of Cleveland on April 5, 1968, *Ideastream*, posted April 4, 2018, https://www.youtube.com/watch?v=Vt7IuKoETEc&feature=emb_logo.

227 Saul McLeod, Ph.D., "Id, Ego and Superego," *Simply Psychology*, 2021, https://www.simplypsychology.org/psyche.html.

228 Ann Weiser Cornell, Ph.D., "Presence Meets Ego," *Focusing Resources*, quoting Michael Butler, "An Overview of Buddhism," https://focusingresources.com/presence-meets-ego/.

229 Saul McLeod, Ph.D., "Carl Jung's Theories: Archetypes, & The Collective Unconscious," *Simply Psychology*, 2018, https://www.simplypsychology.org/carl-jung.html.

230 David Hoffmeister, "What Is the Ego? The Allegiance to Fear and Death," https://spirit-of-love.net/what-is-the-ego-allegiance-fear-death.

231 "Eckhart Tolle : Transcending The Egoic Mind And Tuning Into Cosmic Consciousness," *Psychedelic Adventure*, January 31, 2009, https://www.psychedelicadventure.net/2009/01/eckhart-tolle-transcending-egoic-mind.html.

232 Eckhart Tolle, "Did the Universe Make a Mistake with the Ego?" posted October 9, 2012, video 1:45, https://www.youtube.com/watch?v=bImdyQn43s8; Miki Kashtan, Ph.D., "Ego, Mind, and Culture," *Psychology Today*, November 22, 2013, https://www.psychologytoday.com/us/blog/acquired-spontaneity/201311/ego-mind-and-culture.

233 Mark Gerzon, "The Reunited States of America," *WikiPolitiki*, interview by Steve Bhaerman, November 17, 2020, audio 5:28, https://wikipolitiki.com/the-reunited-states-of-america-how-we-can-close-the-reality-gap-and-create-a-sane-and-sacred-center/.

234 Larry Bush, "The Morphology of a Humorous Phrase: 'We have met the enemy and he is us,'" *Humor in America Blog*, May 19, 2014, https://humorinamerica.wordpress.com/2014/05/19/the-morphology-of-a-humorous-phrase/.

235 Ibid.

236 Carole Parks, "Todays Black Woman Examines Her Role with Black Men," *Jet Magazine*, January 14, 1971, 27.

237 Bush, "The Morphology of a Humorous Phrase."

238 Ibid.

239 Charlotte Alter, Saying Haynes and Justin Worlan, "2019 Person of the Year: Great Thunberg," *Time*, December 23-30, 2019, https://time.com/person-of-the-year-2019-greta-thunberg/.

240 Andrew Freedman, "Pace of climate change shown in new report has humanity on 'suicidal' path, U.N. leader warns," *The Washington Post*, December 2, 2020, https://www.washingtonpost.com/weather/2020/12/02/un-climate-report-2020-warmest-year/.

241 Andrew Freedman, "Hottest Arctic temperature record probably set with 100-degree reading in Siberia," *The Washington Post*, June 23, 2022, https://www.washingtonpost.com/weather/2020/06/21/arctic-temperature-record-siberia/.

242 Freedman, "Pace of Climate Change."

243 Alter et al., "2019 Person of the Year."

244 Parry, *Original Politics*, 261.

245 Ibid., 262.

246 Ibid.

247 Parry, *Original Politics*, 247.

248 Reynard Loki, "IPCC Report: Joining forces and using indigenous knowledge could avert disaster," *Down to Earth*, August 12, 2021, https://www.downtoearth.org.in/blog/climate-change/ipcc-report-joining-forces-and-using-indigenous-knowledge-could-avert-disaster-78434.

249 Parry, *Original Politics*, 281.

250 Somini Sengupta, "Protesting Climate Change, Young People Take to Streets in a Global Strike," *New York Times*, September 21, 2019, https://www.nytimes.com/2019/09/20/climate/global-climate-strike.html

251 Alter et al., "2019 Person of the Year."

252 Peter Russell, "The Mystery of Time," interview by Tami Simon, *Sounds True*, Episode 2, March 4, 2009, https://resources.soundstrue.com/transcript/peter-russell-widespread-awakening/.

253 Ibid.

254 Jonathan M. Katz, *Gangsters of Capitalism: Smedley Butler, the Marines, and the Making and Breaking of America's Empire* (New York: St. Martin's Press, 2021); Jonathan Katz, "Smedley Butler," *Democracy*

Now!, Interview by Amy Goodman, January 28, 2022, https://www.wearenotyoursoldiers.org/smedley-butler-jonathan-katz-on-gangsters-of-capitalism/; Jonathan Katz, "Why Would a Marine Call Himself a 'Racketeer for Capitalism'?" *New York Times*, January 28, 2022, https://www.nytimes.com/2022/01/28/opinion/smedley-butler-wars.html. Smedley Butler was a decorated World War I vet who had great enmity towards President Franklin Roosevelt. He claimed (with later substantiation) that a group of Wall Street magnates approached him due to his past military accomplishments, heroism and dislike of the president, to marshal a half-million soldier force down Pennsylvania Avenue in Washington, D.C. and make FDR surrender to what would be a fascistic dictatorship. The press, some of whom were tangentially connected to the conspirators, derided the story, but Butler's credible evidence and previous ties to capitalist enterprises that meddled in foreign countries for monetary gain, gave credence to the story, which he later revealed in a congressional hearing. Many historians today conclude that the threat was not only plausible, but likely, and provides a chilling parallel to the January 6, 2021, insurrection. In addition, in 1940, there was an alleged plot to overthrow the US government by force by members of the Christian Nationalist Front whose prosecution led to acquittal or were nol-prossed.

255 Jill Lepore, "The Last Time Democracy Almost Died," *The New Yorker*, February 3, 2020, https://www.newyorker.com/magazine/2020/02/03/the-last-time-democracy-almost-died.

256 Ibid.

257 "Democracy Index 2021: less than half the world lives in a democracy," *Economist Intelligence* (UK), February 10, 2022, https://www.eiu.com/n/democracy-index-2021-less-than-half-the-world-lives-in-a-democracy/.

258 The Democracy Index, *Economist Intelligence* (UK), February 10, 2022, https://www.eiu.com/n/campaigns/democracy-index-2021/.

259 Mark A. Cohen, "Vision for 2020: A focus on defending the rule of law," *ABA Journal*, February 20, 2020, https://www.abajournal.com/voice/article/2020-vision-focus-on-defending-the-rule-of-law.

260 Ibid.

261 Ibid.

262 "Hong Kong: First arrests under 'anti-protest' law as handover marked," *BBC News*, July 1, 2020, https://www.bbc.com/news/world-asia-china-53244862.

263 "Hong Kong National Security Law Full Text," *Scribd*, https://www.scribd.com/document/467553047/Hong-Kong-national-security-law-full-text#fullscreen&from_embed.

264 Jason Rezaian, "Press Freedoms Are Fading in Asia," *The Washington Post Weekly*, July 11, 2021, p. 22.

265 Ibid.

266 Former US General R. McMaster, *CNN*, March 7, 2022, video, 10:18am.

267 Lauren Elizabeth, "Brazil, the Rainforest, and the Single Greatest Threat to Earth as We Know It," *Medium Magazine*, August 24, 2019, https://medium.com/swlh/brazil-the-rainforest-and-the-single-greatest-threat-to-earth-as-we-know-it-b0345cce89a0.

268 Ibid.

269 Eric R. Maisel Ph.D., "Why Authoritarians Love Religion," *Psychology Today*, January 18, 2018, https://www.psychologytoday.com/us/blog/rethinking-mental-health/201801/why-authoritarians-love-religion.

270 Ibid.

271 Phillip Perry, "Is There a Link Between Religion and Authoritarianism?" *Big Think*, https://preprod.bigthink.com/politics-current-affairs/is-there-a-link-between-religiosity-and-authoritarianism/.

272 Matthew Wills, "What Links Religion and Authoritarianism?" *JStorDaily*, July 25, 2017, https://daily.jstor.org/what-links-religion-and-authoritarianism/.

273 Paul Wink, Michele Dillion and Adrienne Prettyman, "Religiousness, Spiritual Seeking, and Authoritarianism: Findings from a Longitudinal Study," *Journal for the Scientific Study of Religion*, vol. 46, No. 3 (September 2007), 321-335, cited in *JStorDaily*, https://www.jstor.org/stable/4621983?mag=what-links-religion-and-authoritarianism&seq=1#page_scan_tab_contents.

274 Daniel F. McCleary, Lisa N. Foster, Colin C. Quillivan, "Meta-Analysis of Correlational Relationships Between Perspectives of Truth in Religion and Major Psychological Constructs," *Psychology of Religion and Spirituality*, August 2011, cited in Researchgate, https://www.researchgate.net/publication/232496755_Meta-Analysis_of_Correlational_Relationships_Between_Perspectives_of_Truth_in_Religion_and_Major_Psychological_Constructs.

275 Thomas J. Bouchard, Jr., "Authoritarianism, Religiousness, and Conservatism : Is'Obedience to Authority the Explanation for Their Clustering, Universality and Evolution?'" (2009), In: E.Voland, W. Schiefenhövel, editors, *The Biological Evolution of Religious Mind and Behavior*, The Frontiers Collection. Springer, Berlin, Heidelberg. https://doi.org/10.1007/978-3-642-00128-4_11.

276 Maisel, "Why Authoritarians Love Religion."

277 Ibid.

278 Wink, Dillion and Prettyman, "Religiousness, Spiritual Seeking, and Authoritarianism."

279 Ibid.

280 Ibid.

281 Perry, "Is There a Link Between Religion and Authoritarianism?"

282 Wink, Dillion and Prettyman, "Religiousness, Spiritual Seeking, and Authoritarianism."

283 Parry, *Original Politics*, 272.

CHAPTER 5

284 David McCullough, *John Adams* (New York: Simon & Schuster, 2002), 544.

285 "Americans are somewhat more open to the idea of an atheist president," *Pew Research Center*, May 29, 2014, https://www.pewresearch.org/fact-tank/2014/05/29/americans-are-somewhat-more-open-to-the-idea-of-an-atheist-president/.

286 Gordon-Reed and Onuf, "Jefferson's Bible."

287 Philip Terzian, "Weekly Standard: Bigoted Against Brigham's Faith?" *NPR*, Opinion, November 4, 2011, https://www.npr.org/2011/11/04/142014074/weekly-standard-no-bigotry-for-brigham-followers.

288 "Al Smith Presidential Campaign - Timeline Event, November 6, 1928," *The Association of Religion Data Archives*, citing sources: Oscar Handlin, Al Smith and His America (Boston: Little, Brown and Company, 1958); John T. McGreevy, *Catholicism and American Freedom: A History* (New York: W.W. Norton and Company, 2003); Robert A. Slayton, *Empire Statesman: The Rise and Redemption of Al Smith* (New York: The Free Press, 2001), https://www.thearda.com/timeline/events/event_156.asp.

289 Tim Ott, "How Billy Graham Tried to Prevent JFK From Winning the Presidency," *Biography*, October 15, 2020, https://www.biography.com/news/john-f-kennedy-billy-graham-prevent-presidency.

290 Ibid.

291 Ibid., citing Richard M. Nixon, *Beyond Peace* (New York: Simon and Schuster, 1994).

292 Meacham, *American Gospel*, 141.

293 Yasmine Hafiz, "American Religions Born In The USA. Bring Home The Country's Rich Religious History," *Huffington Post*, May 4, 2017, https://www.huffpost.com/entry/american-religions-born-in-us-a_n_5552873.

294 Ibid.

295 Derek Thompson, "Three Decades Ago, America Lost Its Religion. Why?" *The Atlantic*, September 26, 2019, https://www.theatlantic.com/ideas/archive/2019/09/atheism-fastest-growing-religion-us/598843/.

296 Ibid.

297 Herbert Pankratz, "A Guide to Historical Holdings in the Dwight D. Eisenhower Library: Eisenhower and Religion," *WayBack Machine*, 2001, http://www.eisenhower.archives.gov/research/GUIDES/Eisenhower_and_religion.pdf.

298 Lloyd Grove "Barry Goldwater's Left Turn," *The Washington Post Archives*, July 28, 1994, https://www.washingtonpost.com/wp-srv/politics/daily/may98/goldwater072894.htm.

299 Maria L. LaGanga, "Opinion: Two questions, four answers from Barack Obama," *The Los Angeles Times*, March 2, 2008, https://www.latimes.com/archives/blogs/top-of-the-ticket/story/2008-03-02/opinion-two-questions-four-answers-from-barack-obama.

300 Charles Babington and Darlene Superville, "Obama 'Christian By Choice': President Responds To Questioner," *HuffingtonPost Politics*, November 26, 2011, http://www.huffingtonpost.com/2010/09/28/obama-christian-by-choice_n_742124.html.

301 "Obama's 2006 Speech on Faith and Politics," *New York Times*, June 28, 2006, https://www.nytimes.com/2006/06/28/us/politics/2006obamaspeech.html.

302 Katelyn Sabochik, "President Obama Celebrates Ramadan at White House Iftar Dinner," *The White House President Barack Obama*, August 14, 2010, https://obamawhitehouse.archives.gov/blog/2010/08/14/president-obama-celebrates-ramadan-white-house-iftar-dinner.

303 Peter Wehner, "The Deepening Crisis in Evangelical Christianity," *The Atlantic*, July 5, 2019, https://www.theatlantic.com/ideas/archive/2019/07/evangelical-christians-face-deepening-crisis/593353/.

304 Ibid.

305 Ibid.

306 Diane Winston, "How Can Christians Support Donald Trump?" *USCDornsife*, originally published by *Religion News Service*, December 18, 2018, https://crcc.usc.edu/how-can-christians-support-donald-trump/.

307 Gregory A. Smith, "More White Americans adopted than shed evangelical label during Trump presidency, especially his supporters," *Pew Research Center*, September 15, 2021, https://www.pewresearch.org/fact-tank/2021/09/15/more-white-americans-adopted-than-shed-evangelical-label-during-trump-presidency-especially-his-supporters/.

308 Ibid.

309 PRRI Staff, "Despite Chaos and Controversy, Trump Favorability Stable Throughout 2019," *PRRI*, February 26, 2020, https://www.prri.org/research/despite-chaos-and-controversy-trump-favorability-stable-throughout-2019/.

310 Peter Wehner, "The Great #MeToo Awakening," *New York Times*, Opinion, May 12, 2018, https://www.nytimes.com/2018/05/12/opinion/sunday/the-great-metoo-awakening.html.

311 Laura Turner, "The rise of the star-studded, Instagram-friendly evangelical church," *Vox*, February 6, 2019, https://www.vox.com/culture/2019/2/6/18205355/church-chris-pratt-justin-bieber-zoe-hillsong.

312 Joel Stein, "Hollywood's Holy Hipster Scene," *Vanity Fair*, July 12, 2019, https://www.vanityfair.com/style/2019/07/hollywood-and-religion.

313 Turner, "The rise of the star-studded, Instagram-friendly evangelical church."

314 "Many Americans Say Other Faiths Can Lead to Eternal Life," *Pew Research Center*, December 18, 2008, https://www.pewresearch.org/religion/2008/12/18/many-americans-say-other-faiths-can-lead-to-eternal-life/; "Nones on the Rise," *Pew Research Center*, October 9, 2012, https://www.pewresearch.org/reli-

gion/2012/10/09/nones-on-the-rise/; "Sharp Rise in the Share of Americans Saying Jews Face Discrimination," *Pew Research Center*, April 15, 2019, https://www.people-press.org/2019/04/15/sharp-rise-in-the-share-of-americans-saying-jews-face-discrimination/.

315 Turner, "The rise of the star-studded, Instagram-friendly evangelical church."

316 "Bishop Carlton Pearson opens up the religious message that cost him everything," interview by Meagan Kelly, *The NBC Today Show* video, 2:15, https://www.today.com/video/bishop-carlton-pearson-opens-up-the-religious-message-that-cost-him-everything-1195021891649.

317 Caryle Murphy, "Most Americans believe in heaven … and hell," *Pew Research Center*, November 10, 2015, https://www.pewresearch.org/fact-tank/2015/11/10/most-americans-believe-in-heaven-and-hell/.

318 Albert Winseman, "Eternal Destinations: Americans Believe in Heaven, Hell," *Gallup*, May 25, 2004, https://news.gallup.com/poll/11770/Eternal-Destinations-Americans-Believe-Heaven-Hell.aspx.

319 Carlton Pearson, "Carlton Pearson speaks about Joel Osteen," *Youtube*, posted April 13, 2013, https://www.youtube.com/watch?v=c8Pxx4dVoHg.

320 Ibid., video, 2:12.

CHAPTER 6

321 Horowitz, *New World Radio*, November 10, 2010, 18:19.

322 Thompson, "America Lost Its Religion."

323 Ibid.

324 "In US, Decline of Christianity Continues at Rapid Pace," *Pew Research Center*, October 17, 2019, https://www.pewforum.org/2019/10/17/in-u-s-decline-of-christianity-continues-at-rapid-pace/; "Nones on the Rise," *Pew*.

325 Michael Shermer, "The Number of Americans with No Religious Affiliation Is Rising," *Scientific American*, April 1, 2018, https://www.scientificamerican.com/article/the-number-of-americans-with-no-religious-affil-iation-is-rising/.

326 Jeffrey M. Jones, "US Church Membership Falls Below Majority for First Time," *Gallup*, March 29, 2021, https://news.gallup.com/poll/341963/church-membership-falls-below-majority-first-time.aspx.

327 "Why America's 'nones' don't identify with a religion," *Pew Research Center*, August 8, 2018, https://www.pewresearch.org/fact-tank/2018/08/08/why-americas-nones-dont-identify-with-a-religion/.

328 Shermer, "No Religious Affiliation."

329 "America's 'nones' don't identify," *Pew Research Center*; Dahlia Famy, "Among religious 'nones,' atheists and agnostics know the most about religion," *Pew Research Center*, August 21, 2019, https://www.pewresearch.org/fact-tank/2019/08/21/among-religious-nones-atheists-and-agnostics-know-the-most-about-religion/.

330 Thompson, "America Lost Its Religion."

331 Ibid.

332 Shermer, "No Religious Affiliation is Rising"; Famy, "atheists and agnostics know most about religion."

333 Thompson, "America Lost Its Religion."

334 "The Bill W. - Carl Jung Letters," *Speaking of Jung*, November 14, 2015, citing the *AA Grapevine*, January 1963, https://speakingofjung.com/blog/2015/11/13/the-bill-w-carl-jung-letters.

335 Robert C. Fuller, *Spiritual But Not Religious* (New York: Oxford University Press, 2001), 113.

336 Ibid.,130.

337 Larry Dossey, M.D., *One Mind* (Carlsbad, CA: Hay House, Inc., 2012), 82-83.

338 Fuller, *Spiritual But Not Religious*, 113.

339 Peter Gibbon, "The Thinker Who Believed in Doing," *Humanities*, Winter 2018, vol. 39, no. 1, https://www.neh.gov/humanities/2018/winter/feature/the-thinker-who-believed-in-doing-0.

340 Fuller, *Spiritual But Not Religious*, 131.

341 Ibid.

342 About the Society, *The American Society for Psychical Research*, http://aspr.com/who.htm.

343 Stuart Vyse, "William James and the Psychics," *Skeptical Inquirer*, January 30, 2018, citing Deborah Blum, *Ghost Hunters: William James and the search for scientific proof of life after death* (New York: Penguin, 2007); Linda Simon, *Genuine Reality: A Life of William James* (Chicago: University of Chicago Press, 1999), https://skepticalinquirer.org/exclusive/william-james-and-the-psychics/.

344 Ibid.

345 Robert D. Richardson, *William James: In the Maelstrom of American Modernism* (Boston: Houghton, Mifflin, 2006), 160.

346 Gura, *American Transcendentalism*, 305.

347 Fuller, *Spiritual But Not Religious*, 131.

348 Gura, *American Transcendentalism*, 306.

349 Gibbon, "The Thinker Who Believed in Doing."

350 Bill Wilson, *Alcoholics Anonymous Comes of Age: A Brief History of A. A.* (New York: Alcoholics Anonymous World Services, 1957), 63.

351 John D. McPeake, Ph.D., "William James, Bill Wilson, and the development of Alcoholics Anonymous (A.A.)," *The Dublin Group*, quoting Bill Wilson *Alcoholic Anonymous Comes of Age*, 64, http://dubgrp.com/content/william-james-bill-wilson-and-development-alcoholics-anonymous-aa. .

352 Fuller, *Spiritual But Not Religious*, 114.

353 Ibid.

354 Ibid.

355 Ibid., 115.

356 Shirley MacLaine, *Out on a Limb* (New York: Bantam Books, 1983).

357 Frank Deford, "Shirley MacLaine," *People Magazine*, vol. 20, no. 10, July 18, 1983, retrieved August 22, 2020, https://people.com/archive/shirley-maclaine-vol-20-no-3/; "MacLaine, Letterman Lock Horns on Late Night TV," *Deseret News*, October 7, 1988, https://www.deseret.com/1988/10/7/18780851/maclaine-letterman-lock-horns-on-late-night-tv.

358 Ross Posnock, *The Trial of Curiosity: Henry James, William James and the Challenge of Modernity* (New York: Oxford University Press, 1991), 238.

359 William James, *The Varieties of Religious Experience* (New York: Longman, Green & Co., 1902), Lecture IV.

360 Ibid., 92-93.

361 Malise Ruthven, "The Obituary: The Rev. Norman Vincent Peale," *The Independent* (UK), January 3, 1994, https://www.independent.co.uk/news/people/obituary-the-rev-norman-vincent-peale-1397666.html.

362 Robert C. Fuller, *Mesmerism and the American Cure of Souls* (Philadelphia: University of Pennsylvania Press, 1982),

363 Mitch Horowitz, *Occult America, The Secret History of How Mysticism Shaped Our Nation* (New York: Tarcher/Penguin, 2008), 44-45.

364 "What's a Christian Science Reading Room?" https://christianscience.ab.ca/christian-science-reading-room.htm.

365 Angela King and Kim Shephard, "How do Christian Scientists deal with the pandemic?" *KOUW/NPR* Interview by Angela King of Lance Madison, member of the Church Of Christ, Scientist, https://www.kuow.org/stories/how-do-christ.

366 Val Kilmer, "Mark Twain and Mary Baker Eddy, A Film by Val Kilmer," July 12, 2010, http://www.twaineddyfilm.com/blogs/category/directors-notes/.

367 James R. Lewis and J. Gordon Melton, *Perspectives on the New Age* (New York: SUNY Press, 1992), 16-18.

367 Chris Lehman, "The Self-Help Guru Who Shaped Trump's Worldview," *Moyers*, December 17, 2017, https://billmoyers.com/story/self-help-guru-shaped-trumps-worldview/.

369 "The Oldest US Corporation is a Church in NoMad New York," *Nomad*, May 3, 2012, https://experiencenomad.com/the-oldest-u-s-corporation-is-a-church-in-nomad-new-york/.

370 Horowitz, *New World Radio*, November 10, 2010, audio 36:15.

371 David Maurer, "Yesteryears, Pt. 2, Norman Vincent Peale Speaks," *The Daily Progress*, February 10, 2015, https://dailyprogress.com/entertainment/lifestyles/yesteryears-part-2-norman-vincent-peale-speaks/article_d49c6316-7179-11e2-9aff-0019bb30f31a.html.

372 Fuller, *Spiritual Not Religious*, 147.

373 Horowitz, *New World Radio*, November 10, 2010, audio 39:15.

374 Tamra Keith, "Trump Crowd Size Estimate May Involve the 'Power of Positive Thinking,'" *NPR*, January 22, 2017, https://www.npr.org/2017/01/22/510655254/trump-crowd-size-estimate-may-involve-the-power-of-positive-thinking.

375 Sir Knight Dr. Ivan Tribe, "Sir Knight Norman Vincent Peale: A Powerful Positive Thinker," *Knights Templar*, August 5, 2014, http://www.knightstemplar.org/KnightTemplar/articles/20110521.htm.

376 Horowitz, *New World Radio*, November 10, 2010, audio 41:15.

377 Norman Vincent Peale, "Turn to the Bible to Deepen Your Faith," *Guideposts*, posted in Positive Thinking, Feb 27, 2009, https://www.guideposts.org/better-living/positive-living/positive-thinking/turn-to-the-bible-to-deepen-your-faith.

378 "Ernest Holmes and Life Healing," *A Place for the Heart*, http://aplacefortheheart.co.uk/philosophies/ernest-holmes/.

379 Horowitz, *Occult America*, 94.

380 Jeannette Quinn Bisbee, "The Power of Positive Thinking: How Norman Vincent Peale Was Influenced by Ernest Holmes," *Science of Mind Archives*, https://scienceofmindarchives.com/the-power-of-positive-thinking/.

381 Ibid.

382 Ibid.

383 Bisbee, "Power of Positive Thinking."

384 Raja Bhat, M.D., *A Way Beyond Religion to Our Inner Spirit* (Bloomington: AuthorHouse, 2004), 82.

385 Bisbee, "Power of Positive Thinking."

386 David Cloud, "Norman Vincent Peale: Apostle of Self-Esteem," *Way of Life Literature*, first published April 26, 1997, Republished September 16, 2009, https://www.wayoflife.org/database/peale.html.

387 Tim Stafford, "Peale's Half-Full Christianity," *Christianity Today*, June 21, 1993, https://www.christianitytoday.com/ct/1993/june-21/special-books-section.html.

388 Cloud, quoting Hugh Pyle, *Sword of the Lord*, Dec. 14, 1984, https://www.wayoflife.org/database/peale.html.

389 Michael Kruse, "The Power of Trump's Positive Thinking," *Politico*, October 13, 2017, https://www.politico.com/magazine/story/2017/10/13/donald-trump-positive-thinking-215704.

390 Lehman, "The Self-Help Guru Who Shaped Trump's Worldview."

391 Tara Isabella Burton, "The prosperity gospel, explained: Why Joel Osteen believes that prayer can make

you rich," *Vox*, September 1, 2017, https://www.vox.com/identities/2017/9/1/15951874/prosperity-gospel-explained-why-joel-osteen-believes-prayer-can-make-you-rich-trump.

392 Mariam Sulakian, "Emerson, Self-Reliance and the Sin of Prayer," *MariamSulakian.com*, June 25, 2006, https://mariamsulakian.com/2016/06/25/emerson-self-reliance-and-the-sin-of-prayer/.

393 Kruse, "The Power of Trump's Positive Thinking."

394 Maurer, "Yesteryears, Pt. 2, Norman Vincent Peale Speaks."

395 John D. Chitty, "Positivity Trumps Pauline Truth," *The Misadventures of Captain Headknowledge*, January 18, 2016, https://capthk.com/tag/kenneth-hagin/.

396 Newsweek Staff, "Religion in 1960 Election," *Newsweek*, December 16, 2007, citing "The Religious Issue: Hot and Getting Hotter," *Newsweek* September 19, 1960.

397 Ron Elving, "Norman Vincent Peale Was A Conservative Hero Known Well Beyond His Era," *NPR*, July 24, 2020, https://www.npr.org/2020/07/24/894967922/norman-vincent-peale-was-a-conservative-hero-known-well-beyond-his-era.

398 Joe Carter, "What Kanye Should Know About Joel Osteen," *The Gospel Coalition*, November 24, 2017, https://www.thegospelcoalition.org/article/what-kanye-should-know-about-joel-osteen/.

399 John Osteen, "John Osteen's Win the Battle of the Mind!" 1987, *Youtube*, posting date unknown, https://www.youtube.com/watch?v=ZO4f7HSAsOg.

400 Michael Mooney, "Why Joel Osteen Is the Most Popular Preacher on the Planet," *Success*, October 11, 2016, https://www.success.com/why-joel-osteen-is-the-most-popular-preacher-on-the-planet/.

401 Horowitz, *New World Radio*, February 10, 2010, audio 27:17.

402 Kristi Watts, "Joel Osteen: The Man Behind America's Largest Church," *CBN*, https://www1.cbn.com/700club/joel-osteen-man-behind-americas-largest-church.

403 Carter, "What Kanye Should Know About Joel Osteen."

404 Polite Leader, "Joel Osteen Exposed," *Youtube*, video 00:45, https://www.youtube.com/watch?v=M_kpQ8RgIiI.

405 Jack MacArthur, "John MacArthur Rebukes Joel Osteen," *Youtube*, video 00:20, https://www.youtube.com/watch?v=jDuDN2FtrIo.

406 Ibid., audio 01:46.

407 Joel Osteen interviewed by Larry King, *Larry King Live*, CNN Transcripts, June 20, 2005, http://transcripts.cnn.com/TRANSCRIPTS/0506/20/lkl.01.html.

408 Billy Graham interviewed by Larry King, *Larry King Live*, CNN Transcripts, June 16, 2005, http://transcripts.cnn.com/TRANSCRIPTS/0506/16/lkl.01.html.

409 "Joel Osteen Apologizes for Larry King Appearance," *Carolina Christian Conservative*, June 28, 2005, http://carolinachristianconservative.blogspot.com/2005/06/joel-osteen-apologizes-for-larry-king.html.

410 Polite Leader, "Joel Osteen Exposed," video 4:30.

411 Melissa Barnhart, "Interview: Joel Osteen on Life, Tragedy and Why He Shuns 'Prosperity Gospel' Label," April 21, 2013. *Christian Post*, https://www.christianpost.com/news/interview-joel-osteen-on-life-tragedy-and-why-he-shuns-prosperity-gospel-label-94355/.

CHAPTER 7

412 Staff Writers, "The 500 Greatest Songs of All Time," *RollingStone Magazine*, issue 963, December 9, 2004, https://www.rollingstone.com/news/story/11028260/the_rs_500_greatest_songs_of_all_time; "John Lennon's 'Imagine' is released," *History*, July 18, 2019, https://www.history.com/this-day-in-history/john-lennon-yoko-ono-imagine-released.

413 Julian Lennon, "Julian Lennon's Foundation Was Born Out Of A Special Message From His Father John Lennon," *Youtube*, video 1:14, https://www.youtube.com/watch?v=9V2KrG4yktA.

414 Rebecca Dube, "Julian Lennon on the 'sign' father John Lennon sent to him after death," *NBC Today*, April 11, 2017, https://www.today.com/parents/julian-lennon-sign-he-got-dad-john-lennon-t110285

415 Lennon, "Julian Lennon's Foundation," video 1:47.

416 Dube, "Julian Lennon on the 'sign.'"

417 Ibid.

418 "Within You, Without You" from *Sergeant Pepper's Lonely Hearts Club Band*, "Across the Universe" from *Let It Be*, "Tomorrow Never Knows" from *Revolver*, "The Inner Light" B-Side to the single of "Lady Madonna," "I Am the Walrus" from *Magical Mystery Tour* and others.

419 Jasmine Yeung, "The meaning of 'jai Guru Deva om' from The Beatles' Across The Universe," *The Focus*, 2021, https://www.thefocus.news/tv/jai-guru-deva-om-meaning/; "Jai Guru Deva Om," *Urban Dictionary*, December 22, 2004, https://www.urbandictionary.com/define.php?term=Jai%20Guru%20Deva%20om.

420 John Lennon, "John Lennon's last interview, December 8, 1980," *Beatles Archive*," Interview by Dave Sholin and Laurie Kaye, posted December 21, 2013, http://www.beatlesarchive.net/john-lennons-last-interview-december-8-1980.html.

421 Entrepreneur Staff, "The 15 Most Inspirational John Lennon Quotes," *Entrepreneur*, October 9, 2018, https://www.entrepreneur.com/article/321404.

422 Jan Wenner, *Lennon Remembers* (London: Verso, 2000), 48; Lennon said more or less the same thing years earlier in an interview at Apple Studios: "We're all God. Christ said, 'The Kingdom of Heaven is within you.' And the Indians say that and the Zen people [Buddhists] say that. We're all God. I'm not a god or the

God, but we're all God and we're all potentially divine—and potentially evil. We all have everything within us and the Kingdom of Heaven is nigh and within us, and if you look hard enough you'll see it." John Lennon, "John Lennon & Yoko Ono Interview: Apple Offices, London 5/8/1969," *The Beatles Ultimate Experience*, Interview with David Wigg, May 8, 1969, http://www.beatlesinterviews.org/db1969.0508. beatles.html.

423 Evelyn Underhill, *Mysticism: A Study in the Nature and Development of Spiritual Consciousness,* 12th Edition (Mineola: Dover Publications, 2002), Preface.

424 John Horgan, "Rational Mysticism," *New York Times*, March 23, 2003, https://www.nytimes. com/2003/03/23/books/chapters/rational-mysticism.html.

425 Underhill, *Mysticism*, Preface.

426 James, *Varieties*, Lecture IV.

427 Horgan, "Rational Mysticism."

428 William James, *The Varieties of Religious Experience*, Bradley, Matthew, ed., (New York: Oxford University Press, 2012). 32.

429 Ibid., 293.

430 Julian Huxley, *Aldous Huxley 1894–1963: a Memorial Volume* (London: Chatto & Windus, 1965), 22.

431 Ibid., 54.

432 Signe Toksvig, "Aldous Huxley's prescriptions for spiritual myopia," *New York Times*, September 30, 1945, 117.

433 Aldous Huxley, *The Perennial Philosophy* (New York: Harper & Bros., 1945), back cover.

434 Sara Diane Outhier, "Igor Stravinsky and Aldous Huxley: Portrait of a friendship," *Kansas State University*, December 2009, https://krex.k-state.edu/dspace/handle/2097/2353.

435 Mary Rourke, "Huston Smith, pioneering teacher of world religions, dies at 97," *Los Angeles Times*, January 5, 2017, https://www.latimes.com/local/obituaries/la-me-huston-smith-20170105-story.html.

436 Douglas Martin and Dennis Hevasi, "Huston Smith, Author of 'The World's Religions,' Dies at 97," *New York Times*, January 1, 2017, https://www.nytimes.com/2017/01/01/us/huston-smith-author-of-the-worlds-religions-dies-at-97.html.

437 Rourke, "Huston Smith."

438 Ibid.

439 Martin and Hevasi, "Huston Smith."

440 Rourke, "Huston Smith."

441 Ibid.

442 Christoper J.R., Armstrong, *Evelyn Underhill: An Introduction to Her Life and Writings* 1875-1941 (London–Oxford: A.R. Mowbray & Co., 1975), Introduction.

443 Charles Williams, ed., *The Letters of Evelyn Underhill* (New York: Longman, Green & Co., 1943), 122–23.

444 Armstrong, *Evelyn Underhill*, xiii-xiv.

445 Ibid.

446 Margaret Cropper, *Life of Evelyn Underhill* (New York: Harper & Brothers, 1958), 47.

447 Evelyn Underhill, *Mysticism: A Study in the Nature and Development of Spiritual Consciousness* (Mineola, New York: Courier Dover Publications, 2002, first published 1911), xiv.

448 Jerome Gellman, "Mysticism," *The Stanford Encyclopedia of Philosophy*, Summer 2011 Edition, Edward N. Zalta, ed., substantive revision June 29, 2022.

449 Underhill, *Mysticism: A Study in the Nature and Development of Spiritual Consciousness*, xiv-xv.

450 Cropper, *Life of Evelyn Underhill*, 47.

451 *The Dorothy Day Guild*, http://dorothydayguild.org.

452 Casey Cap, "Dorothy Day's Radical Faith," *The New Yorker*, April 6, 2020, https://www.newyorker.com/magazine/2020/04/13/dorothy-days-radical-faith.

453 "Meet a Mystic: Dorothy Day," *Monastery of St. Gertrude*, June 27, 2016, https://stgertrudes.org/meet-mystic-dorothy-day/.

454 Ibid.

455 "The Question of God: Dorothy Day," *PBS*, compiled from articles in America and Preservation of the Faith. Reprinted courtesy of Dorothy Day Library on the Web, www.catholicworker.org/dorothyday/, http://www.pbs.org/wgbh/questionofgod/voices/day.html

456 "Meet a Mystic: Dorothy Day," *Monastery of St. Gertrude*.

457 Cap, "Dorothy Day's Radical Faith."

458 Matthew Fox, "Dorothy Day and the Darkness that Accompanies Glory," *Daily Meditations with Matthew Fox*, December 30, 2020, https://dailymeditationswithmatthewfox.org/2020/12/30/dorothy-day-and-the-darkness-that-accompanies-glory/.

459 Ibid.

460 "Meet a Mystic: Dorothy Day," *Monastery of St. Gertrude*.

461 *The Dorothy Day Guild*.

462 "Meet a Mystic: Dorothy Day," *Monastery of St. Gertrude*.

463 Charles C. McCauley, *Zen And the Art of Wholeness: Developing a Personal Spiritual Psychology* (Google Book Search, iUniverse, 2005), 54, cited from https://en.wikipedia.org/wiki/Rational_mysticism.

464 Henry W. Clark, "Rational Mysticism and New Testament Christianity," *The Harvard Theological Review*, vol. 4, Issue 3, 311–329.

465 Jeffrey J. Kripal, *Roads of Excess, Palaces of Wisdom: Eroticism and Reflexivity in the Study of Mysticism* (Chicago: University of Chicago Press, 2001), 3.

466 John Horgan, "'Rational Mysticism,'" *New York Times*, March 23, 2003, https://www.nytimes.com/2003/03/23/books/chapters/rational-mysticism.html.

467 Ibid.

468 Ibid.

469 John Horgan, "Why I Don't Dig Buddhism," *Scientific American*, December 11, 2011, https://blogs.scientificamerican.com/cross-check/why-i-dont-dig-buddhism/.

470 Noah's Dove, "Mystical Deception File," *Darkness to Light*, https://www.zeolla.org/christian/cults/article/mystical.htm.

471 William Harmless, *Mystics* (New York: Oxford University Press, 2007), 14.

472 Home page, *Center for Action and Contemplation*, https://cac.org/living-school/program-details/the-perennial-tradition/#gsc.tab=0:.

473 Aldous Huxley, Gerald Heard, ed., *Prayers and Meditation* (Eugene: Wipf & Stock Publishers, 2008), 21.

474 Dove, "Mystical Deception File."

475 Matthew Fox, "Meister Eckhart: A Mystic Warrior for Our Times," *Youtube*, posted June 19, 2014, video 1:20m, https://www.youtube.com/watch?v=LLk2VcUIH8I.

476 Jacob Needleman, *Lost Christianity* (New York: Tarcher Perigree, 2003, first published 1980), 242.

477 Ibid., 112.

478 Matthew Fox, "A review of 'The Martyrdom of Thomas Merton: An Investigation,'" *Welcome From Matthew Fox*, July 2018, https://www.matthewfox.org/blog/a-review-of-the-martyrdom-of-thomas-merton-an-investigation.

479 David Van Biema, "Rhythm of the Saints," *Time*, http://content.time.com/time/specials/packages/article/0,28804,1850894_1850898_1850891,00.html.

480 Margalit Fox, "Rabbi Philip Berg, Who Updated Jewish Mysticism, Dies at 86," *New York Times*, September 20, 2013, https://www.nytimes.com/2013/09/21/us/rabbi-philip-berg-who-updated-jewish-mysticism-dies-at-86.html?pagewanted=all.

481 Joseph Telushkin, "Kabbalah: An Overview," *Jewish Virtual Library*, https://www.jewishvirtuallibrary.org/kabbalah-an-overview.

482 Deborah Kerdeman and Lawrence Kushner, *The Invisible Chariot: An Introduction to Kabbalah and Jewish Spirituality* (North Adams MI: Out of the Way Books, 1999), 90.

483 Pinchas Giller, *Kabbalah - A Guide for the Perplexed* (London: Bloomsbury Academic, 2011), 1-7.

484 Lisa Barr, M.D., "A Perspective on Kabbalah," Interview by Christopher Naughton, August 8, 2020.

485 Rabbi Geoffrey W. Dennis, "What is Kabbalah?" *ReformJudaism.org*, https://reformjudaism.org/what-kabbalah.

486 Joseph Telushkin, *Jewish Literacy: The Most Important Things to Know About the Jewish Religion, Its People and Its History* (New York: William Morrow and Company, 1991).

487 Mitch Horowitz, "We Cannot Hide These Things from the World," *Medium Magazine*, January 26, 2020, https://medium.com/@mitch.horowitz.nyc/we-cannot-hide-these-things-from-the-world-946803af0d72.

488 Arthur Kurzweil, "Kabbalah is the Official Theology of the Jewish People," *Arthur Kurzweil*, July 25, 2012, https://arthurkurzweil.com/2012/07/kabbalah-is-the-official-theology-of-the-jewish-people/.

489 Jonathan Garb, "How Kabbalah Went Viral," *Fifteen EightyFour, Academic Perspectives from Cambridge University Press*, September 17, 2020, http://www.cambridgeblog.org/2020/09/how-kabbalah-went-viral.

490 Fox, "Rabbi Berg."

491 Ibid.

492 D.T. Suzuki, *Mysticism: Christian and Buddhist* (London: Routledge, 2002, 2nd edition); *Mysticism: Christian and Buddhist* book description, https://www.routledge.com/Mysticism-Christian-and-Buddhist/Suzuki/p/book/9780415285865.

493 "Sufism and Zen in the modern Western world: Spiritual marriage of East and West or Western cultural hegemony?" *University of Glasgow*, 2017, https://www.gla.ac.uk/media/Media_562126_smxx.pdf.

494 "Black Women Mystics: Gifts of Power," *The Center for Action and Contemplation*, August 1, 2019, citing Rebecca Jackson, *Gifts of Power: The Writings of Rebecca Jackson, Black Visionary, Shaker Eldress*, ed. Jean McMahon Humez (Amherst: University of Massachusetts Press,1981), 72, https://cac.org/daily-meditations/gifts-of-power-2019-08-01/.

495 Ibid., citing Joy Bostic, *African American Female Mysticism: Nineteenth-Century Religious Activism* (London: Palgrave Macmillan: 2013), 96-97, 102, 117.

496 "People & Events: Rebecca Cox Jackson," *PBS*, http://www.pbs.org/wgbh/aia/part3/3p247.html.

497 Bostic, "African American Female Mysticism," 96.

498 Joy R. Bostic, "Look What You Have Done: Sacred Power and Reimagining the Divine," *Springer Link* citing *African American Female Mysticism*, 95-117, https://link.springer.com/chapter/10.1057/9781137375056_5.

499 Jackson, "Black Women Mystics: Gifts of Power."

500 "People & Events: Rebecca Cox Jackson."

501 Lillian Faderman, *To Believe in Women: What Lesbians Have Done for America - A History* (New York: Mariner Books, 1999), 264–265.

502 "People & Events: Rebecca Cox Jackson."

503 Ibid.

504 Jackson, "Black Women Mystics: Gifts of Power."

505 Clara Endicott Sears, *Gleanings from Old Shaker Journals*, compiled by Clara Endicott Sears (Boston: Houghton Mifflin, 1916), 7.

506 "Shakers," *Wikipedia*, https://en.wikipedia.org/wiki/Shakers.

507 "Black Women Mystics: Gifts of Power."

508 Ibid., quoting Jackson, *Gifts of Power*, 174-5.

509 "Black Women Mystics: Gifts of Power."

510 Stephen W. Angell, "Howard Thurman and the Quakers," *Quaker Theology*, https://quakertheology.org/howard-thurman-and-quakers/.

511 Ibid.

512 Ibid., citing Gary Dorrien, *The Making of American Liberal Theology: Idealism, Realism, and Modernity, 1900-1950* (Louisville: Westminster John Knox Press, 2003), 565.

513 Alton Pollard III, *Mysticism and Social Change: The Social Witness of Howard Thurman* (New York: Peter Lang Publishing, 1992), 163.

514 Angell, "Howard Thurman," quoting Howard Thurman, *With Head and Heart: The Autobiography of Howard Thurman* (San Diego: Harcourt Brace Jovanovich, 1979), 76-77

515 Zalman Schachter-Shalomi, Reb Zalman and Gropman, Daniel, *The First Step: A Guide For the New Jewish Spirit* (Toronto: Bantam, 1983), 3-6.

516 John Blake, "He was MLK's mentor, and his meeting with Gandhi changed history. But Howard Thurman was largely unknown, until now," *CNN*, February 1, 2019, https://www.cnn.com/2019/02/01/us/howard-thurman-mlk-gandhi/index.html.

517 Ibid., quoting Thurman.

518 Ibid.

519 Quinton Dixie and Peter Eisenstadt, *Visions of a Better World: Howard Thurman's Pilgrimage to India and the Origins of African American Nonviolence* (Boston: Beacon Press, 2011), 95–115.

520 Howard Thurman, *Jesus and the Disinherited* (Boston: Beacon Press, 2012, originally published 1949), 29.

522 Blake, "MLK's mentor."

523 Ibid., quoting filmmaker Martin Dobelmeier "Backs Against the Wall: The Howard Thurman Story."

523 Brent Powell, "Henry David Thoreau, MLK Jr. and the American Tradition of Protest," *OAH Magazine of History*, vol. 9, issue 2, Winter 1995, 26; https://academic.oup.com/maghis/article-abstract/9/2/26/1035789?login=false.

524 Fuller, *Spiritual Not Religious*, 80.

525 "Alternative Altars," *The Pluralism Project*, Harvard University, https://pluralism.org/alternative-altars.

526 Fuller, *Spiritual Not Religious*, 80.

527 Helena Petrovna Blavatsky, "Theosophy—The Essence of Philosophy and Science," Collected Writings, Volume II, 1879, p. 209, https://play.google.com/books/reader?id=028sDwAAQBAJ&pg=GBS.PA14&hl=en.

528 Horowitz, *Occult America*, 5.

529 Louis Fischer, *The Life of Mahatma Gandhi* (New York: Harper & Row, 1950), 416-17.

530 John L. Crow, "The Strange Theosophical Connection to the US Civil Rights Movement," *Religion in American History*, January 30, 2013, http://usreligion.blogspot.com/2013/01/the-strange-theosophical-connection-to.html.

531 Powell, "Thoreau, MLK."

532 Dixie and Eisenstadt, *Howard Thurman's Pilgrimage*, xii.

533 Nick Tasler, "Four Intriguing Decisions From Martin Luther King— Success lessons from the life and legacy of Martin Luther King, Jr.," *Psychology Today*, January 20, 2014, https://www.psychologytoday.com/us/blog/strategic-thinking/201401/4-intriguing-decisions-martin-luther-king

534 Martin Luther King, Jr., "Out of the Long Night," *The Gospel Messenger*, 1958 February 8, 14, https://archive.org/details/gospelmessengerv107mors/page/n177/mode/2up.

535 Ibid.

536 John Craig, "Wesleyan Baccalaureate Is Delivered by Dr. King," *Hartford Courant*, June 8, 1964, as cited in footnote 9, https://quoteinvestigator.com/2012/11/15/arc-of-universe/#f+4794+1+8.

537 Ibid., footnote 10.

538 Ibid., footnote 1, citing Theodore Parker, *Ten Sermons of Religion*, "Of Justice and the Conscience," (Boston: Crosby, Nichols and Company, , 1853), 84-85; https://books.google.com/books?id=sUUQA-AAAYAAJ&.

539 "The Arc of the Moral Universe Is Long, But It Bends Toward Justice," *Quote Investigator*, https://quoteinvestigator.com/2012/11/15/arc-of-universe/.

540 Cara Herbert, "Am I a Mystic?" *Gaia*, February 6, 2020, https://www.gaia.com/article/am-i-a-mystic-10-signs.

541 Caroline Myss, "Why Write a Book on Prayer?" *Venture Inward* magazine, Fall 2020, p. 21.

542 Ibid.

CHAPTER 8

543 "History," *American Atheists*, https:// www.atheists.org/about/history/.

544 Michael Lipka, "10 facts about atheists," *Pew Research Center*, December 6, 2019, https://www.pewresearch. org/fact-tank/2019/12/06/10-facts-about-atheists/.

545 Derek Thompson, "Elite Failure Has Brought Americans to the Edge of an Existential Crisis," *The Atlantic*, September 5, 2019, https://www.theatlantic.com/ideas/archive/2019/09/america-without-family-god-or-patriotism/597382/.

546 "In US, Decline of Christianity Continues at Rapid Pace," *Pew Research Center*, October 17, 2019, https:// www.pewresearch.org/religion/2019/10/17/in-u-s-decline-of-christianity-continues-at-rapid-pace/.

547 Sam Harris, "The Four Horsemen: The Conversation That Sparked an Atheist Revolution," *Sam Harris*, October 2019, https://samharris.org/books/the-four-horsemen/.

548 Barack Obama, "Yesterday, President Obama delivered his Inaugural Address, calling for a 'new era of responsibility,'" January 22, 2009, https://obamawhitehouse.archives.gov/realitycheck/the_press_office/ President_Barack_Obamas_Inaugural_Address.

549 Steve Prothero, "Atheists Need a Different Voice," *United Coalition of Reason*, https://unitedcor.org/atheists-need-a-different-voice/.

550 Ibid.

551 "A Kinder, Gentler (Mostly Feminine) Atheism?" *New World Radio*, WTAR-850 AM Norfolk, VA., Unity Online Radio, audio 14:40, October 29, 2010, referencing Real Time with Bill Maher, *HBO*, Episode #184, airdate May 14, 2010.

552 Meacham, *The National Constitution Center*.

553 "Decline of Christianity," *Pew Research*.

554 Laura Barrett Bennett, "A Kinder, Gentler (Mostly Feminine) Atheism?" *New World Radio*, audio 17:55.

555 Ibid., Rev. Diane Scribner-Clevinger audio 18:45.

556 Steve Bhaermann, "Life After Death Informs Life BEFORE Death," interviewing Bruce Greyson, MD, *Wikipolitiki*, April 20, 2021, audio 15:17.

557 Richard Rohr, "Doubt: A Necessary Tool for Growth," *Center for Action and Contemplation*, Richard Rohr's Daily Meditation, Feb. 1, 2021, https://email.cac.org/t/ViewEmail/d/4D7DDEDAC-915C3B22540EF23F30FEDED/D3834B5B987AF82E46778398EADC2510.

558 "Atheism: A Belief in the Here and Now," *ExChristian.Net*, December 28, 2007, https://news.exchristian. net/2007/12/atheism-belief-in-here-and-now.html.

559 "Religious Landscape Study: Atheists," *Pew Research Center*, 2014, https://www.pewforum.org/ religious-landscape-study/religious-family/atheist/#frequency-of-feeling-wonder-about-the-universe.

560 Sam Harris, *Waking Up: A Guide to Spirituality Without Religion* (New York: Simon & Schuster, 2015), 228.

561 Sam Harris, "Why Sam Harris is trying to rehabilitate the word 'spirituality,'" *Big Think*, video 1:58, https://bigthink.com/videos/sam-harris-on-spirituality.

562 *Wikipedia*, quoting Sam Harris, *The End of Faith: Religion, Terror, and the Future of Reason* (New York: W.W. Norton, 2004), https://en.wikipedia.org/wiki/The_End_of_Faith.

563 Prothero, "Atheists Need."

564 Ibid.

565 George Yancey, "How Should an Atheist Think About Death?" *New York Times*, October 20, 2020, https:// www.nytimes.com/2020/10/20/opinion/philosophy-death-atheism.html.

566 Giovanni Aquilecchia, "Giordano Bruno," *Brittanica*, https://www.britannica.com/biography/Giorda-no-Bruno.

567 Ibid.

568 Horgan, "'Rational Mysticism.'"

569 John Horgan, "Science Will Never Explain Why There's Something Rather Than Nothing," *Scientific American*, April 23, 2012, https://blogs.scientificamerican.com/cross-check/science-will-never-explain-why-theres-something-rather-than-nothing/.

570 Vincent Bugliosi, *New World Radio*, Christopher Naughton interviewing Bugliosi, May 13, 2011, audio 4:42.

571 Ibid., audio 19:56.

572 Carly Sitrin, "Making Sense: Decoding Gertrude Stein," *Boston University (B.U.) Arts and Sciences*, http://www.bu.edu/writingprogram/journal/past-issues/issue-6/sitrin/.

573 Dana Tanner-Kennedy, "Gertrude Stein and the Metaphysical Avant-Garde," *MDPI*, Religions, vol. 11, issue 4, March 12, 2020, https://www.mdpi.com/2077-1444/11/4/152.

574 Susan Blackmore and Emily Troscianko, *Consciousness: An Introduction* (Oxfordshire, UK: Taylor & Francis, 2018, 3rd ed.), Introduction.

575 Clifford N. Lazarus Ph.D., "Does Consciousness Exist Outside of the Brain?" *Psychology Today*, June 26, 2019, https://www.psychologytoday.com/us/blog/think-well/201906/does-consciousness-exist-out-side-the-brain?fbclid=IwAR3LnAFYI560cTq6njdJkpZ2tcUrklhSf588hJPzzUXfaXY5_d5jt6KVz1w.

576 John Horgan, "David Chalmers Thinks the Hard Problem Is Really Hard," *Scientific American*, April 10, 2017, https://blogs.scientificamerican.com/cross-check/david-chalmers-thinks-the-hard-problem-is-really-hard/.

577 Dossey, *One Mind*, 113.

578 Mario Beauregard and Denyse O'Leary, *The Spiritual Brain: a Neuroscientist's Case for the Existence of the Soul* (San Francisco: HarperOne, 2007), Introduction, xi.

579 Ibid.

580 Ibid.

581 Tim Ventura, "Deepak Chopra on Freedom Beyond Symbols & Understanding Reality," *Medium Magazine,* July 23, 2020, based on an interview of Chopra by Ventura, https://medium.com/@timventura/ deepak-chopra-on-freedom-beyond-symbols-understanding-reality-63a3d5cf7abf.

582 Lazarus, "Exist Outside the Brain?"

583 Ibid.

584 Susan Blackmore, "Near-Death Experiences on TV: Why quantum coherence cannot explain the NDE," *Sceptic Magazine,* vol. 17, issue 1, Spring 2004, 8-10, https://www.susanblackmore.uk/articles/near-death-experiences-on-tv/.

585 Ibid.

585 Tim Ventura, "Radin on Global Consciousness, Parapsychology, and Psychic Research," *Medium Magazine,* March 24, 2020, https://medium.com/predict/dean-radin-on-global-consciousness-parapsychology-and-psychic-research-685b4d3b7382.

587 Maureen Seaberg, "Real Magic: Prominent researcher and synesthete says real magic is frontier science," *Psychology Today,* March 29, 2018, https://www.psychologytoday.com/us/blog/sensorium/201803/real-magic.

588 Ibid.

589 Ibid.

590 Fernando Alvarez, "An Experiment on Precognition with Planarian Worms," *Researchgate* citing *Journal of Scientific Exploration,* 30(2), 2016, 217-226, https://www.researchgate.net/publication/304412781_An_ Experiment_on_Precognition_with_Planarian_Worms; Raymond Trevor Bradley, "The Psychophysiology Of Intuition: A Quantum-Holographic Theory Of Nonlocal Communication," *Taylor & Francis Research Online* citing *The Journal of New Paradigm Research,* vol. 63, is-sue 2, 2007, https://www.tandfonline.com/ doi/abs/10.1080/02604020601123148?journalCode=gwof20.

591 "Interconnected Mind and the Global Consciousness Project feat. Roger Nelson," *Youtube,* posted August 26, 2010, video 3:45, https://www.youtube.com/watch?v=RojTua3coto&feature=player_embedded#%21.

592 *Wikipedia,* "The Global Consciousness Project," citing "Terry Schiavo and the Global Consciousness Project," *Skeptic News,* 27 April 2005 and "A disturbance in the Force . . . ?" *Boundary Institute,* December 2001. Archived from the original on 2011-07-17, https://en.wikipedia.org/wiki/Global_ Consciousness_Project.

593 Claus Larsen, "An evening with Dean Radin," *Skeptic Report,* https://www.skepticreport.com/an-evening-with-dean-radin/.

594 "Terry Schiavo," *Skeptic News.*

595 "Larry Dossey on the Healing Power of Prayer," *DownloadForAll,* December 17, 2020, https://dl4all.us/ courses/79020-larry-dossey-on-the-healing-power-of-prayer.html.

596 Dossey, *One Mind,* book cover.

597 Aldous Huxley, *The Doors of Perception* (New York: Harper & Row, 1954), 6.

598 "Larry, Dossey," M.D., "Nonlocal Mind: A (Fairly) Brief History of the Term," aapsglobal.com/wp-content/ uploads/2018/04/Dossey-Nonlocal-Mind.pdf.

599 Ibid.

600 Dossey, *One Mind,* 85.

601 J.W.N. Sullivan, "Interviews with Great Scientists, VI - Max Planck," *The Observer,* January 25, 1931, 17, as quoted in *Newspapers*.com, https://archive.ph/AqT80.

602 James Jeans, *Mysterious Universe* (Cambridge: Cambridge University Press, 1931), 137.

603 Richard Conn Henry, "The Mental Universe," *Nature,* July 6, 2005, https://www.nature.com/ articles/436029a.

604 "Erwin Schrödinger: There is only one mind," *Hendrik-Wintjen,* https://www.hendrik-wintjen.info/ consciousness/erwin-schroedinger-one-mind/.

605 Sam Harris, "The Mystery of Consciousness II," *Sam Harris,* October 19, 2011, https://samharris.org/the-mystery-of-consciousness-ii/.

606 "People on TV Shows Live Inside the Television," *I Used to Believe,* https://www.iusedtobelieve.com/media/ tv/people_on_tv_live_in_it/.

607 Graham Hancock, "The Consciousness Revolution," *Shift Frequency,* March 24, 2015, https://www.shiftfrequency.com/consciousness-revolution/.

608 Ibid.

609 Mark Gober, *Where Is My Mind?* podcast, August 8, 2019, Ep. 1, https://podcasts.apple.com/us/podcast/ where-is-my-mind/id1470129415?i=1000519266697.

610 Hancock, "Revolution."

611 Dean Radin, *The Conscious Universe: The Scientific Truth of Psychic Phenomena* (New York: Harper Collins, 1997), 324-325.

612 Larry Dossey, MD, "Counterclockwise: When Biology Is Not Destiny," *Reality Sandwich,* March 26, 2015, https://realitysandwich.com/counterclockwise-when-biology-is-not-destiny/.

613 "Scientific Evidence for Reincarnation by Dr Ian Stevenson," *Youtube*, https://www.youtube.com/watch?v=PbWMEWubrk0.

614 Jim Tucker, M.D., *Before: Children's Memories of Past Lives* (New York: St. Martin's Press, 2021).

615 Ibid.

616 Dossey, *One Mind*, 114 quoting Ian Stevenson, *Where Reincarnation and Biology Intersect* (Goleta, CA: Praeger Publishers, 1997), 181.

617 Tucker, *Before*, 211.

618 Jim B. Tucker, M.D., "Children Who Claim to Remember Previous Lives: Past, Present, and Future Research," *Journal of Scientific Exploration*, vol. 21, no.3, 2007, 546, https://med.virginia.edu/perceptual-studies/wp-content/uploads/sites/360/2016/12/REI35.pdf.

619 Bruce Greyson, MD, "Is There Life After Death?" moderated by John Cleese at the 2018 Tom Tom Festival, Charlottesville, VA., *Youtube*, posted May 30, 2018, video 44:14, https://www.youtube.com/watch?v=4R-GizqsLumo&t=2653s.

620 Ibid., video 44:35.

621 Ibid., Emily Williams Kelly, Ph.D., video 1:07:02. 39:24, https://www.youtube.com/watch?v=4RGizqsLumo&t=2653s.

622 Blackmore and Troscianko, *Consciousness*, 3rd ed., Introduction.

623 Susan Blackmore, "First Person—Into the Unknown," *New Scientist*, November 4, 2000, 55, https://www.susanblackmore.uk/journalism/first-person-into-the-unknown/.

624 Susan Blackmore, *Dying To Live* (Buffalo: Prometheus Books, 1993), preface.

625 "The Dying Brain Theory," https://www.near-death.com/science/articles/dying-brain-theory.html.

626 Susan Blackmore, "Why I no longer believe religion is a virus of the mind," *The Guardian*, September 16, 2010, https://www.theguardian.com/commentisfree/belief/2010/sep/16/why-no-longer-believe-religion-virus-mind.

627 Ibid.

628 Blackmore and Troscianko, *Consciousness*, 3rd ed., 6.

629 Ibid.

630 Ibid., xii.

631 Ibid., 6.

632 *Wikipedia* citing Peter Roennfeldt, "Near Death Experiences," *Mariah Ministries Australia*, http://www.moriah.com.au/textarchive/nde.htm.

633 Maria Popova, "The Dalai Lama on Science and Spirituality," *The Marginalian*, https://www.brainpickings.org/2018/10/16/dalai-lama-science-spirituality-destructive-emotions/.

634 Ibid., quoting the Dalai Lama from Daniel Goleman, *Destructive Emotions: A Scientific Dialogue with the Dalai Lama* (New York: Bantam Books, 2004), preface.

635 Dalai Lama, *The Universe in a Single Atom: The Convergence of Science and Spirituality* (New York: Morgan Books, 2005), Prologue, 3.

636 Deepak Chopra, "Debunking 'The God Delusion,' Part 1," *Beliefnet*, 2006, https://www.beliefnet.com/wellness/2007/02/debunking-the-god-delusion-part-1.aspx.

CHAPTER 9

637 Richard Moe, "The train ride that brought Lincoln to D.C.—and introduced him to the nation," *The Washington Post*, April 24, 2020, https://www.washingtonpost.com/outlook/the-train-ride-that-brought-lincoln-to-dc--and-introduced-him-to-the-nation/2020/04/23/afef2192-4f58-11ea-bf44-f5043eb3918a_story.html.

638 Ibid.

639 Lina Mann, "Spies, Lies and Disguise: Abraham Lincoln and the Baltimore Plot," *White House Historical Association*, https://www.whitehousehistory.org/spies-lies-and-disguise-abraham-lincoln-and-the-baltimore-plot.

640 Moe, "Train Ride."

641 Mann, "Spies, Lies."

642 Ibid.

643 Ibid.

644 Ted Widmer, "The Capitol Takeover That Wasn't," *New York Times*, Opinion, January 8, 2021, https://www.nytimes.com/2021/01/08/opinion/capitol-protest-1861-lincoln.html.

645 Ibid.

646 Ibid.

647 Dan Gilgoff, "Abraham Lincoln's Religious Uncertainty," *US News and World Report*, February 12, 2009, https://www.usnews.com/news/history/articles/2009/02/12/abraham-lincolns-religious-uncertainty.

648 Bret Stephens, "Lincoln Knew in 1838 What 2021 Would Bring," *New York Times*, January 18, 2021, https://www.nytimes.com/2021/01/18/opinion/trump-lincoln-mobs-democracy.html.

649 Joseph Campbell, *Thou Art That: Transforming Religious Metaphor* (New York: Joseph Campbell Foundation, 2002), 11.

650 Stephen Flurry, "Lincoln and the Bible," *The Trumpet*, August 12, 2019, https://www.thetrumpet.com/21110-lincoln-and-the-bible.

651 Josiah Gilbert Holland, *Holland's Life of Abraham Lincoln* (Lincoln: University of Nebraska Press, 1998), 542.

652 Widmer, "The Capitol Takeover That Wasn't."

653 Franklin Steiner, *Religious Beliefs of Our Presidents* (Girard, KS: Haldeman-Julius Publications, 1936), *Positive Atheism,* quoting Chapter VIII, "Abraham Lincoln, Deist, and Admirer of Thomas Paine," citing J.G. Holland, *The Life of Abraham Lincoln* (New York: Dodd, Mead, 1887), 492, http://celestiallands.org/library/lincoln.htm.

654 Douglas Wilson, "William H. Herndon and Mary Todd Lincoln," *Journal of the Abraham Lincoln Association,* vol. 22, issue 2, Summer 2001, 26, quoting William Herndon "Lincoln's Religion," Illinois State Register, Dec. 1873, http://hdl.handle.net/2027/spo.2629860.0022.203.

655 Stephen Mansfield, "The maddeningly untraditional and modern faith of Abraham Lincoln," *Religion News,* August 12, 2019, https://religionnews.com/2019/08/12/the-maddeningly-untraditional-and-modern-faith-of-abraham-lincoln/.

656 Steiner, "Religious Beliefs."

657 Mark Noll, "The Puzzling Faith of Abraham Lincoln," *Christianity Today,* https://www.christianitytoday.com/history/issues/issue-33/puzzling-faith-of-abraham-lincoln.html.

658 *Wikipedia,* citing "Christian Flag," *The Christian Advocate,* (New York: T. Carlton & J. Porter, 1909), 84, https://en.wikipedia.org/wiki/Christian_Advocate.

659 Franklin Schaeffer quoting Thomas B. Edsell, "The Capitol Insurrection was as Christian Nationalist as it Gets," *New York Times* as cited in *The Franklin Schaeffer Blog,* posted January 28, 2021, https://frankschaefferblog.com/2021/01/via-new-york-times-the-capitol-insurrection-was-as-christian-nationalist-as-it-gets/.

660 Rev. Keith A. Haemmelmann, "The Threat of Christian Nationalism," *The PAG Church,* January 17, 2021, https://pagchurch.org/blog/the-threat-of-christian-nationalism/.

661 Schaeffer, *The Franklin Schaeffer Blog,* January 28, 2021, quoting Katherine Stewart, "The Power Worshippers: Inside the Dangerous Rise of Religious Nationalism."

662 John Fea, "New video: January 6 insurrectionists pray in the Senate chamber," *Current,* January 17, 2021, https://thewayofimprovement.com/2021/01/17/new-video-january-6-insurrectionists-pray-in-the-senate-chamber/

663 Schaeffer, *The Franklin Schaeffer Blog,* January 28, 2021, quoting Samuel L. Perry, professors of sociology, University of Oklahoma,"Taking America Back for God," https://frankschaefferblog.com/2021/01/via-new-york-times-the-capitol-insurrection-was-as-christian-nationalist-as-it-gets/.

664 Phyllis Tickle, "The Great Emergence," *Youtube.com,* posted October 8, 2008, video, 00:27, https://www.youtube.com/watch?v=YRtQM5lO0aw.

665 Graham Pemberton, "Why Christianity Must Change or Die—John Shelby Spong," *Medium Magazine,* April 16, 2020, https://medium.com/@graham.pemberton/why-christianity-must-change-or-die-john-shelby-spong-6db9563168b2.

666 Frank Zindler, "Did Jesus Exist?" *American Atheists,* https://www.atheists.org/activism/resources/did-jesus-exist.

667 Bill Maher, "Did CBS Censor Bill Maher?" *The O'Reilly Factor* with Bill O'Reilly, September 26, 2006, published January 27, 2017, https://www.foxnews.com/transcript/did-cbs-censor-bill-maher.

668 "Gandhi's Message to Christians," *MahatmaGandhi.org,* https://mkgandhi.org/africaneedsgandhi/gandhis_message_to_christians.php.

669 M.K. Gandhi, *An Autobiography or The Story of My Experiments with Truth* (Ahmedabad: Navjivan Publishing House, 1927), 49.

670 Gandhi, *Autobiography,* 49.

671 M.K. Gandhi, *My Religion* (Ahmedabad: Navjivan Publishing House, 1955), edited by Bharatan Kumarappa, 25.

672 Cynthia Bourgeault, "Putting on the Mind of Christ," *Center for Action and Contemplation,* January 14, 2019, https://cac.org/daily-meditations/putting-on-the-mind-of-christ-2019-01-14/.

673 Endrina Tay, "The Philosophy of Jesus of Nazareth," *Th. Jefferson Monticello,* https://www.monticello.org/research-education/thomas-jefferson-encyclopedia/philosophy-jesus-nazareth/.

674 Elaine Pagels, *The Gnostic Gospels* (New York: Vintage Books, 1989, orig. published 1979), Introduction, xii.

675 "Jefferson's Bible: A Revolutionary Act," *Smithsonian,* November 11, 2011-July 15, 2012, https://americanhistory.si.edu/documentsgallery/exhibitions/jefferson/4.html.

676 Mitch Horowitz, "My Take: How Jefferson's Secret Bible May Have Changed History," *CNN,* January 11, 2012, horowitz https://religion.blogs.cnn.com/2012/01/11/my-take-how-thomas-jeffersons-secret-bible-might-have-changed-history/.

677 Ibid.

678 Ibid.

679 James Lyons, *The Cosmic Christ in Origen and Teilhard de Chardin: a Comparative Study* (Oxford: Oxford University Press, 1982), 202–203.

680 Anodea Judith, "Teihard de Chardin 1881-1955," *GaiaMind,* December, 1996, https://www.gaiamind.com/Teilhard.html.

681 Peter Medawar, *Critical Notice* (Oxford: Oxford University Press, 1961), 99–106.

682 Richard Dawkins, *Unweaving the Rainbow: Science, Delusion and the Appetite for Wonder* (Boston: Hough-ton Mifflin Harcourt, 2000), 320.
683 Gerard O'Connell, "Will Pope Francis remove the Vatican's 'warning' from Teilhard de Chardin's writings?" *America, The Jesuit Review,* November 21, 2017, https://www.americamagazine.org/faith/2017/11/21/will-pope-francis-remove-vaticans-warning-teilhard-de-chardins-writings.
684 Pierre Teilhard de Chardin, *Cornent Je Crois* (English translation by Bernard P., New York: Harper and Row Publishers, 1965), 150; trans., 130, cited in "Teilhard deChardin and the Religious Phenomenon," *Unesco,* http://www.crossroad.to/Quotes/science/teilhard-Unesco.htm.
685 Pierre Teilhard de Chardin, *The Phenomenon of Man* (New York: Harper Perennial, 1976, originally published 1955), 226.
686 Matthew Fox, *The Coming of the Cosmic Christ: The Healing of Mother Earth and the Birth of a Global Renaissance* (San Francisco: Harper & Row, 1988), inside cover.
687 Molly O'Neil, "At Supper with Matthew Fox; Roman Catholic Rebel Becomes Cause Celebre," *New York Times,* March 17, 1993, https://www.nytimes.com/1993/03/17/garden/at-supper-with-matthew-fox-roman-catholic-rebel-becomes-a-cause-celebre.html.
688 "Why doesn't the Roman Catholic church defrock Richard Rohr?" *Christianity,* https://christianity.stackexchange.com/questions/43057/why-doesnt-the-roman-catholic-church-defrock-richard-rohr.
689 "The Cosmic Christ with Richard Rohr," *Youtube,* posted September 12, 2014, video 00:25, https://www.youtube.com/watch?v=IabeHxwSlWU.
690 Cynthia Bourgeault, "Cynthia Bourgeault on The Universal Christ by Richard Rohr," video 04:04, https://vimeo.com/315749554.
691 Fox, *Coming Cosmic Christ,* 240.
692 Thomas Merton, *Ishi Means Man* (Greensboro, NC: Unicorn Press, 1976).
693 Parry, *Original Politics,* 163.
694 Ibid., 33.
695 Ibid., 27.
696 Ibid., 56.
697 Ibid., 34.
698 Ibid., 56.
699 Ibid., 63.
700 Ibid., 57.
701 Fuller, *Spiritual But Not Religious,* 93.
702 Parry, *Original Politics,* 163.
703 Ibid.
704 Ibid., 61.
705 Ibid., 33.
706 Ibid., 99.
707 Needleman, *The American Soul,* 215.
708 Ibid., 202.
709 Parry, *Original Politics,* 116.
710 Fuller, *Spiritual But Not Religious,* 93.
711 Parry, *Original Politics,* 26.
712 Ibid., Preface.
713 Needleman, *The American Soul,* 21.
714 Frank Waters, *Book of the Hopi* (New York: Penguin Books, 1977).
715 Ellen Pages, "Return Of Pahana–The Lost White Brother Of The Hopi And The Sacred Tablet," March 15,2018, https://www.ancientpages.com/2018/03/05/return-of-pahana-the-lost-white-brother-of-the-hopi-and-the-sacred-tablets/.
716 Ibid.
717 Richard Rohr, "Order, Disorder, Reorder: Part One, The Universal Pattern," *Center for Action and Contemplation,* August 9, 2020, https://email.cac.org/t/ViewEmail/d/711151553F-90BA9F2540EF23F30FEDED/D3834B5B987AF82E46778398EADC2510.
718 Thompson, "America Lost Its Religion."
719 Michelle Boorstein, "A Shift in Religious Identity," quoting from the forthcoming *The Secular Surge, The Washington Post* Weekly, July 11, 2021, 3.
720 Thompson, "America Lost Its Religion."
721 Fox, *Cosmic Christ,* inside cover.
722 Caroline Myss, "Why Write a Book on Prayer?" *Venture Inward,* Fall 2020, 21.
723 Marianne Williamson, *A Politics of Love* (San Francisco: HarperOne, 2019) 59.
724 Thom Hartmann, "Has the Fourth Turning Begun?" *Medium Magazine,* November 10, 2022, https://medium.com/@thomhartmann/has-the-fourth-turning-begun-d0ddc8f792ab.
725 Ibid.
726 Parry, *Original Politics,* 216.
727 Thom Hartmann, "The Fourth Turning: An American Prophecy," *The Thom Hartmann Program,* citing William Strauss and Neil Howe, *The Fourth Turning: What the Cycles of History Tell Us About America's*

Next Rendezvous with Destiny (New York: Crown Publishing, 1997), July 8, 2004, https://www.thomhartmann.com/blog/2004/07/fourth-turning-american-prophecy.

728 Rohr, "Order, Disorder."

729 Sidney Kirkpatrick, *An American Prophet* (New York: Riverhead Books, 2000).

730 The Edgar Cayce Readings, 3976-2 Series, https://www.edgarcayce.org/.

731 Ibid.., Reading #1152-11, https://www.edgarcayce.org/.

732 Ibid., Reading #3976-13, https://www.edgarcayce.org/.

733 Ibid., Reading #2167-1, https://www.edgarcayce.org/.

734 Jacob Needleman, "The American Soul," interview by Krista Tippet, *On Being*, NPR, Oct 26, 2006, audio, 6:16.

735 Ibid., at 7:25.

736 Henry, "The Mental Universe."

737 Mitch Horowitz, "The Man Who Destroyed Skepticism," *BoingBoing*, October 26, 2020, https://boingboing.net/2020/10/26/the-man-who-destroyed-skepticism.html.

738 Blanche Marie Gallagher, *Meditations with Teilhard de Chardin* (Santa Fe: Bear & Co., 1988), 105.

739 Ibid., 99.

GRAPHICS

p. xiii
caption: Why the Seven Pointed Star?
Sources: Emily Carding, "The Septagram: Seven Directions and Seven Qualities," Llewellyn, October 22, 2012, https://www.llewellyn.com/journal/article/2320; William G. Fellows, "The Stars in Freemasonry," http://www.md-mrs.com/library/Stars%20in%20Freemasonry.pdf; "The Bennington Flag," Revolutionary War and Beyond, October 21, 2011, https://www.revolutionary-war-and-beyond.com/bennington-flag.html; Chris-Anne, "7 Pointed Star Symbolism," Chris-Anne's Curio: Tarot & Sacred Business, chris-anne.com; Chris Deziel, "Cherokee Indian Symbols and Meanings," The Classroom, October 18, 2022, https://www.theclassroom.com/cherokee-symbols-and-what-they-mean-12078903.html.

p. 21
caption: Washington's Vision: The First Union Story Ever Written
attribution: "Washington's Vision: The First Union Story Ever," Edward Everett, Alexander & Co., Philadelphia, PA, ca. 1864. Booklet, Digital Collections, Indiana University. http://fedora.dlib.indiana.edu/fedora/get/iudl:1212086/OVERVIEW.

p. 39
caption: A History of Early Opinions Concerning Jesus Christ by Joseph Priestly
attribution: Priestley, Joseph, 1733-1804: An history of early opinions concerning Jesus Christ, compiled from original writers; proving that the Christian church was at first Unitarian, (Birmingham [Eng.] Printed for the author, by Pearson and Rollason, 1786).

p. 52
caption: Washington as Freemason
attribution: Washington as a Freemason, Library of Congress, Strobridge & Gerlach lithographers, Pike's Opera House, Cincinnati, O., ca. 1866. Photograph. https://www.loc.gov/item/96518222/.

p. 57
caption: Eye of Providence, Reverse of the Great Seal of the United States
attribution: Eye of Providence: Annuit Coeptis, iStock Photo 92085706, uploaded by Paul Paladin, licensed (assigned to Christopher W. Naughton) June 18, 2010. https://www.istockphoto.com/photo/pyramid-on-one-dollar-bill-gm92085706-9435463?clarity=false.

p. 76
caption: The Caning of Sen. Charles Sumner
attribution: Public Domain-Wikimedia https://commons.wikimedia.org/wiki/File:Southern_Chivalry.jpg.

p. 95
caption: Pogo, "We Have Met the Enemy"
attribution: © Okefenokee Glee & Perloo, Inc. Used by permission. Contact mailto:permissions@pogocomics.com.

p. 124
caption: Get Out of Hell Free
attribution: Adapted from Hasbro's Monopoly game; numerous renditions online, including thisistrue.com, Secular Humanist Society of New York SHSNY.org, and others.

p. 173
caption: The Tree of Life, Kabbalah
attribution: "Tree of Life" (Kabbalah), Wikimedia commons, public domain.

p. 231
caption: Christian flag, designed by Charles Overton in 1897
attribution: Wikimedia, public domain, https://commons.wikimedia.org/wiki/File:Christian_flag.svg

p. 2367
caption: Jefferson's "cut and paste" of the Canonical Gospels, King James Bible
attribution: Wikimedia Commons, Scanned by The Smithsonian, The Smithsonian National Museum of American History, https://commons.wikimedia.org/wiki/File:Jefferson_Bible.jpg.

p. 236
caption: "The Jefferson Bible" in the author's handwriting
attribution: The Life and Morals of Jesus of Nazareth (Jefferson Bible; c. 1820) by Thomas Jefferson (1743 – 1826); Wikimedia Commons, Scanned by The Smithsonian, The Smithsonian National Museum of American History, https://commons.wikimedia.org/wiki/File:Jefferson_Bible.jpg.

ACKNOWLEDGMENTS

My thanks to so many who inspired and supported me on this journey. Friends and colleagues gave valuable feedback and didn't shy away from speaking their minds in order to make this project what it is today: from my lifelong friends Bill Hoffman and Chuck Cuttic, fellow history majors who weighed in with critiques and encouragement early on; my "radical brotherhood salon" of Chris Ryan and Jake Balderson, men with great interests in politics, history and ecumenical spirituality who were kind enough to slog through the early versions with all of my "down-the-rabbit-hole-research"; my dear friend Henrietta Bertelsman who helped me change my approach early on; New Thought ministers Laura Barrett Bennett, Diane Scribner-Clevinger and Paula Mekdeci, whose words and inspiration are found on these pages; Eileen Naughton who consistently supported the project and provided essential insights right before publishing, especially with the cover design concept; and my longtime friend and mentor Alan Cohen whose kind, loving philosophy is a template for succeeding generations and provides foundational concepts found in these pages. And of course, my lifelong partner Valerie, whose love defies description but shows up everywhere.

Also, much thanks is owed to John Koehler and those at Koehler Publishing for their diligence in getting this right: from the CMS "dictates" of Joe Coccaro, the friendly and fastidious editing of Hannah Woodlan and the magnificence and dedication of Christine Kettner whose fine-tune editing skills, design and layout acumen, as well as her personal interest in the subject, were a boon to this project.

To those who inspired me whose names are not included, I thank you for your presence in my life and know that the final outcome is imbued with your love and wisdom.

INDEX

Page numbers in *italics* indicate illustrations.

A

CHRISTOPHER NAUGHTON has merged his passions for American history and constitutional law with his keen interest in comparative spirituality and metaphysics that are the core inspirations for this book. He is a former New Jersey trial attorney and the six time Emmy® award winning host and executive producer of the twenty-five-plus years *The American Law Journal* airing on the CNN affiliate for Philadelphia, accepted by American Public Television (APT) for distribution to PBS stations. His *New World Radio* program examining holistic health and world spiritualities has aired on NPR affiliates, AM and FM commercial stations and Unity Online Radio. Christopher has conducted series, classes, multi-media lectures and moderated panels on related topics. He and this longtime partner Valerie Jones live in Virginia Beach, Virginia.